EURODÉLICES

DESSERTS

EURODÉLICES

DESSERTS

DINE WITH EUROPE'S
MASTER CHEFS

KÖNEMANN

Acknowledgements

We want to thank the following persons, restaurants and companies for their contribution to this book:

Ancienne Manufacture Royale, Aixe-sur-Vienne; Baccarat, Paris; Chomette Favor, Grigny; Christofle, Paris; Cristalleries de Saint-Louis, Paris; Grand Marnier, Paris; Groupe Cidelcem, Marne-la-Vallée; Haviland, Limoges; Jean-Louis Coquet, Paris; José Houel, Paris; Lalique, Paris; Les maisons de Cartier, Paris; Maîtres cuisiniers de France, Paris; Philippe Deshoulières, Paris; Porcelaines Bernardaud, Paris; Porcelaine Lafarge, Paris; Puiforcat Orfèvre, Paris; Robert Haviland et C. Parlon, Limoges; Société Caviar Petrossian, Paris; Villeroy & Boch, Garges-les-Gonesse; Wedgwood Dexam-International, Coye-la-Forêt.

A special thank you goes to: Lucien Barcon, Georges Laffon, Clément Lausecker, Michel Pasquet, Jean Pibourdin, Pierre Roche, Jacques Sylvestre und Pierre Fonteyne.

Difficulty of a recipe

★	easy
★★	advanced
★★★	difficult

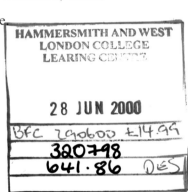

Photos: Studio Lucien Loeb, Maren Detering

© Fabien Bellhasen and Daniel Rouche

© 1998 for the English-language edition
Könemann Verlagsgesellschaft mbH
Bonner Str. 126, D - 50968 Köln

Translation from German: Fiona Hulse
Coordinator for the English-language edition: Tammi Reichel
English-language editor: Tammi Reichel
Jacket design: Peter Feierabend
Series project manager: Bettina Kaufmann
Assistant: Stephan Küffner
Typesetting: Goodfellow & Egan
Proofreading: Jacqueline Dobbyne
Production manager: Detlev Schaper
Assistant: Nicola Leurs
Reproduction: Reproservice Werner Pees
Printing and binding: Leefung Asco Printing Co., Ltd.

Printed in China

ISBN 3-8290-1130-x

10 9 8 7 6 5 4 3 2 1

Contents

Foreword

The Eurodélices series brings a selection of European haute cuisine right into your kitchen. Almost 100 professional chefs, many of them recipients of multiple awards and distinctions, associated with renowned restaurants in 17 countries throughout Europe, joined forces to create this unique series. Here they divulge their best and their favorite recipes for unsurpassed hot and cold appetizers, fish and meat entrees, desserts, and pastry specialties.

The series as a whole, consisting of six volumes with over 1,900 pages, is not only an essential collection for gourmet cooks, but also a fascinating document of European culture that goes far beyond short-lived culinary trends. In a fascinating way, Eurodélices explores the common roots of the different "arts of cooking" that have developed in various geographic locations, as well as their abundant variety.

For eating is much more than the fulfillment of a basic bodily need; cooking is often elevated to the level of an art, especially in association with parties and celebrations of all kinds, in private life and in the public sphere. Young couples plan their futures over a special dinner at an elegant restaurant, partners gather at table to launch new business ventures, heads of state are wined and dined. Every conceivable celebration involves food, from weddings to funerals, from intimacies shared over coffee and cake to Sunday dinners to Passover and Thanksgiving feasts.

We often have our first contact with the cultures of other lands, whether nearby or across an ocean, through their food. Precisely because the various contributing chefs are rooted in their distinct traditions, some flavors and combinations will be new to North American readers, and occasionally ingredients are called for that may be unfamiliar or even difficult to locate. The texts accompanying each recipe help elucidate and, wherever possible, suggest substitutes for ingredients that are not readily available in North America. A glossary is also included to explain terms that may not be obvious, listing some ingredients.

Because precision is often crucial to the success of recipes of this caliber, a few words regarding measurements and conversions are in order. In Europe, it is customary to use metric units of liquid volume or weight, that is, milliliters or grams. Every household has a kitchen scale and solid ingredients are weighed, rather than measured by volume. Converting milliliters to fluid cups and grams to ounces is straightforward, if not always neat. More problematic are ingredients given in grams that North Americans measure by volume, in tablespoons and cups. Throughout the Eurodélices series, the original metric measurement follows the North American equivalent. The conversions are painstakingly accurate up to 100 ml and 100 g (which necessitates some awkward-looking amounts). Thereafter, they are more neatly, and thus less accurately, rounded off. As with all recipes, measurements are approximate for many ingredients, and a wide variety of factors ranging from temperature and humidity to accuracy of kitchen implements to the way food is sold will affect the amount actually used. If the reader wants to recreate the recipes as given, however, the use of a kitchen scale is strongly recommended.

The unique collection of around 750 recipes contained in Eurodélices aims to excite its readers' curiosity. Classic dishes, which have been enjoyed for generations and thus form the foundations of modern cookery, are liberally presented. But there are also new and surprising pleasures, familiar foods prepared in novel ways, as well as culinary delights composed of ingredients from far away places that we experience for the first time. Allow yourself to be inspired by the European master chefs to try and, perhaps, try again.

Coconut and Chocolate

Preparation time: 2 hours
Cooking time: 30 minutes
Difficulty: ★★★

Serves 4

For the caramelized bananas:
1 banana
6¹/₂ tbsp / 100 g sugar

For the curry jelly:
1¹/₂ sheets of gelatin
1 cup / 250 ml water
a pinch of curry
2 tbsp / 30 g sugar

For the cylinders:
chocolate
grated coconut

For the chocolate sauce:
³/₄ cup / 200 ml each sugar, coconut water
3¹/₂ oz / 100 g each cocoa butter, chocolate

For the curry mousse:
1 cup / 250 ml cream
4 egg yolks
2¹/₂ tbsp / 40 g sugar
a pinch of curry

Coconut and curry, this combination of such very different flavors, is now broadly accepted by chefs.

The Indians have been masters of the combination of coconut and curry in all imaginable variations for centuries, as proven by the menus in the best Indian restaurants.

There one finds curry, or "cary" as the mixture of spices is known in India, equally often in sweet and savory recipes. It can be bought as a powder or paste. When selecting curry, the mixture should at the very least contain turmeric, ginger, cumin, coriander, and pimento. The spices need to be well-balanced so that no one flavor stands out. This fine balance is all the more important for the success of this particular recipe, as the flavor of both the mousse and the jelly depend on it.

Originally the dish was meant to be a savory one with only curry and coconut water. There is something quite bold about the idea of transforming it into a dessert by combining it with chocolate, and our chef may well have broken out in a cold sweat when he first served it to an illustrious group of top international chefs. However, he passed this test with style, and is now willing to reveal that for this recipe to succeed it is absolutely essential to use chocolate with a very high level of cocoa (at least 70%).

This recipe is a good example of the increasing importance of spices in the preparation of desserts: cinnamon, poppy, nutmeg, and star anise are by now popular ingredients in fine pastries and desserts, and gourmets consider them to be tasteful in the truest sense of the word.

1. Peel the banana, cut it into large pieces and caramelize with the sugar for 5 minutes. For the curry jelly, dissolve the gelatin in cold water. Bring the water, curry, and sugar to a boil. Remove from heat, stir in the gelatin and allow to cool.

2. To make the cylinders, warm the chocolate. Using a plastic strip and adhesive tape, form a chocolate cylinder measuring 3¹/₂ × 2 in / 8 x 4 cm. Place this on the plate, fill with grated coconut and cover well with a lid of chocolate. For the chocolate sauce, boil the sugar, coconut water, and cocoa butter, then add the chocolate.

Dessert with Curry

3. To make the curry mousse, bring the cream to a boil in a pan. In a bowl, beat the egg yolks with the sugar until the mixture is foamy and add the hot cream. Pour everything back into the pan and cook like a custard (see basic recipes). Pour into a bowl and add the curry powder. Refrigerate for one day, then beat again with a mixer.

4. Arrange some pieces of banana at the edge of each plate, add the curry jelly and curry mousse and decorate it with a little chocolate sauce. Garnish with mint leaves.

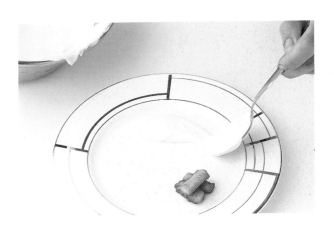

Mango and

Preparation time: 1 hour 20 minutes
Cooking time: 50 minutes
Difficulty: ★

Serves 4

3 lb 4 oz / 1¹/₂ kg mangoes
1 cup plus 2 tbsp / 400 g honey
1 sheet of gelatin

14 oz / 400 g quark
1 lemon
  ³/₄ cup plus 1 tbsp / 200 g   sugar
10¹/₂ oz / 300 g black currants, pureed
  sprigs of mint

Mango sorbet (see basic recipes)

While this book was being prepared, Alberto Adría, the brother of our chef Fernando Adría, demonstrated the masterly, experienced movements of the professional pastry chef using this recipe. The original intention was to use avocados in the recipe; but because their flesh rapidly becomes brown when exposed to air, making them unsightly, it was decided to use mangoes instead.

This tropical fruit possesses all the qualities necessary for the rolls to be a success: an aromatic flesh that is rich in vitamin A, a smooth surface, and a firm consistency.

The honey serves to intensify the sweetness and exquisite flavor of the dish. It must be good quality so that it does not

burn while being caramelized, and unfortunately this can only be tested by trying it out beforehand. Its dark color and intense flavor form an ideal contrast to the quark, which is neutral in taste.

If you would like to use other fruits than those suggested here, our chef suggests bananas, which fit in with the exotic context of the dessert, or alternatively peaches. Apples and pears are not recommended, as they are scarcely suited to the play of flavors in this recipe. The dessert's success depends on the fruit having reached perfect ripeness.

1. Peel the mangoes and cut into wafer-thin slices. Create a honey jelly using the honey and soaked gelatin. Place a small amount of quark on half of the mango slices. Fold the slices twice and top with a small amount of the honey jelly.

2. Caramelize the other half of the mango slices. Dry them in a warm oven (175 °F / 80 °C) for 40 minutes, then place in a syrup (made of equal parts water and sugar) at 30 °Beaumé and put in a 320 °F/160 °C oven for 7 minutes. Finally fold the slices up into rolls and prepare the sorbet.

Honey Rolls

3. Fill the rolls with mango sorbet using a pastry bag.

4. Place the rolls on a plate, then arrange the mango slices filled with quark and honey jelly and the pureed black currants around them. Garnish with sprigs of mint.

Puff Pastry with

Preparation time: 1 hour
Cooking time: 1 hour
Difficulty: ✶✶

Serves 6

9 oz / 250 g puff pastry (see basic recipes)

For the creamy rice pudding:
6 tbsp / 85 g short grain rice
³/₄ cup / 190 ml milk
³/₄ cup / 190 ml crème fraîche
peel of 1 untreated lemon
2 tsp sugar
¹/₂ cinnamon stick

For the rice pudding mousse:
11¹/₂ oz / 335 g rice pudding
2 egg yolks

3¹/₂ sheets of gelatin
5 oz / 135 g meringue (see basic recipes)
³/₄ cup / 200 ml cream

For the glazed cherries:
juice of 3 lemons
5 tbsp / 85 ml water
thyme
4¹/₂ tbsp / 70 g sugar
3 oz / 85 g cherries, stoned

For the apple sorbet:
1 lb 7 oz / 660 g apples (e.g. Rennets)
1 cup / 250 ml syrup (³/₄ cup / 170 ml water,
    ¹/₃ cup / 80 g sugar)
juice of 3 lemons

Next to wheat, the most familiar grain is rice, which is prepared in countless fashions throughout the world. It fulfills many functions, being a cleaning product (rice powder), the basic material used in the production of sculptures and white earthenware, and above all an essential basic foodstuff. It has been known in Spain since the 7th century, when it was introduced by the Moors who conquered the country. The long presence of the Arabs, until the 15th century, made rice a permanent part of the traditional cuisine of the Iberian peninsula. From there rice appears to have spread to northern Italy to the Po plain, so we can indirectly thank the Moors for dishes such as the generally popular risotto.

Here, Hilario Arbelaitz tempts us with a classically prepared, European-style creamy rice pudding. Genuine rice pudding is made with short grain rather than long grain rice; it soon cooks and expands in the milk, producing an even mass that is firm enough to be spread between sheets of pastry without oozing away.

To add to people's enjoyment of this dessert, something refreshing should be served as a contrast to the sweetness of the rice pudding. For this purpose, our chef recommends an apple sorbet made with sweetish-sour apples, which has precisely the desired effect.

1. For the creamy rice pudding, combine the rice, milk, crème fraîche, lemon peel, sugar, and cinnamon stick in a pan. Cook over a low heat until the mixtures thickens to a creamy consistency.

2. For the rice pudding mousse, mix the creamy rice pudding, egg yolks, and the gelatin (that has been soaked in water). Add the meringue and, as the final step, fold in the cream, which has been whipped to a stiff consistency.

Creamy Rice Pudding

3. Roll out the puff pastry as thinly as possible and cut out rounds with a diameter of 4¹/₂ in / 10 cm. Place the rounds in an oven preheated to 300 °F / 150 °C and bake until golden brown. Place one thin round on a plate and put a spoonful of rice pudding mousse onto it. Repeat three times, finishing with a piece of pastry.

4. For the glazed cherries, boil the lemon juice, water, thyme, and sugar for 2 minutes. Add the cherries and cook at 185 °F / 85 °C in a double boiler for 30 minutes. To make the apple sorbet, chop the apples in a juice extractor, then pour the sugar syrup and lemon juice into the apple puree. Thoroughly mix everything in a ice cream machine. Place sorbet on the plates next to the pastry and garnish with the cherries.

Sloe Gin Soufflé

Preparation time: 30 minutes
Cooking time: 2 minutes
Cooling time: 6 hours
Difficulty: ★★

Serves 4

8 egg yolks
1 egg
4 cups / 1 l crème fraîche
10¹/₂ oz / 300 g meringue (see basic recipes)

6¹/₂ tbsp / 100 ml Patxaran (or sloe gin)
1 mango
blueberry syrup
peel of 1 untreated orange
¹/₂ cup plus 2 tbsp / 100 g blueberries
seasonal fruits

One must differentiate between the ordinary plum tree and the wild sloe tree, and between their fruits as well. Sloes are not harvested until after the first frosts, and are immediately pickled in alcohol because they are so sour that it is impossible to eat them raw. They are used to make several liqueurs and a transparent fruit schnapps with fine nuances of flavor, called Patxaran in Spain. Our chef uses this very special schnapps to flavor his exquisite cold soufflé, which is then crowned with mango. If you are not able to obtain Patxaran, ordinary sloe gin is perfectly acceptable.

As this is a cold dessert, there is no need to worry about baking times – one can linger over dinner and take one's time serving the dish. Very important, however, is that the eggs and meringue are carefully blended to form an even mixture to achieve the best possible texture.

One of the virtues of the perfect chef is still patience. The soufflés must be cooled for at least 6 hours to prevent difficulties when removing them from the molds. Small, varying molds for each portion are an attractive means of making this dessert more individual.

The decorative mango crowns each little soufflé. Choose a ripe, tasty fruit whose flesh gives a little under pressure, and which can be easily cut into thin slices.

1. In a bowl, beat the egg yolks and egg. In another, stir the crème fraîche to a creamy consistency. Prepare the meringue, allow to cool and mix with the eggs.

2. Add the crème fraîche and sloe gin to the egg and meringue mixture and combine.

with Mango

3. Pipe the mixture into the molds and allow to set in the freezer for 6 hours. (This step should be carried out a day in advance.)

4. Peel the mango and cut into slices. Pour a little blueberry syrup, in which the orange peel has been soaked, into a pan and heat the blueberries in it for 1 minute. Remove the soufflés from the molds, and arrange the mango slices on them attractively. Garnish using the blueberries, seasonal fruits, and orange peel.

Preparation time: 45 minutes
Cooking time: 1 hour 20 minutes
Difficulty: ★★

Serves 4

For the dough:
1 egg yolk
6¹/₂ tbsp / 100 g sugar
³/₄ cup plus 1 tbsp / 100 g flour
3¹/₂ tbsp / 50 g butter, softened
2¹/₂ tbsp / 20 g ground almonds
¹/₄ oz / 5 g yeast

1 tsp rum
¹/₂ tsp vanilla sugar
a pinch of salt

For the pastry cream:
1 cup / 250 ml milk
¹/₂ vanilla bean
5 tbsp / 75 g sugar
2 egg yolks
1 tsp rum
3¹/₂ tbsp / 25 g flour
2 eggs, beaten

Many people are familiar with the three crowning elements of Basque cuisine: the Basque hen, an egg dish with Bayonne ham, and Basque cake. The latter, a traditional dessert, keeps for a few days, making it a thoughtful gift.

Of course, this dessert is more than just a simple cake filled with cream or cherry preserves. It is a real delight, soft and crisp at the same time, and combines a sweet, dry butter dough with the gentle flavors of orange flowers and rum or the local herbal liqueur Izarra.

This dessert occupied a very special place in the childhood memories of our chef. It was a cake baked in folded paper, crumbled up and eaten at the school entrance, with the name of the baker printed on the paper folds.

Today, this specialty is still one of the favorite homemade cakes in the Basque country of northern Spain and southwest France: a favorite charitable gift in those homes that continue the traditional ways.

Firmin Arrambide recommends preparing the cake on the previous evening and allowing it to rest in the refrigerator, covered with plastic wrap so that the surface does not become hard. As is often the case when baking, it is most important to use precisely the quantities given. Also, the cake should be taken out of the pan immediately after baking and cooled on a cooling rack for about 20 minutes to allow steam to escape. This will help the cake remain crisp for longer.

1. A day in advance, mix the ingredients for the dough (do not overwork). Refrigerate for at least 4 hours. To make the pastry cream, warm the milk with the vanilla bean in it. In a separate bowl, combine the sugar, egg yolks, rum, and flour. Remove the vanilla bean from the milk. Bring the milk to a boil and add the egg mixture to it. Bring everything to a boil while stirring continuously, then allow to cool.

2. Use butter to grease a cake pan of about 10 in / 22 cm diameter. Use a rolling pin to roll half of the dough to a thickness of ¹/₄ in / 3 mm or less. Cover the bottom and sides of the pan with the dough.

Cake

3. Spread the cold pastry cream onto the dough in the cake pan.

4. Cover the cream with the other half of the dough. Pour the beaten eggs over the cake. Bake for 1 hour in a moderate oven (320 °F / 160 °C). Serve lukewarm or cold.

Fruit Terrine with

Preparation time: 2 hours
Cooling time: 8 hours
Difficulty: ★★

Serves 8

2 lb 3 oz / 1 kg strawberries
7 kiwis
4 mangoes
7 oz / 200 g sponge cake

For the almond mousse:
1³/₄ cups / 200 g almonds, finely ground
10 tbsp / 150 g butter
1¹/₃ cups / 200 g confectioners' sugar
3¹/₂ tbsp / 50 ml Grand Marnier
1 cup / 250 ml cream, whipped

Our chef was inspired to produce this colorful dessert by a vegetable terrine. Its exceptional quality lies in the combination of the almond mousse and Grand Marnier, light and flavorful, making the juxtaposition of fruits possible.

It is precisely this combination, which is produced by mixing butter, confectioners' sugar, ground almonds, and Grand Marnier, that is the main difficulty in making this recipe. The mixture must be at the right temperature, so that the cream does not harden the butter. If the use of gelatin can be avoided, this will guarantee the lightness of the dessert and make it even more delicate.

The first step is to prepare the fruit. After selecting nicely ripe but not overly soft mangoes, tender medium-sized kiwis, and reasonably large strawberries, they should be cut into pieces of approximately equal size. One might want to substitute tasty peaches for the mangoes, whose fibrous flesh frequently makes them rather difficult to cut.

The sponge cake base must be thinly sliced with a serrated knife or bread slicer. This is facilitated by placing the sponge cake in the freezer for a few moments. It will be easier to turn the finished terrine out of the pan if the pan is lined with aluminum foil before lining with sponge cake.

The terrine comprises three layers altogether, and a spoon is used to press the fruits into the almond cream so that no air spaces remain. The resulting contrast of fruits and colors is most effective if one has cut them into pieces of relatively equal size, as described above.

1. Prepare the almond mousse by beating the ground almonds, butter, confectioners' sugar, and Grand Marnier with a mixer. Carefully fold in the whipped cream.

2. Peel the fruit and remove the stems from the strawberries. Quarter the mangoes and kiwis lengthwise.

Almond Mousse

3. Line the bottom and sides of a porcelain rectangular baking dish with the sliced sponge cake.

4. To make the terrine, place alternating layers of almond mousse and fruits into the dish so that the fruits produce a pattern. Finish off with a layer of sponge cake. Refrigerate at least overnight. Cut into slices and serve with raspberry sauce, if desired.

Preparation time: 10 minutes
Cooking time: 1 hour
Difficulty: ✶

Serves 4

7 oz / 200 g cherries
butter
kirsch
2¹/₂ tbsp / 40 ml Chartreuse (herbal liqueur)

For the sugar syrup:
1¹/₂ cups / 350 g sugar
1 cup / 250 ml water

For the pistachio ice cream:
(see basic recipes)
2 cups / 500 ml milk
6 egg yolks
¹/₂ cup / 125 g sugar
pistachio cream (or ground pistachios)

There were centuries in which cherries were one of the most highly prized fruits. They were already cultivated in the Middle Ages, and early-ripening cherries were first grown during the Renaissance. Louis XIV was particularly fond of cherries, and during the 19th century, when cherries were enormously popular, the orchards of Montmorency were almost taken by storm. Nobility went so far as to rent the trees by the hour or the day, so as to be able to pick the fruit in peace.

Today, there are at least 2,000 recorded varieties of cherries in existence. They are classified according to such characteristics as tree size, self- or cross-pollination, growing season and harvest time, fruit size, and of course, the fruit itself: every nuance of flavor from sweet enough to eat off the tree to sour enough to be used only for canning or baking, and all variations of color from dark red to yellow. Without a doubt, North America's favorite variety is the Bing cherry. The dark red,

almost black fruits are harvested mid-summer: large, firm, juicy, sweet, and irresistible. One can, however, use other sorts of cherries, some of which are available from markets as early as May.

The sauce must be prepared a day in advance so the cherries can marinate in it overnight. They go well with ingredients with strong flavors, such as the pistachio ice cream used in this recipe. Of course the ice cream melts when the hot cherries are poured over it; this should obviously be done immediately before serving.

Chartreuse is an herbal liqueur made in the French Alps by Carthusian monks. According to a top-secret recipe, 53 herbs are distilled to produce a liqueur with 55% alcohol by volume. In addition to the little glassful that is poured over the hot cherries you can, of course, serve another to be drunk with the dessert.

1. Make a syrup from the sugar and water. Add to it the cherries with the stems removed, but not yet stoned, and bring to a boil. Remove from heat, cover, and allow to cool. Mix the pistachio ice cream and allow to harden in an ice cream machine.

2. Melt the butter in a pan. Heat and toss the stoned cherries in it, allowing about 12 cherries per person. Sprinkle them with sugar.

Cold Cherries

3. Once the cherries are hot but still firm, add a little kirsch to the pan and flambé.

4. Pour 3¹/₂ tbsp / 50 ml of the cherry syrup into a pan and slowly boil down to the consistency of a sauce. Stir in the Chartreuse. Place 2 balls of pistachio ice cream on each plate and pour the hot cherries over them. Serve immediately.

Delicate

Preparation time: *1 hour*
Cooking time: *2 hours*
Difficulty: ★★

Serves 4

For the Italian meringue:
5 tbsp / 75 g sugar
2 egg whites, lightly beaten

For the parfait:
5 tbsp / 75 g sugar
4 egg yolks, beaten
coffee extract
2 cups / 500 ml cream, whipped

For the baked meringue:
2 egg whites
¼ cup / 60 g sugar
1 tsp freeze-dried coffee

For the sauce:
5 tbsp / 75 g sugar
4 egg yolks
rum
2 cups / 500 ml cream, whipped

confectioners' sugar for dusting

One could eat this delicious dessert at any time of day for the sheer pleasure of it. The preparation does, however, require a degree of effort and care.

Meringue is a devilish invention that, according to some sources, was imported from Poland in the 18th century by Stanislas Leczinsky, the father-in-law of King Louis XV. There are three different sorts of meringue: piped, baked, and the smoother Italian meringue, which is made with lightly beaten egg white. It is important to add the boiled sugar syrup last and at the prescribed temperature. The same is true of the parfait; the sugar must reach a temperature of 250 °F / 118 °C before it is poured over the egg yolks. The mixture then has to be beaten continuously close to the edge of the bowl until it cools.

Generally, the dessert is composed of three layers and is served on a plate with sauce. In this case our chef has enriched the sauce with cream. In contrast to the other ingredients, which can be kept for a day, the sauce has to be prepared on the day of serving.

The last step is to beat the egg whites until they are so stiff that the dessert will not collapse, but not so stiff that the parfait's texture becomes grainy.

After baking, the dessert is served immediately. One can add another flavor to this dessert by using high-quality chocolate, if desired, without altering the recipe in the process.

1. To make the Italian meringue, cook the sugar with water at 250 °F / 118 °C. Add to 2 egg whites that have been lightly beaten, and beat continuously until completely cooled. Next, prepare the parfait. Again, heat the sugar with water to 250 °F / 118 °C, and this time pour onto the 4 beaten egg yolks. Beat until cooled.

2. Combine the parfait with the Italian meringue and add the coffee extract. Finally, fold in the whipped cream. Pour onto a baking tray with a high edge and place in the freezer.

Coffee Parfait

3. For the baked meringue, beat the egg whites and sugar until they are stiff, then mix in the freeze-dried coffee. Spread the stiff egg whites onto a sheet of baking paper to a thickness of ¹/₂ in / 1 cm and steam at 175 °F / 80 °C for 2 minutes. For the sauce, heat the sugar to 250 °F / 118 °C, then carefully add the 4 egg yolks. Beat until the mixture has cooled, then stir in the rum and cream.

4. For each portion, cut out 2 circles of meringue and 1 circle of parfait with a diameter of ca. 3 in / 6.5 cm. Place some sauce on each plate and glaze. Layer a slice of meringue, a slice of coffee parfait and another meringue slice. Place on top of the sauce. Sprinkle with confectioners' sugar. Glaze again.

Meringue with

Preparation time: 30 minutes
Cooking time: 4 hours
Difficulty: ★★

Serves 4

For the meringue:
2 egg whites
a pinch of salt
¹/₃ cup/80 g superfine sugar
¹/₃ cup/80 g vanilla sugar

For the filling:
9³/₄ oz / 280 g mascarpone
20 oz / 600 g red forest fruits

For the strawberry sauce:
20 oz / 600 g strawberries

Our ancestors recognized very early on the harmonious combination of sugar and fruit that has given rise to so many delicious variations over the centuries. Here you can discover the flavors and scents of various red forest fruits, which are also known for their wealth of vitamins and minerals. Of course, the ripest and most succulent strawberries, raspberries and red currants are found in the summer, though at different times, which makes it somewhat difficult to serve them as a mixture.

Mascarpone, used to give this delicacy its creaminess and spicy flavor, is an Italian cheese made of cream cheese and fresh cheese that combine to produce its creamy, firm consistency and, above all, its refined taste. It is equally well-suited to presentation as part of a cheese board as in a dessert.

The main difficulty in this recipe is making the meringue. Stiffly whisked egg whites are called for, to which first superfine sugar and then vanilla sugar are added. The meringue must bake for 4 hours at 210 °F / 100 °C in a pan with a steamer insert. It can also be baked in the oven in a water bath (a pan of boiling water placed in the oven). This is vital in order to prevent discoloration of the meringues and to give them the firmness necessary for decorating. When preparing meringues, patience and precision are of the utmost importance.

Light, aromatic and refreshing, one could imagine serving this dessert for breakfast in summer, with a strawberry sauce prepared at the last minute.

1. To make the meringue, whisk the egg whites with a pinch of salt. Gradually add the superfine sugar and then the vanilla sugar.

2. Use forms to cut out 8 circles of ca. 3¹/₂ in / 8 cm diameter from the egg white mixture.

Forest Fruits

3. Bake the meringues for 4 hours at 210 °F / 100 °C in a water bath, being careful to avoid discoloration. After the meringues have cooled, use a pastry bag to apply a thin layer of mascarpone on four of the slices.

4. Place the forest fruits on top of the layer of mascarpone, cover with another circle of meringue and sprinkle with confectioners' sugar. Serve with a sauce made of pureed strawberries.

Zabaglione with Dessert Wine

Preparation time: 1 hour 15 minutes
Cooking time: 30 minutes
Difficulty: ★★

Serves 4

For the zabaglione:
8 egg yolks
4 tbsp superfine sugar
³/₄ cup / 200 ml dessert wine from Liguria (or another dessert wine)

For the fried dough:
4 cups / 500 g flour
3¹/₂ tbsp / 50 g soft butter
3 eggs
6¹/₂ tbsp / 100 g superfine sugar
6¹/₂ tbsp / 100 g confectioners' sugar
3 tbsp cognac
a pinch of salt
6 cups / 1¹/₂ l oil for deep-frying
grated peel of 1 untreated lemon

Ligurian cuisine is characterized by simplicity, but it would be a great mistake to think that it is too humble to be interesting. Even though this region in northwestern Italy has a very dry climate, its difficult location between the Alps and the Mediterranean does not prevent certain varieties of vegetables and fruit being cultivated here, as they are protected from the winds from the north and east. Wines cultivated in this region are the perfect accompaniment to a gastronomy with refined taste.

After the harvest in the latter part of September, grapes that have spent the whole summer soaking up southern European sunshine are hung for a few weeks in the open air. A unique dessert wine is created from these grapes, which is used in diverse recipes and here gives its special character to the zabaglione.

It is said that the Ligurian zabaglione was invented during the carnival season, the raucous pre-Lenten festivities celebrated in parts of Europe. The chefs must have kept their cool during the celebration, or they might not have had much success preparing the delicate wine cream in a double boiler. The chemical reaction created by the use of a copper bowl gives the egg yolks a better consistency for the dessert.

The dough can only be prepared using soft butter, to ensure an even texture. It should be left to rest for several hours before continuing or, if desired, it can be prepared the previous day. The dough strips must be narrow enough to be knotted before being deep-fried.

This dessert can be eaten hot or cold. In the unlikely event that there should be some left over, the knots can be kept in an airtight container.

1. For the zabaglione, place the egg yolks and sugar in a copper bowl. Beat for 5 minutes with a whisk. Add the wine. Place the bowl in a double boiler and stir over low heat until the mixture has a thick, creamy consistency. Keep lukewarm.

2. To make the dough, mound the flour on a work surface. Make a well in the middle and place all the other ingredients in it; then mix everything thoroughly until a smooth dough forms. Wrap in plastic wrap and allow to rest for several hours.

and Fried Dough Knots

3. Roll the dough out to a thickness of ¹/₂ in / 1 cm, and use a serrated pastry cutter to cut the dough into 5 x 1 in / 10 x 2 cm strips. Knot each of them once.

4. Deep-fry the knotted strips in boiling oil. Drain thoroughly and dust with confectioners' sugar. Serve warm or cold with the zabaglione.

Chocolate

Preparation time: 2 hours
Cooking time: 30 minutes
Difficulty: ★★★

Serves 4

For the milk & white chocolate mousses:
3¹/₂ oz / 100 g each milk & white chocolate, grated
1 cup / 240 ml cream for each mousse

For the chocolate sorbet:
3¹/₂ oz / 100 g chocolate coating
¹/₃ cup / 35 g cocoa powder
2 tsp / 15 g honey
¹/₂ cup plus 2 tbsp / 150 g sugar
1²/₃ cups / 400 ml water

For the chocolate cake:
3 oz / 85 g bittersweet chocolate
3¹/₂ tbsp / 50 g butter
3 eggs, separated

3 tbsp / 20 g cocoa powder
6¹/₂ tbsp / 100 g sugar

For the bittersweet chocolate mousse:
7 oz / 200 g bittersweet chocolate, grated
1¹/₄ cups / 300 ml each milk, cream
¹/₄ cup / 60 g sugar, 3 egg yolks

To garnish:
3¹/₂ oz / 100 g raspberry sauce
¹/₃ cup / 70 g candied orange peel
²/₃ cup / 70 g grated chocolate
2 tsp coffee extract
a little pistachio or bitter almond extract

9 oz / 250 g custard (see basic recipes)

Though the wide range of ingredients in this recipe may at first seem daunting, the preparation is by no means as difficult as one might suppose. If you follow our chef's instructions step by step, you will certainly succeed in creating an array of desserts of the very highest quality.

When making the mousses, it is essential that the chocolate be at the proper temperature: it must be warm enough for the ingredients to combine, but not hot enough to melt the whipped cream. It is best to prepare the sorbet immediately before serving. Stirring it while it is cold will give it a nice sheen.

When preparing the sponge cake, make sure that the mixture of chocolate and butter is not heated for too long, as this would impair the flavor of the chocolate. After baking, handle the sponge cake as little as possible, and then very gently.

As soon as the boiling custard has reached the right consistency, it is advisable to dip the bottom of the bowl in cold water to prevent the custard from continuing to cook. It must be beaten thoroughly after cooking and cooling; only then should the custard be divided, one third to be flavored with coffee, and another third with pistachio extract. This method results in three custards with the same consistency, but different colors and flavors, which supplement each other nicely.

When creating this gourmet recipe, Michel Blanchet certainly had chocolate enthusiasts in mind: it is well known that chocolate is useful in alleviating stress and generally lifting spirits.

1. For the milk chocolate mousse, whip the cream until stiff. Melt the milk chocolate in a double boiler, then stir in the whipped cream and leave to cool. Repeat these steps to prepare the white chocolate mousse. For the sorbet bring water, sugar and honey to a boil. Then dissolve the chocolate coating and cocoa powder in it. Leave to cool and blend in an ice cream machine.

2. To make the sponge cake, break the chocolate into pieces and melt in a double boiler with the butter. Beat the egg yolks with half of the sugar until they are light yellow. Add the cocoa. Beat the egg whites with the remaining sugar until stiff. Add the egg yolk mixture and the chocolate mixture to the egg whites. Pour into a springform pan and bake for 6 to 8 minutes at 355 °F / 180 °C.

Variations

3. Make 9 oz / 250 g custard according to the basic recipe. Separate the custard into three portions; flavor one part with coffee and another with pistachio extract. To make the bittersweet chocolate mousse, mix the milk and cream and bring to a boil. Whisk the egg yolks with the sugar until foamy and pour the hot milk mixture over them. Simmer while stirring, then add the grated bittersweet chocolate. Allow to set.

4. Divide the sponge cake horizontally and layer with the milk chocolate mousse. Dust with cocoa powder. Use forms to cut the sponge cake into small pieces. Arrange and decorate the various elements according to taste.

Burgundy Pear with

Preparation time: 30 minutes
Cooking time: 45 minutes
Difficulty: ★

Serves 4

For the Burgundy pears:
4 pears
4 cups / 1 l Burgundy wine
³/₄ cup plus 1 tbsp / 200 g sugar
1 cinnamon stick

For the licorice ice cream:
3 sticks licorice root
2 cups / 500 ml milk
6¹/₂ tbsp / 100 g sugar
4 eggs
4 tsp / 20 ml cream
2 tsp / 10 ml pastis (aniseed liqueur)
custard (see basic recipes)

To garnish:
4 mint leaves
almonds, tinted pink and roasted

In the Far East in ancient times, pears were not shared with friends in order to avoid causing major arguments: the Chinese name for the pear is *li*, which also means separation. The Greeks considered it to be a fruit of divine origins, and six varieties were known to them. Increased by means of hybridization, there were already 1,000 different varieties in the 19th century. Now there are almost 5,000. However, only about twelve of these are commonly found in stores. Pears are mainly eaten in the late summer and autumn, though some fruit merchants offer them into the winter. For this recipe one should choose pears that remain firm when cooked, and that

give slightly when touched. Their consistency will be similar to that of the licorice ice cream with which they will be served.

The choice of Burgundy wine is left to individual preference. Our chef recommends avoiding the least expensive alternatives, instead using a quality wine with a pronounced bouquet. Heavy Burgundies are particularly suitable for heating, which releases the full spectrum of their tempting aromas. They go well with the tender pears, which soak up the flavors, promising a real delight for the taste buds.

1. Peel the pears but do not remove the stems. Poach at a low temperature for 30 minutes in a mixture of the red wine, sugar and the cinnamon stick.

2. While the pears are cooking, prepare the ice cream. Cut up the sticks of licorice root and place in the milk. Then use the milk, sugar, and eggs to prepare a custard according to the basic recipe. When it has cooled, pour the custard into the ice cream machine. Before the ice cream has frozen, add the cream and aniseed liqueur. After stirring thoroughly, freeze and allow to set.

Licorice Ice Cream

3. Strain the pears, cut off the ends with the stems and cut in half lengthwise. On a chopping board, cut into slices so that they are still connected at one end, and arrange on a plate in a fan shape. Sprinkle with sugar and grill briefly under a hot grill.

4. Reduce the cooking juices. Arrange two pear halves to form a butterfly on each plate and pour the reduced liquid over them. Sprinkle with the crushed, roasted almonds and serve with a ball of licorice ice cream.

Bread and

Preparation time: 35 minutes
Cooking time: 1 hour 45 minutes
Difficulty: ★★

Serves 4

1 cup plus 2 tbsp / 270 ml milk
2 tbsp / 30 g salted butter
¹⁄₄ cup / 60 g sugar
3 eggs
¹⁄₂ vanilla bean
¹⁄₄ cup / 55 g currants and sultanas
confectioners' sugar for sprinkling

For the bread:
2 cups / 250 g bread flour
¹⁄₂ oz / 10 g yeast
6¹⁄₂ tbsp / 100 ml milk
3 tbsp / 45 g sugar
1 egg
¹⁄₄ cup / 65 g butter
1 tbsp / 10 g baking powder
6 tbsp / 75 g currants
4 tbsp / 65 g candied cherries
1 tsp / 5 g salt

It used to be unimaginable to throw away stale bread. Instead, leftover pieces were used to prepare other hearty dishes. Today we have this practice to thank for a delicious dessert that can be prepared in all sorts of ways. Several versions of such delicious casseroles or puddings with a golden-brown crust are known in southern France, where they are traditionally eaten at Easter. It is perhaps most renowned as "bread and butter pudding" in England, where pudding is a rather general term for all desserts. Bread pudding should not be confused with the famous, sumptuous plum pudding made of beef fat, prunes and various preserved fruits, which is prepared in English homes several months before Christmas specially for the holiday.

When cooks had to be economical, they prepared the pudding with a lot of bread and a little butter and eggs. Since this dessert is not intended to be a filling meal for many hungry mouths, the recipe has been refined by changing the proportions of the ingredients.

Ideally, the pudding should be completely prepared a day in advance and refrigerated overnight, uncooked, so that it can soak thoroughly. After it has cooled, very impatient people should allow it to rest for a minimum of three hours in order to develop the ideal consistency and its characteristic crust. If you want to give the pudding a little additional refinement, use slightly salted instead of unsalted butter – both varieties are equally tasty. Serve the pudding lukewarm with fresh fruit.

1. Scatter the currants and sultanas in a casserole dish. To make the bread, prepare a yeast dough using the yeast, baking powder, milk and a quarter of the flour, and let rise. Place the remaining flour, sugar and salt in a mixing bowl; stir in the egg and yeast dough with a mixer. Knead the butter soft by hand, and add to the dough. Mix in the currants and cherries. Let the dough rise. Place in pans and bake in a 390 °F / 200 °C oven for 45 minutes.

2. For the liquid mixture, bring the milk to a boil. Use a whisk to beat the eggs, sugar and pulp from the vanilla bean until foamy. Pour in the hot milk a little at a time and stir thoroughly. Pour through a sieve.

Butter Pudding

3. Cut the bread into round slices about ¼ in / 0.5 cm thick and arrange evenly in the casserole dish. Cut the salted butter into three pieces and spread out across the bread.

4. Pour the egg milk over the bread. Simmer the pudding in a water bath at 300 °F / 150 °C for about 1 hour, until the mixture is firm and has a golden-brown color. Sprinkle with confectioners' sugar and glaze under a hot grill. Serve warm.

Cherry Trifle

Preparation time: 30 minutes
Cooking time: 15 minutes
Difficulty: ★★

Serves 4

For the sponge cake:
$^1/_2$ cup plus 2 tbsp / 150 g sugar
5 eggs
$1^1/_4$ cups / 150 g flour
$1^1/_4$ cups / 450 g sour cherry jam

To soak the sponge cake:
1 tbsp / 15 ml rum
$2^1/_2$ tbsp / 35 ml cherry brandy
5 tbsp / 70 ml sugar syrup at 30 °Beaumé

For the pudding:
$1^1/_2$ cups / 375 ml milk
2 tbsp / 30 g sugar
4 tsp / 10 g pudding powder
2 egg yolks
1 egg

To garnish:
2 cups / 500 ml cream
$3^1/_2$ tbsp / 50 g superfine sugar
almonds, blanched and roasted
pistachios, chopped
raspberry jelly
fresh strawberries

Perfection in cooking is achieved only through attention to detail: who could exemplify this more clearly than the master pastry chefs at the Connaught Hotel in London?

This dessert, made with soaked sponge cake, is a typical English dish. It combines the flavors of rum and cherry brandy, the latter drink being particularly popular with the English upper classes and only mistakable for sherry by the completely uninitiated. As one can well imagine, the two potent alcoholic drinks have to be measured very carefully. The invention of rum, by the way, dates back to the French missionary Jean-Baptiste Labat: he worked in the Antilles in the 18th century and succeeded in producing rum from sugar cane, which at the time was a bone of contention between the French, British, and Dutch. The priest also distinguished himself in battle against the British, which in hindsight is not without a certain irony...

When preparing the sponge cake, one must work with precision during the decisive stage: it must retain its light consistency when mixed with the other ingredients. The sponge cake must be allowed to cool completely before continuing. It can even be prepared a day in advance, so that it is a little firmer. When soaking the cubes of sponge cake, it is important to insure that the liquid is distributed evenly over all the cubes.

The whipped cream used to decorate the trifle must be foamy and light. Our chef says the cream will be even lighter if an egg white is folded in at the last moment. One can use raspberry jam in place of cherry to fill the sponge cake.

1. To make the sponge cake, sprinkle the sugar on a baking tray covered with waxed paper and heat in the oven. Beat the eggs with a mixer until foamy. Add the heated sugar, continuing to stir until the mixture has cooled. Stir in the sifted flour. Pour the mixture into a greased cake pan, and bake at 390 °F / 200 °C until golden brown, then reduce the heat to 320 °F / 160 °C and bake until finished.

2. Allow the sponge cake to cool, cut in half horizontally and fill with cherry jam. Combine the rum, cherry brandy, and syrup. Dice the sponge cake and fill a bowl half full with the cubes (this will be the serving bowl). Pour the alcohol and syrup mixture over the cubes and allow to soak in.

"Wally Ladd"

3. To make the pudding, bring the milk to a boil. Beat the sugar and eggs with a whisk. Stir in the pudding powder (instant pudding mix). While stirring, add a little boiling milk, then pour the mixture into the hot milk and continue cooking as for a custard (see basic recipes). Pour through a pointed sieve and whisk thoroughly again.

4. When the syrup has been thoroughly soaked up by the sponge cake, pour the custard over it. Allow to cool. Garnish with sweetened whipped cream, blanched almonds, pistachios, raspberry jelly, and strawberries.

Crème

Preparation time: 10 minutes
Cooking time: 5 minutes
Cooling time: 2 hours
Difficulty: ★★

Serves 4

1³/₄ cups / 425 ml heavy cream (48 % fat)
²/₃ cup / 150 ml light whipping cream (40 % fat)
1 vanilla bean
8 egg yolks

¹/₄ cup / 60 g sugar
2 cups wild strawberries
¹/₂ cup plus 1 tbsp / 100 g brown sugar

The desserts that we are familiar with nowadays have been part of our gastronomic culture since about 1850. The term "dessert" is derived from the French word *desservir*, which means "clear (the table)." So a dessert was evidently what was served after the previous meal had been cleared away. In those days, it was customary to prepare the dessert at the head of the table at the beginning of the meal, and the lavish compositions positively enticed people to overindulge. These days top chefs create sweet temptations in more moderate portions: they invite us to indulge without damaging our health.

The pastry chefs at the Connaught Hotel in London, the Power twins, are masters in their field and convincingly demonstrate every day that an exceptional meal may only be followed by an equally exceptional dessert. Our crème brûlée is also based on this maxim.

As the quality of dairy products has improved, keeping cream fresh and storing it is much less of a problem than it used to be, and as a result it is less difficult to work with. However, it is important that the proportions of the different varieties of cream in our recipe are precisely reproduced.

Wild strawberries are extremely well suited to this recipe because of their small size; but other small strawberries could also be used. It is essential that the crème cools down completely before it is glazed, so that the sugar sprinkled over it can be caramelized without re-heating the crème. The contrast between the heat of the Bunsen burner, used in professional kitchens, and the coolness of the crème from below, creates a smooth, shining sugar glaze. Afterwards, the crème must be refrigerated again so that it can set slightly and form a homogeneous whole.

1. Combine the heavy and light creams in a pan with the opened vanilla bean and bring to a boil. Using a whisk, beat the egg yolks and sugar until they are light yellow, then mix in a little of the hot cream. Pour the mixture back into the pan and bring everything to a boil while stirring constantly. Pour through a pointed sieve.

2. Place a layer of wild strawberries in the dessert bowls and hold them in place with some of the crème. Refrigerate the bowls. Also refrigerate the remaining crème, then fill the bowls completely. Refrigerate for 2 to 3 hours.

Brûlée

3. Take the dessert bowls out of the refrigerator, sprinkle on a generous layer of brown sugar and glaze under a hot grill without heating the crème.

4. Finally, heat the glaze with a Bunsen burner, so that it becomes smooth and shiny. Alternatively, the dessert can be briefly re-glazed under a hot grill. Place in the refrigerator again until the glaze has reached the desired firmness. Serve very cold.

British

Preparation time: 45 minutes
Cooling time: 12 hours
Difficulty: ★

Serves 4

1 loaf English toast bread (white sandwich
  bread)
1 sheet of gelatin
6¹/₂ tbsp / 100 ml sugar syrup
1 cup blackberries

1 cup blueberries
1 cup black currants
1 cup red currants
1 cup raspberries
1 cup strawberries
1 cup cranberries
1 tsp sugar

For the raspberry sauce:
1 lb / 500 g raspberries
¹/₂ cup / 125 g sugar

This British classic made with red fruits is usually prepared in summer. It provides a wealth of vitamins and minerals in the form of berries of all kinds: almost transparent red currants (or alternatively gooseberries, though their color would make the dessert as a whole lighter), nicely dark-colored blackberries, tart cranberries and gleaming purple blueberries, black currants and wild strawberries (which one should not wash before use). Raspberries can also be used; in England a yellow variety is even available.

If possible, the summer pudding should be made with English white bread, which has a slightly "rubbery" consistency that makes it particularly well-suited to soaking up the juices of the fruit mixture. This bread has a very soft dough and almost no crust. British people eat vast quantities of it, which has unfortunately done nothing to prevent the gradual disappearance of traditional bakeries in England (there are less than a thousand). To line the pudding mold, the bread should be cut in medium-sized slices.

The majority of the berries used in this pudding are quite sensitive, and therefore require very careful handling. The fruits should never be bruised. The different kinds of berries should be combined to produce a balanced blend of their varying flavors. They should be served as cold as possible, with a little whipped cream.

1. Line the pudding mold with cut slices of white bread. Soak the gelatin in cold water, prepare the syrup and then add it to the gelatin.

2. Remove the stems from the fruit and then blanch them together. While still warm, drain the berries in a sieve and sugar them. Add the liquid that drains away to the syrup. Stir carefully into the fruit. Allow the fruit to drain again and pour the resulting syrup through a pointed sieve.

Summer Pudding

3. Fill the bread-lined pudding mold with the berries. Fill carefully, so that as much fruit as possible can be fitted in. Finish by placing a slice of bread on top.

4. Carefully pour the fruit syrup between the inside of the mold and the bread. Soak the top slice of bread with the syrup. Allow to set in the refrigerator overnight. Remove from the mold and decorate with raspberry sauce and summer fruits.

Cassata alla

Preparation time: 2 hours
Cooling time: 12 hours
Difficulty: ★★

Serves 4

For the Pan di Spagna sponge cake (see basic recipes):
4 eggs
$^1/_2$ cups / 125 g sugar
1 cup / 125 g flour

For the ice cream:
$^3/_4$ cup / 180 g sugar
6 egg yolks

1 vanilla bean
2 cups / 500 ml milk
grated peel of 1 untreated lemon

For the cream:
2 egg whites
$^1/_2$ cup / 75 g sugar
4 tbsp candied fruit, soaked in rum
$3^1/_2$ tbsp / 50 ml crème fraîche

For the sauce:
strawberries or similar fruit

To garnish:
seasonal red fruits

On the island of Sicily, a true paradise for gourmets, almost all the fruits one can imagine are grown. Many are preserved by being candied, and thus available for use in refined dishes year-round. It is equally well known that the Sicilians have an exceptional talent for making cakes and desserts, and are internationally admired for specialties such as exquisite cheese-filled cannoli pastries and, of course, the frequently imitated cassata. Cassata has a permanent place on Carlo Brovelli's menus, and the chef has been praised by many a Sicilian who visited him on the mainland and appreciated his consciousness of tradition.

The quantity and variety of crunchy, colorful fruit that make this dessert so special are considered to be a sign of respect for the guests. A cassata is a vital part of any festive occasion or banquet in Sicily.

The preparation of a genuine cassata requires a great deal of time and experience, so the instructions should be followed step by step. Begin your preparations a day in advance, for the ice cream needs to be very firm before the remaining steps are taken to complete the cassatas.

The finished dessert is chilled overnight so that it achieves the required firm consistency.

The name of the sponge cake, *Pan di Spagna* (It. Spanish bread), may be surprising. Actually, numerous Italian desserts are originally derived from bread (pane), and these terms have been retained up to the present day out of respect for the country's traditional cuisine. This is also true of the "Pan di Natale," or Christmas bread, which is traditionally made and served at Christmas.

1. Make the Pan di Spagna sponge cake. Line small hemispherical forms with aluminum foil, then line each mold with a 1 in / 2 cm layer of sponge cake.

2. Mix all the ingredients for the ice cream and prepare in an ice cream machine. Spread a layer of vanilla ice cream onto the sponge cake layer lining the molds and freeze.

Siciliana

3. Beat the egg whites and sugar with a whisk until stiff. Add the rum-soaked candied fruits. Stir the crème fraîche until smooth. Combine both mixtures in one bowl and mix with a spatula for about 10 minutes until it becomes a homogeneous cream.

4. Completely fill the individual molds with the cream and smooth with a knife. Allow to set overnight in the freezer. Turn each mold out onto a plate, garnish with some red fruits and serve with a strawberry sauce made of strained strawberries.

Preparation time: 45 minutes
Cooking time: 45 minutes
Difficulty: ✳

Serves 4

For the apple compote:
2 lb 3 oz / 1 kg apples (e.g. Golden Delicious)
3/4 cup / 200 ml white wine
3/4 cup plus 1 tbsp / 200 g sugar
grated peel of 1/2 untreated lemon

For the short pastry:
2 cups / 250 g flour, sifted
1 tbsp water
6 1/2 tbsp / 100 g butter
1 egg
4 1/2 tbsp / 70 g sugar
1 pinch of salt

Optional:
custard (see basic recipes)

This apple cake would certainly have provided any *giovanotto* (It. "young rascal") with a moment of pleasure on his way to school. It used to be made as large as a pizza and cut into individual portions. Although the cake is now served in restaurants in individual-size portions, it is just as crunchy and tasty as ever. It can be served with a ball of ice cream or a custard sauce.

Our chef prefers to use a type of apple grown in Lombardy that is not well known elsewhere. This is unfortunate, as it is both very sweet and remains firm when cooked. If you cannot go to Lombardy, you can make do with Golden Delicious apples, which are universally available. They should not be too green, however, as too much acidity would detract from the flavor of the cake. After cooking the apples should be tender, sweet, but still firm.

The lattice decoration made with strips of dough on top of the apple filling is a little reminiscent of the *Linzertorte* widely available in Austria. The strips can be arranged any way one likes.

These tarts are particularly delightful when enjoyed over an afternoon cup of coffee with friends, a wonderful European tradition. They can also be served with tea, cappuccino or a fruity muscatel. Other fruit, such as pears, are equally suitable for use as a filling.

1. Peel, core and cut the apples into eight pieces, then cover them with water, and bring them to a boil over moderate heat. Add the white wine, sugar and lemon peel. Cook for about 15 minutes.

2. Make a short pastry using the flour, water, butter, egg, sugar and salt. Refrigerate for 1 hour, then roll it out evenly and use it to line the molds.

Tarts

3. Fill the molds with the apple compote.

4. Cover each tart with a lattice of pastry strips cut with a serrated pastry cutter and bake at 355 °F / 180 °C for 30 minutes. Dust with confectioners' sugar. Serve with custard or whipped cream.

Shortbread with Oranges

Preparation time: 2 hours
Cooking time: 10 minutes
Difficulty: ★★

Serves 4

10 oranges

For the shortbread (see basic recipes):
1¼ cups / 150 g flour
½ cup / 120 g butter
1 egg yolk
½ cup / 60 g chopped almonds
6 tbsp / 60 g confectioners' sugar

For the Grand Marnier cream:
10 tbsp pastry cream (see basic recipes)
3 tbsp cream, whipped and flavored with vanilla
1 cup / 250 ml Grand Marnier

For the chocolate sauce:
9 oz / 250 g bittersweet chocolate coating

To garnish:
cream
chopped pistachios

Can one ever tire of singing the praises of the orange? This citrus fruit, full of vitamin C and available all year round, is an inexhaustible source of energy. Ripe, firm fruits that are heavy in the hand are best to use, and keep in mind their one shortcoming: they do not retain their freshness long.

In Belgium there are many traditional uses for oranges. One example is the pre-Lenten festival in Binche, in the Hennegau province, where paraders called *gilles* march along the streets in jester costumes and hats decorated with gigantic ostrich feathers, bombarding the public with oranges.

For this particular recipe, it is best to use very juicy oranges and allow them to drain for several hours before use.

The whipped vanilla cream is prepared using vanilla sugar or, better yet, vanilla extract, though this could cause the cream to collapse. One must make the addition very carefully. The pastry cream keeps quite well; it need only be refrigerated and covered with plastic wrap to keep out the air. The dessert should be assembled just before serving, as the sandcakes would otherwise become saturated with orange juice.

1. Take the dough, prepared the previous day, and roll it out to a thickness of ¼ in / 0.5 cm. Cut out circular pieces with a diameter of 3½ in / 8cm, allowing 2 pieces per serving. Place on a greased baking tray sprinkled with sugar. Bake for 5 to 6 minutes at 440° / 225 °C. Keep at room temperature.

2. To make the Grand Marnier cream, start with the pastry cream (see basic recipes). Beat the whipping cream until stiff and fold into the cooled pastry cream. Finally, add the Grand Marnier.

3. Peel the oranges, cut into segments and allow to drain in a sieve. Melt the chocolate in a double boiler. When it is nicely smooth, poor onto the deep plates, wait a few moments and then decorate with a little lightly beaten cream.

4. To assemble the dessert: place a spoonful of the Grand Marnier cream on the center of one circle of shortbread and arrange orange pieces in a circle around the edge. Then place another circle of shortbread, dusted with confectioners' sugar and sprinkled with chopped pistachios, on top. Place on the plate with the chocolate sauce.

Normandy

Preparation time: 45 minutes
Cooking time: 18 minutes
Difficulty: ★★

Serves 4

4 apples (Rennets and Granny Smiths)
3¹/₂ tbsp / 50 g butter
3¹/₂ tbsp / 50 g sugar

Puff pastry (see basic recipes):
4 squares measuring 3 × 3 in / 6 × 6 cm

Apple sorbet (see basic recipes):
1 cup / 250 ml

For the pastry cream (see basic recipes):
3¹/₂ tbsp / 50 ml kirsch
4 tbsp cream, whipped and sweetened

For the apple sauce:
several apples
6¹/₂ tbsp / 100 g sugar
juice of 1 lemon

2 tbsp / 20 g almonds, roasted

Our chef considers this hot and cold dessert the quintessence of his commitment to the preservation of the traditional dishes and produce of Normandy. The apples of Pays d'Auge, the region where the best Calvados is made, are legendary, both the varieties that no longer exist and those that are still cultivated. Michel Bruneau singles out Napoleon apples, which are just the size of a cherry, as those he considers the very best.

In this varied dessert, however, other sorts of apples are used. It is best to use a mixture of apples, such as the tart Granny Smiths which give taste and color to the sorbet, and sweeter Rennets for the sauce. It is precisely this interplay of flavors that make this dessert an unforgettable delight.

Entirely in keeping with Norman tradition, the cream filling is made with dairy cream. Combined with the aroma of cherries,

it enriches the entire composition. To make the sorbet, cut the apples into thin slices, place them in the freezer the previous day in order to make the flesh firmer, and then pour very hot syrup over them before placing them in the ice cream machine.

One should be particularly careful when cooking apples that have been cut lengthwise: while the exterior becomes shiny and caramelized in the butter and sugar, the interior should still be crisp and hot.

The finished dessert can also be decorated with caramel lattice made using brown sugar, or, if desired, one can pour some cider or pommeau – a mixture of Calvados and new cider – over it.

1. Prepare the puff pastry, pastry cream and apple sorbet according to the basic recipes. Bake the puff pastry in the oven for 12 minutes. Meanwhile, peel the apples and cut into lengthwise pieces (6 to 8 pieces per person).

2. Cook the apple segments with the butter and sugar in a frying pan for 4 to 5 minutes, or until golden brown. In a mixing bowl, flavor the pastry cream with kirsch and blend in the sweetened whipped cream.

Delight

3. Remove the pieces of puff pastry from the oven and, while they are still warm, fill them with the cream and top with several cooked apple segments. For the apple sauce, place apples in a juicer, then bring the juice to a boil with the sugar and reduce to the desired consistency. Allow to cool, then stir in the lemon juice.

4. Arrange the puff pastry pieces with the apple sorbet on the plates. Scatter the roasted almonds on top, decorate with the apple sauce, and if desired garnish with a perfect strawberry.

Symphony of Tomatoes

Preparation time: 30 minutes
Cooking time: 4 minutes
Difficulty: ★

Serves 4

2 cups / 500 ml mineral water
2 cups / 500 g brown sugar
4 round tomatoes

4 cups raspberries
royal icing (see glossary)
12 mint leaves
pink peppercorns
fresh basil

This dessert is reminiscent of stuffed Provençal tomatoes. Our chef was inspired to create this unusual dessert by his Parisian colleague Alain Passard, and by the fact that the tomato is, after all, a fruit and can be equally enjoyable when served sweet.

It would be ideal to prepare this recipe using two different varieties of raspberries: firm, tasty fruits for the filling and ripe, soft fruits for the sauce. The final choice is up to the individual, however, and one could also use wild strawberries.

The tomatoes should be very round and firm enough to withstand cooking. Fruits with irregular shapes would not be suitable for this dessert. The stems should definitely not be removed, as the tomatoes are opened at the side to remove the seeds. The stem holds the fruits together, so they can survive the cooking process unscathed.

The flavorings also play an important role in this recipe: glazed mint, basil and pink pepper each make their unique contributions to the perfect interplay of the various flavors.

1. Blanch, skin, and carefully hollow out the tomatoes. Make a syrup using the mineral water and brown sugar.

2. Glaze the tomatoes for 2 minutes in half of the syrup. Use 2 cups of raspberries and the remaining syrup to make a sauce.

and Raspberries

3. To make the icing, thoroughly mix the confectioners' sugar and egg white in a bowl, adding the lemon juice at the end.

4. Fill the tomatoes with the remaining raspberries. Pluck off 8 sprigs of mint and add to the syrup with the pink peppercorns and basil. Glaze the tomatoes for another 2 minutes, spooning the syrup over them a few times. Place the tomatoes on the cold raspberry sauce and garnish the dessert with mint and icing.

Crème Brûlée with Gentian

Preparation time:	20 minutes
Cooking time:	1 hour
Difficulty:	★★

Serves 4

8 egg yolks
3/4 cup / 150 g brown sugar
1 pinch of salt
2 tbsp vanilla extract
4 cups / 1 l cream

6 1/2 tbsp / 100 ml Suze (gentian liqueur)
8 pink grapefruit
sprigs of mint

One has to be very fond of the bitter taste of gentian to mix such generous quantities of it into a creamy dessert. That is certainly true of Alain Burnel, who confesses to a certain predilection for the inimitable Suze and the gentian (*gentiana lutea*), or great yellow gentian, a pretty plant that grows in southern Europe. Although the recipe for Suze is a secret, it is rumored that the root of the plant is pickled in alcohol, and this liquid is distilled twice. Our chef recommends preparing the crème on the previous day but leaving the final glazing until shortly before the dessert is served, as this gives the crème its character. The overnight rest also intensifies the créme's flavor and allows its various elements to combine more thoroughly. The addition of brown sugar produces a nice amber color.

The attractive crowning with pink grapefruit segments calls for a few words about this fruit, which is being used by pastry chefs more and more often.

No matter what the variety (and new varieties are constantly being created), whether a grapefruit or a pomelo, it contains lots of vitamin C and calcium. Ripe fruits should be firm and heavy in the hand. They are usually very juicy, and separate into distinct segments with a whitish skin that should be peeled off for aesthetic reasons. The pink grapefruit, with its pastel color, is particularly well-suited to garnishing and decorating desserts. Before placing the fruit segments on the crème brûlée, one should blot off the excess juice with a paper towel.

1. In a mixing bowl, beat the egg yolks with one-third of the sugar, the salt and vanilla extract until foamy.

2. Bring the cream to a boil in a small saucepan. Pour it onto the egg mixture. Combine well in order to produce a smooth liquid. Pour through a pointed sieve.

Liqueur and Grapefruit

3. Add the gentian liqueur to the crème. Spoon off the foam and discard and pour the crème into four ovenproof dishes. Bake in the oven at 190 °F / 90 °C for 1 hour.

4. Allow to cool, sprinkle on the remaining brown sugar and glaze in the oven or under a hot grill. Arrange the skinned grapefruit segments on the crème and garnish with fresh mint leaves.

Tarte Tatin with Figs

Preparation time: 45 minutes
Cooking time: 15 minutes
Difficulty: ★

Serves 4

6 lb 9 oz / 3 kg fresh figs
6 tbsp acacia honey
1 tbsp pectin
14 oz / 400 g puff pastry
juice of 1 lime
6¹/₂ tbsp / 100 g butter

For the syrup at 30 °Beaumé:
4 cups / 1 kg sugar
4 cups / 1 l water

To garnish:
roasted almonds
red currants

It is not entirely clear whether the Mesdemoiselles Tatin, who were born in the small French town of Neung-sur-Beuvron, invented this small, inverted, intensely sweet cake themselves, or simply brought it home with them from a trip to Provence. If possible, the Tatin should be served lukewarm. Though it is traditionally made with apples, it is certainly no crime to replace the "holy apple" with figs, as they are also highly regarded by gastronomes throughout the world. Indeed, the Hanging Gardens of Babylon, one of the Seven Wonders of the Ancient World, is said to have been mainly populated with fig trees.

It would, of course, be ideal to pluck the figs straight from the tree. They are increasingly available even far from their indigenous areas; in northern Europe one can usually get lovely dark figs with a very red, tasty flesh in the markets. Ripe figs are easy to peel and caramelize with honey. If the figs are very fresh, according to our chef, they should be caramelized the previous evening, placed in the molds and then refrigerated, so that the cake can be completed with the puff pastry at the last minute.

The aroma and color of the acacia honey blends exceptionally well with figs. Alain Burnel favors honey produced in Provence, for he finds it to have a richer taste and a truly astonishing transparency. Rivers of honey with nectar and ambrosia are said to have flown at the banquets of the Olympian Gods. Those lucky enough to be served this lukewarm dessert with vanilla ice cream will surely feel that they have been transported to that very place.

1. Carefully peel the figs. Caramelize half of the honey in a saucepan, then add the figs and pectin, making sure the figs are coated on all sides with the caramelized honey.

2. Place the cooled figs in ovenproof molds. Make sure that the bottom of the dish is completely covered. Cover with a layer of sliced figs.

and Acacia Honey

3. After filling all the molds, cover each with a thin layer of puff pastry and bake for a few minutes in the oven.

4. Pour the remaining honey into a pan, bring to a boil and deglaze with the lime juice. Add the sugar syrup and beat with the butter. Invert the individual cakes onto the center of the plates and glaze with the honey butter. Decorate with a finely sliced fig, and with lukewarm roasted almonds or red currants.

Meringue Tarts

Preparation time: 30 minutes
Cooking time: 1 hour 30 minutes
Difficulty: ★★

Serves 4

9 oz / 250 g blackberries
1 lb / 500 g raspberries
¹/₄ cup / 40 g confectioners' sugar
1 lb / 500 g small, ripe strawberries
2 cups / 500 ml cream, whipped
³/₄ cup / 200 ml raspberry sauce

For the meringue tarts:
5 egg whites
³/₄ cup / 125 g confectioners' sugar
¹/₂ cup / 125 g superfine sugar

For the glaze:
¹/₃ cup / 125 g apricot jelly

To garnish:
red currants or blueberries
sprigs of mint

During the summer, you should allow yourself to be carried away by the variety and splendid colors of red berries: they lend themselves to conjuring up all sorts of enchanting jellies, desserts, and sorbets. However you prepare the fruits, the same basic rule applies: use only completely ripe fruit without any spoiled or bruised spots.

Strawberries should be picked shining red complete with their stems, so that the flesh remains fresh and undamaged. Blackberries have a lovely dark, even color and plump, juicy berries; the same is true of the light red raspberries. Berries, which are very rich in vitamins, are quite sensitive and do not store well; they need to be eaten very soon after being bought. Ideally, they should not be washed, since this causes them to lose much of their flavor.

The base of our tart is made of light whipped egg whites and sugar. It is vital that the bowl in which the egg whites are whipped is absolutely dry and free of fat. A metal bowl is most suitable. Jan Buytaert recommends rinsing the bowl with a solution of vinegar and salt, rinsing it again with clear water and then drying it with a clean dishcloth. The tarts need to be baked a long time at a very low temperature, and afterwards are best stored in a cool, dry place. If you follow these guidelines, you will be able to make the tarts on the previous day.

Perhaps the glorious colors of this dessert will remind you of those sumptuous banquets with lively guests and lavishly laid tables immortalized in the paintings of Flemish artists such as Rubens.

1. For the tarts, whip the egg whites with a pinch of confectioners' sugar until stiff. Mix the remaining confectioners' sugar with the superfine sugar, add to the whipped egg whites and stir for a few seconds. Using a pastry bag, pipe spirals of the meringue mixture onto a greased and floured baking sheet to form 4¹/₂ in / 10 cm circles.

2. Bake the meringue tarts for 90 minutes at 190 °F / 90 °C. Allow to cool. Pipe a mound of whipped cream onto the center of each meringue tart.

with Berries

3. To make the fruit sauce, press some of the raspberries through a sieve and mix in ¼ cup / 40 g confectioners' sugar. Arrange a dome of strawberries, blackberries and raspberries, over the whipped cream. Place red currants or blueberries on top.

4. Glaze the fruits with warmed apricot jelly. Garnish with a sprig of mint. Place on dessert plates and pour raspberry sauce around the tarts.

Preparation time: 35 minutes
Cooking time: 45 minutes
Difficulty: ★★

Serves 4

For the short pastry:
3¹/₂ tbsp / 50 g butter
2¹/₂ tbsp / 25 g confectioners' sugar
1 small egg
³/₄ cup plus 1 tbsp / 100 g flour
a pinch / 1 g dried yeast

For the chocolate filling:
³/₄ cup / 175 ml heavy cream
5¹/₄ oz / 150 g chocolate
1 egg
2 egg yolks

For the almond cookie:
4 tsp / 20 g butter
¹/₄ cup / 40 g confectioners' sugar
4 tsp / 20 ml orange juice
1 tbsp / 10 g flour
¹/₃ cup / 40 g almonds, roasted and chopped

The excellence of this dessert depends on the quality and cocoa content of the chocolate used. For chef Jacques Cagna, chocolate with a cocoa content of less than 70% does not come into question. Excellent good producers of chocolate include, for example, the Caribbean and Venezuela, which is not only known for exporting oil but also produces the very best cocoa – the rare and expensive criollo.

However, one must be aware that chocolate with more than 70% cocoa has a bitter flavor, which could destroy the balance of the dessert. It is equally important to make sure that the short pastry does not become too tough and compact. It should be kneaded using the tips of the fingers only, like a masseur. If desired, the short pastry and the dough for the almond cookies can be made beforehand and keep overnight in the refrigerator. However, the preparation of the chocolate filling should be left until the last minute.

The orange juice gives the almond cookies a pleasant flavor. The combination of chocolate and orange has tempted gourmets for generations. Though the quantity is small, it is best to use fresh-squeezed orange juice, and be aware that contact with air causes vitamins to be lost.

Served lukewarm, these tarts are the perfect opportunity to pay one's respects to Hernan Cortés, who is attributed with bringing cocoa to Europe from Mexico in 1519.

1. To make the short pastry, mix the butter and sugar, add the egg, and finally the flour and dried yeast. Allow to rest for 1 hour.

2. Roll out the pastry very thinly and use to line individual baking forms with a diameter of 4¹/₂ in / 10 cm and a height of 1 in / 2 cm. Fill with baking beans and bake blind for 10 minutes at 320 °F / 160 °C.

Tart

3. To make the chocolate filling, melt the heavy cream and chocolate, remove from the heat and then stir in the egg yolks and egg. Fill the pastry shells with the mixture. Bake until firm at 300 °F / 150 °C, then reduce the heat to 250 °F / 120 °C and bake for another 15 minutes.

4. To make the almond cookies, combine the confectioners' sugar, flour and almonds with the orange juice, and then add the melted butter. Spoon small quantities of the mixture onto baking paper and bake at 390 °F / 200 °C. Place one chocolate tart on each plate and garnish with an almond cookie.

Crunchy Pastries with Sweet

Preparation time: 50 minutes
Cooking time: 10 minutes
Difficulty: ★★★

Serves 4

8 candied sweet chestnuts
8 sweet chestnuts in syrup
2 tsp / 10 g butter
4 slices of phyllo pastry

For the pastry cream:
$^1/_2$ cup / 125 ml whole milk
$^1/_2$ vanilla bean
2 egg yolks
3 tbsp / 40 g sugar
$4^1/_2$ tsp / 12 g flour

For the almond cream:
$3^1/_2$ tbsp / 50 g butter
$^1/_3$ cup / 50 g confectioners' sugar
$^1/_2$ cup / 50 g ground almonds
1 egg

For the chocolate sauce:
$^1/_4$ cup / 25 g cocoa powder
2 oz / 60 g chocolate
1 tbsp whole milk
$4^1/_2$ tbsp / 70 ml water
1 pinch of salt
2 tbsp / 30 g butter
1 tbsp / 15 g sugar
2 tsp / 15 g dextrose
4 tsp / 20 ml Grand Marnier

What could be more delightful in winter than an exceptional dessert made of chocolate and sweet chestnuts?

That, at any rate, is the opinion of Jacques Cagna, who is particularly concerned with reflecting the rhythm of the seasons in cooking, and works only with absolutely fresh ingredients. But chestnuts and chocolate also go exceptionally well together from an aesthetic point of view: the harmonious combination of the various shades of brown on the plate is a pleasure for the eye even before the tastebuds have started to enjoy this noble combination.

It is important to Jacques Cagna to know where the fresh sweet chestnuts come from. He prefers to gather them in Piedmont, beneath the famous vineyards of Asti, in the province in northeastern Italy that was the site of vehement clashes between the French and Italians toward the end of the 15th century. Also noteworthy are the first-class sweet chestnuts from Corsica as well as those from the French regions of Var and Ardèche, whose names sound as sweet as the names of chestnut varieties such as Comballe and Marigoule (the latter is renowned for its marvelous mahogany color).

In France, however, the majority of candied sweet chestnuts are imported from Spain. The means by which chestnuts are conserved continues to be a tricky matter. Each fruit should be examined individually before it is used.

The chocolate sauce tastes particularly rich when made with Caribbean chocolate, with its typically high cocoa content. A dash of Grand Marnier gives the sauce that special touch.

1. To make the pastry cream, bring the milk to a boil with the vanilla bean. Beat the egg yolks and sugar together until the mixture becomes light; add the flour, stir in the hot milk and bring everything to a boil. Let cool. To make the almond cream, whisk the softened butter and confectioners' sugar, add the ground almonds and egg, and finally stir in $3^1/_2$ oz / 100 g of the pastry cream.

2. Line individual forms with a diameter of $2^3/_4$ in / 6 cm, with a sheet of phyllo pastry. The pastry should generously overlap the edges of the form.

Chestnuts from Piedmont

3. Place a spoonful of almond cream and two of the syrup-soaked sweet chestnuts into each form, then top with some pastry cream. To make the chocolate sauce, mix all the ingredients except the butter, bring to a boil and then stir in the butter.

4. Close the prepared pastries with the overlapping phyllo pastry to form pouches. Place in a preheated 390 °F / 200 °C oven, then reduce the temperature to 300 °F / 150 °C and bake for 5 minutes. Pour a little chocolate sauce onto each plate and arrange a pastry and two candied sweet chestnuts on it.

Cake with Heather Honey

Preparation time: 2 hours
Cooking time: 40 minutes
Difficulty: ★★★

Serves 4

9 oz / 250 g white chocolate
30 each: raspberries, blackberries, blueberries
  or red currants

For the orange sponge cake:
1½ untreated oranges
apricot jam
8 egg whites; 9 egg yolks
¾ cup / 175 g sugar
1 cup / 125 g flour
7 tbsp / 50 g cornstarch

For the fruit basket dough:
¾ cup plus 1 tbsp / 200 g sugar
7 tbsp / 50 g flour
⅓ cup / 75 ml orange juice

5 tbsp / 75 g butter
3 tbsp / 25 g almonds, blanched and chopped
9 tbsp / 75 g flaked almonds

For the honey mousse:
5 tsp / 25 ml brandy (cognac)
3½ tbsp / 50 ml white wine
5 tbsp / 125 g heather honey
1½ cups / 350 ml cream
3 egg yolks, beaten
2 egg whites
3½ sheets of gelatin

For the blackberry sauce:
juice of 30 blackberries (⅔ cup / 150 ml)
juice of 1 lemon
⅓ cup / 50 g confectioners' sugar

The many different types of heather do not grow exclusively in Scotland, but they do thrive particularly well in its barren countryside. Heather is used to feed livestock and its pink and violet flowers are visited by bees. Heather honey is produced in Scotland, and Stewart Cameron, who is keen to introduce the specialties of his native land, recommends it for this lavish cake.

Since ancient times honey has been given all sorts of symbolic meanings, and has been used to produce diverse foodstuffs and drinks. Nowadays, honey is used to make lebkuchen, brittle, pralines and many other things, but also in many spicy Asian recipes, where the combination of meat and honey is a classic. Honey is thought to bring good fortune and prosperity, as in "the land of milk and honey."

As far as the recipe at hand, its complexity requires a degree of organization: it is recommended to prepare the sponge cake and fruit baskets a day in advance, so that one can concentrate on the honey and brandy mousse on the day of serving.

As always, choose the best quality oranges possible for the sponge cake and a flavorful apricot jam to spread on it after baking.

1. For the sponge cake, beat the egg yolks and 5 tbsp / 75 g sugar until foamy. Use the egg whites and remaining sugar to make a meringue. Add the juice and zest of the oranges to the egg yolks. Then blend a quarter of the meringue into the egg yolk mixture, followed by the flour, cornstarch and finally the rest of the meringue. Bake for 10 to 12 minutes at 355 °F / 180 °C.

2. Line the molds with the orange sponge cake, which has been layered with apricot jam. To make the dough for the fruit baskets, mix the sugar and flour, add the orange juice, flaked almonds, chopped almonds and melted butter, and combine thoroughly. Allow to rest for 2 hours. Form small balls, and bake them for 8 to 10 minutes at 390 °F / 200 °C. Using brioche forms, shape into little baskets.

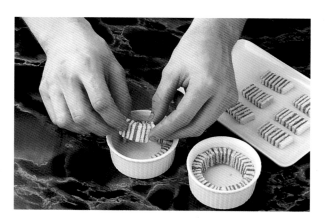

and Brandy Mousse

3. For the mousse, bring the wine and 1 tbsp / 25 g honey to a boil, pour onto the beaten egg yolks and prepare like a custard (see basic recipes). Add the soaked gelatin and allow to cool. To prepare the meringue, bring 4 tbsp / 100 g honey to a boil and pour onto the beaten egg whites. Whip the cream until stiff and add the brandy. Gently combine the cooled cream, whipped cream, and meringue.

4. To make the sauce, press the blackberries through a sieve and bring the juice to a boil with the lemon juice and confectioners' sugar. Reduce to the desired consistency and strain through a pointed sieve. Fill the orange sponge cakes with mousse and place on the center of each plate; garnish with grated white chocolate. Add three fruit baskets filled with red berries. Serve with blackberry sauce.

Chocolate Teardrops

Preparation time: 2 hours
Cooking time: 15 minutes
Cooling time: 3 hours
Difficulty: ★★★

Serves 4

For the chocolate teardrops:
9 oz / 250 g bittersweet chocolate coating

For the pear mousse:
4 sheets of gelatin
6$^1/_2$ tbsp / 100 g sugar
1 cup / 250 ml cream, whipped
9 oz / 250 g pear puree
3$^1/_2$ tbsp / 50 ml pear schnapps

For the caramel sauce:
$^1/_2$ cup / 125 g sugar
2 tbsp / 30 g butter
1 cup / 250 ml cream
$^1/_2$ cup / 125 ml milk
1 tsp vanilla sugar
5 egg yolks
3$^1/_2$ tbsp / 50 ml caramel

For the pear glaze:
6$^1/_2$ tbsp / 100 ml pear juice
3$^1/_2$ tbsp / 50 g sugar
1$^1/_2$ sheets of gelatin

To garnish:
chopped pistachios

These tears are little more than crocodile tears, for there is certainly no reason to cry where such a dessert is concerned! Chocolate, caramel sauce, and pear mousse – elegantly presented so as to be a treat for the eyes as well as the tastebuds.

Pears appear in three different forms in this composition: as a puree, a fruit schnapps for the mousse and a juice for the pear glaze. This is a lovely way of using this fruit, whose praises were sung by Homer and Virgil and of which several thousand varieties now exist. This multitude need not be confusing, for the pears most widely available are perfectly suitable for this recipe. Pear schnapps is produced by fermenting fresh fruit in a sealed container.

Not everyone can prepare chocolate teardrops on their first attempt: they require a little skill, if only to be able to recog-

nize the optimal consistency of melted chocolate needed to form the teardrops. However, with a little practice and perseverance, one can succeed.

It is best to use strips of plastic to shape the teardrops as depicted in the first picture below, and they should then be allowed to set in the refrigerator for several hours. When you are ready to continue, remove the plastic, and if necessary smoothen and straighten the teardrops a bit. Of course, the chocolate used must match the pears in quality, in other words only the finest. It is easier to produce teardrops with high quality chocolate, and the taste makes its own contribution to the effect of the dessert.

1. To make the chocolate teardrops, melt the chocolate coating in a double boiler. Apply a thin layer of chocolate to three plastic strips of different lengths and form teardrop shapes. Allow to set in the refrigerator.

2. For the pear mousse, soak the gelatin in cold water. Mix the sugar and pear puree; bring to a boil until the sugar melts. Add the gelatin and simmer until the mixture is the color of caramel. Allow to cool, then blend in the whipped cream and pear schnapps. Refrigerate the mousse for three hours.

with Pear Mousse

3. To make the sauce, melt the sugar over medium heat, then carefully add half of the cream and the butter. Bring to a boil and simmer until caramel-colored. In another pan bring the remaining cream, milk, and vanilla sugar to a boil. Beat the egg yolks with a little sugar and stir into the mixture. Prepare like a custard (see basic recipes) and pass through a pointed sieve. Add the caramel.

4. Prepare the pear glaze by bringing the sugar and pear juice to a boil, adding the previously soaked gelatin and passing the mixture through a pointed sieve. Fill the teardrops with pear mousse and use a pastry brush to coat them with glaze. Arrange the tears on a plate, pour some caramel sauce next to them and garnish with chopped pistachios.

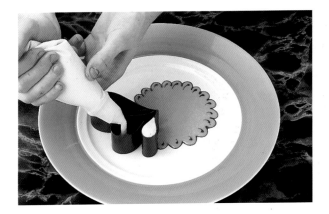

Cassata

Preparation time: 1 hour
Cooling time: 5 hours
Difficulty: ★

Serves 4

10¹⁄₂ oz / 300 g ricotta cheese
1¹⁄₄ cups / 300 g sugar
2¹⁄₂ tbsp / 30 g candied fruits, diced
1 oz / 30 g chocolate coating
a little butter

5 tbsp / 50 g crushed hazelnuts
6¹⁄₂ tbsp / 100 ml crème fraîche
10¹⁄₂ oz / 300 g mixed berries

The Italians have a vast array of delicious dessert recipes at their disposal. Cooks in the north of the country have created a wide range of varieties of *budino* (custards), *cassola* (pancakes), *crostata* (pastries), *fritelli* (fried cakes), *pinocatte* (tarts) and *timbalo* (puddings). Desserts and cakes from Sicily, Sardinia and southern Italy have long enjoyed a good reputation, both in Italy and far beyond its borders throughout Europe.

In the Romagna region in northern Italy, the ricotta cake is very popular. The basis for this crunchy, tasty cassata is a fresh sheep's milk cheese called ricotta. Nowadays, cassatas are usually made in cone-shaped or other small forms. If it is prepared in the traditional loaf shape, however, the dessert is cut into individual portions for serving.

The choice of candied fruits, which are visible on the surface of the finished cassata, is left to you. It is important that they are diced into pieces of just the right size: neither tiny pieces nor chunks of fruit belong in a cassata. One should still be able to recognize the firm texture of the fruit, as it and the grated chocolate create a contrast to the soft ricotta mixture; however, the diced fruit pieces should not conceal the flavor of the other ingredients. For the same reason, the grated chocolate and the nuts, which should not be over-caramelized, are added toward the end. In fact, the trick in producing this composition is to retain a careful balance between the ingredients. You could also use some lemon to flavor the dish, as is customary in Sicily, which lends the dessert a very special taste.

1. In a bowl, combine the ricotta with two-thirds of the sugar, then carefully fold in the diced candied fruits.

2. Using a knife, chop the chocolate coating into very fine pieces. Melt some butter in a pan with the remaining sugar. Caramelize the hazelnuts, which have previously been crushed with a pestle and mortar, in the butter and sugar. Stir the crème fraîche until smooth, then fold it into the ricotta mixture along with the grated chocolate and caramelized nuts. Mix well.

all'Italiana

3. Pour the mixture into individual forms and refrigerate for 3 to 4 hours. Meanwhile, puree the berries with the remaining sugar in a blender.

4. Turn the forms out onto dessert plates, and garnish with fruit sauce and some whole berries. Serve with cookies.

Panna Cotta with

Preparation time: 1 hour
Cooking time: 1 hour
Difficulty: ★★

Serves 4

For the panna cotta:
3 whole eggs
2 egg yolks
$^1/_2$ cup / 125 g sugar
2 cups / 500 ml crème fraîche
$1^3/_4$ cups / 50 g amaretti biscuits (almond macaroons)

For the caramel:
$^1/_2$ cup plus 2 tbsp / 150 g sugar
1 cup / 250 ml water

For the cake dough:
$^2/_3$ cup / 75 g ground almonds
$^1/_2$ cup plus 2 tbsp / 75 g flour
5 tbsp / 75 g sugar
5 tbsp / 75 g butter
1 pinch of salt

For the zabaglione:
2 tbsp sugar
2 egg yolks
$^3/_4$ cup / 200 ml dry Marsala

To garnish:
vanilla sugar
red fruits
sprigs of mint

Don Pellegrino Artusi, in honor of whom this dessert was invented, was a 19th-century Italian gourmet who collected many traditional recipes. Inspired by Renaissance chefs and the age of the great duchies, his main work, *The Art of Eating Well*, was reprinted 120 times and is still considered the most complete treatment of Italian cuisine. Although Artusi was particularly fond of the Romagna region and Tuscany, he gathered recipes from all over Italy and contributed to making them well known.

Artusi was also the first to prepare zabaglione (wine cream) with Marsala, and suggested using a pure, dry variety of this amazingly light Sicilian dessert wine. Marsala is now produced in a controlled environment, eliminating any unpleasant surprises when drinking it.

Panna cotta is simple to make, as long as one is careful when cooking it. The use of small amaretti biscuits, which are mixed into the cream, provides the almond flavor and macaroon-like consistency. They should be used in preference to gelatin. The difficulty is only to resist the temptation to eat these delicious cookies before adding them to the panna cotta.

In addition, our chef recommends that the almond cake be prepared like a dry sponge cake, which makes it possible to use it as a sort of edible spoon for the zabaglione.

1. To make the panna cotta, whisk the eggs, egg yolks, and sugar, then add the crème fraîche. Mix thoroughly, pass through a sieve and add the crumbled amaretti biscuits.

2. For the caramel, dissolve the sugar in boiling water until it turns brown. Coat the bottom of an ovenproof dish with a little caramel, add the panna cotta cream and bake in the oven for 45 minutes at 265 °F / 130 °C in a water bath. Allow to cool.

Zabaglione à la Artusi

3. Prepare the almond cake by combining all the cake ingredients and roll out the dough to form a ¹/₂ in / 1 cm thick circle. Bake for 10 minutes at approximately 340 °F / 170 °C.

4. To make the zabaglione, mix the sugar into the egg yolks, beat in a double boiler with a whisk and add the Marsala. Place the panna cotta, cut into teardrop shapes, onto plates and cover with the caramel. Arrange wedges of cake dusted with vanilla sugar next to them and pour on some zabaglione. Garnish with fruits and a sprig of mint.

Almond Crackers

Preparation time: 1 hour
Cooking time: 15 minutes
Difficulty: ★★

Serves 4

1 cup / 150 g wild strawberries
1 cup / 150 g raspberries
1/2 cup / 80 g red currants
1/2 cup / 80 g blackberries
4 sprigs of peppermint

For the almond crackers:
5 tbsp / 75 g butter
1/2 cup / 75 g confectioners' sugar
3 egg whites
1/2 cup plus 2 tbsp / 75 g flour
1/4 tsp / 3 g aniseed
1/3 cup / 50 g almonds, colored pink and
   roasted

Pastry cream (see basic recipes):
1 1/4 cups / 300 ml cream, whipped until stiff

This dessert with a touch of aniseed flavor is an ideal combination of crunchy crackers and creamy, smooth pastry cream. The colors of the fruits and their slightly sour taste complete the composition, which should tempt even sophisticated gourmets.

The dough for the crackers is as sensitive as the similarly prepared cigarette batter. One should use the aniseed sparingly so that its flavor does not overpower that of the pastry cream. A baking sheet with a non-stick coating should be used to bake the crackers; placing it in the refrigerator beforehand will help prevent the thin layer of dough from running too quickly. After baking, the crackers have to be bent carefully using a rectangu-

lar strainer. These steps look difficult at first, but really only require some practice.

In our recipe, the classic pastry cream is combined with whipped cream to make it even frothier and lighter. However, the pastry cream must cool a little before the whipped cream is added.

Select your berries according to season and availability: black currants, red currants, blueberries, blackberries, and strawberries are all wonderful choices, either individually or combined.

1. To make the crackers, mix the softened butter with the confectioners' sugar in a bowl. Gradually stir in the egg whites, then the sifted flour and the finely crushed aniseed.

2. Using a spatula, spread flat teardrop shapes of dough onto a non-stick baking sheet. Sprinkle the finely crushed almonds over them. Bake at 320 °F / 160 °C until the crackers are brown.

with Berries

3. Allow the crackers to cool in a rectangular strainer; they should take on irregular bent shapes. Make a pastry cream according to the basic recipe. After it has cooled, carefully fold in the stiffly whipped cream.

4. Using a pastry bag, pipe some cream into each dessert bowl, garnish with the mixed berries and a few peppermint leaves, and then arrange the almond crackers decoratively in it.

Grapefruit and Fig Gratin

Preparation time: *1 hour*
Cooking time: *10 minutes*
Difficulty: **★★**

Serves 4

4 grapefruit
4 figs
4 sprigs of rosemary

For the ice cream with rosemary honey:
1 cup / 250 ml milk
6$^{1}/_{2}$ tbsp / 100 ml cream
4$^{1}/_{2}$ tbsp / 100 g rosemary honey
2 egg yolks

For the almond cream:
4$^{1}/_{2}$ tbsp / 65 g butter
$^{3}/_{4}$ cup / 125 g confectioners' sugar
1 cup / 125 g flaked almonds
1 egg
6$^{1}/_{2}$ tbsp / 100 ml cream, whipped

In this recipe we have a delightful combination of figs, rosemary, grapefruit, and almonds. It is a dish that brings to mind long afternoons spent in idle bliss and the countryside of Provence in France.

Particularly well suited to this dessert are very sweet figs, not too small, that give to the touch and have a firm flesh that can be cut easily to make decorative pieces.

In addition, one needs pink grapefruit with a smooth, firm peel. Their taste provides a delicious contrast to the flavor of the rosemary honey, which is a major ingredient in the ice cream. The honey replaces sugar and makes the ice cream a good deal creamier. The intense, refined taste of rosemary in the honey gives the dessert an unexpectedly interesting note.

So that the presentation is also a feast for the eyes, a thin layer of almond cream is poured onto a plate. One should drain and blot the grapefruit segments with a cloth so that they remain juicy after they are placed under a hot grill.

One could use other citrus fruits instead of grapefruit, such as oranges or mandarins, though these yield smaller fruit segments. Lemons are definitely not suitable, however, as their very intense sourness would destroy the balance of the ingredients.

Finally, the plates are decorated with figs and lavender flowers or rosemary. These decorations are also edible; their crispiness provides a pleasant contrast to the tender gratin.

1. For the ice cream, combine the milk, cream, and honey and bring to a boil. Beat the egg yolks, then pour the hot milk onto them while stirring. Pour into a pan and simmer at a low temperature, stirring continuously, until the mixture has thickened. Pass through a sieve and allow to cool, stirring occasionally. Mix in an ice cream machine and allow to harden.

2. In a bowl, stir the butter until soft, then rapidly mix in first the confectioners' sugar and then the flaked almonds. Add the egg and stir to produce an even mixture. Carefully fold in the stiffly whipped cream.

with Almond Cream

3. Cover flat plates with a thin layer of almond cream. Peel the grapefruit, divide into segments, and drain. Arrange them evenly on the cream and briefly brown under a hot grill.

4. Cut each fig into 5 pieces. Carefully arrange the figs on the grilled almond cream in the shape of a tulip. Place a generous ball of honey ice cream in the center of the fig pieces and top with a sprig of rosemary.

Stripped Strawberries

Preparation time: 30 minutes
Cooking time: 10 minutes
Difficulty: ☆

Serves 4

7 oz / 200 g bittersweet chocolate coating
  (55 % cocoa)
10$\frac{1}{2}$ oz / 300 g quark (20 % fat)
2$\frac{1}{2}$ tbsp / 40 ml Armagnac

$\frac{1}{4}$ cup / 60 g superfine sugar
4 very large strawberries
2 sprigs of mint
9 oz / 250 g medium-sized strawberries
$\frac{1}{2}$ untreated lime
1$\frac{1}{2}$ tbsp / 15 g confectioners' sugar

waxed paper or plastic wrap for spreading the
  chocolate coating

Both the French and Italian names for the strawberry (*fraise*, *fragola*) are derived from the Italian word *fragare*, or "smell." The aroma of strawberries is indeed exquisite, but is only produced by fresh and ripe fruits. Therefore, a conscientious chef uses strawberries only when they are in season, and certainly never makes use of the very poor substitutes that are available year round.

As a proud citizen of Grasse, the town of smells and perfumes, our chef can well withstand the temptation of the market, which tries to entice consumers to buy strawberries for 10 months out of the year. This dessert should really be made only when strawberries are in season locally, and one should choose nice, shining red fruits, such as the Pajaro variety, in which one can positively taste the summer sunshine.

The quark with which they are served should have a perfectly smooth texture. When gently flavored with sugar and Armagnac, its subtle flavor will successfully highlight the taste of the previously sweetened strawberries. This refreshing and yet sweet combination is given extra tang by means of the contrast with the lime, which is even sourer than a lemon.

In a recipe such as this, where the chocolate coating stands alone, it is well worth using high-quality chocolate coating with a high cocoa content (55–70 %). In our recipe, it is prepared in three stages: first, it is carefully melted at 130 °F / 55 °C, then it is cooled to 70 °F / 20 °C, and finally reheated to 85 °F / 31 °C before being poured onto wax paper and spread out thinly.

1. Melt the chocolate coating, let cool and then warm to the correct temperature (see above). Pour onto waxed paper or plastic wrap and spread out thinly with a spatula. Cut out rectangles 3 in / 7 cm wide and 5$\frac{1}{2}$ in / 12 cm long, allowing two pieces per serving.

2. Using a whisk, mix the quark with 3 tbsp / 40 g of sugar and the Armagnac. Hollow out the large strawberries, retaining the stems for garnishing, and fill the berries with quark. Using a sharp tipped knife, cut the mint leaves into very fine strips.

with Chocolate

3. Cut the medium-sized strawberries into small pieces. Using a sharp knife, shave off the lime peel very thinly, chop finely and mix with the remaining sugar. Combine the strawberries and lime peel with the juice of the same lime half.

4. Arrange the dessert on the plates. Spoon a small amount of the quark mixture in the center (4½ in / 10 cm diameter). Place a rectangular piece of chocolate on it, cover with chopped strawberries, and cover with a second piece of chocolate. Place a filled strawberry on each serving and dust everything with confectioners' sugar. Garnish with the mint strips.

Warm Soufflé

Preparation time: 20 minutes
Cooking time: 8 minutes
Difficulty: ✳

Serves 4

3 egg whites
a pinch of salt
3¹/₂ tbsp / 50 g sugar

For the soufflé:
7 tsp / 35 g butter
5 tbsp / 35 g flour
¹/₂ cup plus 3 tbsp / 165 ml milk
3 egg yolks
6¹/₂ tbsp / 100 ml Grand Marnier

The purpose of desserts is to balance out the previous courses. If the preceding meal was a rich one with a lot of flour, one should plan a fresh, light dessert with fruit. On the other hand, after a lighter meal one can serve a more lavish creation, such as this soufflé with Grand Marnier, which will create a great impression. The most difficult aspect of it is surely judging the precise moment at which it has risen perfectly and should be served.

For our chef, the key to a soufflé lies in the preparation of the beaten egg whites. The extent to which the souffle rises during baking depends on their firmness. Another important detail: the flour and butter mixture created at the beginning has to brown slowly over a moderate heat and form a consistency like the skin on heated milk. All these preparations can be made a few hours before the final stages of work.

One must not forget to preheat the oven well in advance of baking the soufflé. If the oven is not hot enough, the soufflé may rise less impressively than it otherwise would.

We have every reason to be grateful to Louis-Alexander Marnier-Lapostolle for producing an elegant and subtle liqueur, very widely used today, using exotic oranges, orange peel, and cognac. As is true of many successful businesses, the secret of the production of Grand Marnier has not been revealed.

1. Separate the eggs. Make a roux by melting the butter, then adding the flour. Cook over low heat until just golden and thin with the milk, then stir in the egg yolks and Grand Marnier.

2. Beat the egg whites until stiff in a copper bowl that is completely clean and dry. Add the salt and sugar.

with Grand Marnier

3. Combine the beaten egg whites with the roux mixture and fold in carefully. Using a spatula, work them in from top to bottom.

4. Grease the soufflé dishes, sprinkle in some sugar, and fill with the mixture. Bake for 8 minutes in an oven preheated to 480 °F / 250 °C. Once the soufflé has risen, serve immediately.

Citrus Fruit Terrine with

Preparation time: 45 minutes
Cooking time: 15 minutes
Cooling time: 2 hours
Difficulty: ★★

Serves 4

²/₃ cup / 150 ml orange juice
3¹/₂ tbsp / 50 ml grapefruit juice
6 tbsp / 90 g sugar
8 sheets of gelatin
¹/₂ vanilla bean
a little freshly ground pepper
fresh mint, shredded
²/₃ cup / 150 ml muscatel

6 oranges
2 grapefruit

For the tea sauce:
4 tea bags
2 cups / 500 ml water
¹/₂ cup / 125 g sugar
4 sheets of gelatin

For the glazed orange peel:
2 tbsp grenadine
1 tbsp water
3¹/₂ tbsp / 50 g sugar
peel of 1 untreated orange

Playing with the flavor and appearance of fruit is a pleasure known since classical times. The development of certain products has made it possible to create stylish fruit terrines whose composition flatters the gourmet's tastebuds.

It is citrus fruits that have inspired our chef to create this dessert, more precisely the orange and the grapefruit, which are similar to each other in appearance and taste. The orange is a winter fruit, and we have the seafarer Vasco da Gama (1469–1524) to thank for its introduction to Europe. The grapefruit was cultivated from the pomelo or shaddock, native to warmer regions of North America, and was not exported to Europe from Florida until the 19th century. By now, so many different varieties exist that they can be classified both by their

country of origin and their color, so one has to compare the various types of oranges and grapefruit and decide which complement each other best. Blood oranges, however, should be avoided, as their coloring is too intense. Whichever you select, please make sure that all the seeds have been carefully removed. It can be quite unpleasant to bite down on a seed when enjoying a refreshing slice of citrus fruit terrine.

The jelly that forms the basis of this recipe contains muscatel, or more precisely muscatel from Rivesaltes, if the choice were left to our chef. This is a fine, highly aromatic wine that has been produced in Roussillon for centuries. Its intoxicating aroma provides an excellent contrast to the English tea sauce.

1. Slightly warm the orange juice and grapefruit juice. Add the sugar, soaked gelatin and the pulp of the vanilla bean to the juices. Add a little pepper and the shredded mint. Heat everything at a low temperature, then allow to cool. Stir in the muscatel.

2. Peel the oranges and grapefruit, and cut out segments without seeds or skin. Cut the peel of one orange into thin strips.

Muscatel and Tea Sauce

3. Use a ladle to pour a layer of the orange and grapefruit jelly into a rectangular baking dish, and allow to set in the refrigerator for about 15 minutes. To make the tea sauce, bring 2 cups / 500 ml of water to a boil, then add the sugar, tea bags, and soaked gelatin. Allow to steep until completely cooled. Remove the teabags and pass through a pointed sieve.

4. Once the jelly has set, place a layer of fruits flat onto it. Cover with another layer of jelly and again allow to set in the refrigerator. Continue this process until all the ingredients have been used. Bring the water to a boil with the sugar and grenadine, and glaze the orange peel in the resulting syrup. Simmer for 10 minutes. Serve the terrine in slices. Garnish with the tea sauce and orange peel.

Nougat Parfait

Preparation time: 30 minutes
Cooling time: 12 hours
Difficulty: ★★

Serves 6

¹/₂ cup / 100 g candied fruits, diced
6¹/₂ tbsp / 100 ml Grand Marnier

For the pine nut brittle:
6¹/₂ tbsp / 100 g sugar
4 tsp / 30 g dextrose
¹/₂ cup / 80 g pine nuts

For the meringue:
2 tbsp / 50 g dextrose
3¹/₂ tbsp / 50 g sugar
4¹/₂ tbsp / 100 g heather honey
5 egg whites
2 cups / 500 ml cream

For the strawberry sauce:
1 lb 12 oz / 800 g strawberries
juice of ¹/₂ untreated lemon

Heath landscapes have many delights to offer visitors, such as extensive plains and woodlands of natural beauty in which the two main varieties of heather grow in glorious abundance: winter heath (erica) and ling (calluna). Interestingly, these two species of heather never grow and flower at the same time.

This explains the truly remarkable extent of heather honey production, a trade in which many regions are specialized. For this recipe, a dark winter heath honey, with its distinctive aroma and strong flavor, would be ideal. Heath only grows in the spring, while the ling variety flowers in the autumn and produces a lighter honey. Instead of winter heath honey, another dark honey could be used as an alternative.

Some skill is required to make the meringue, as the temperature of the honey and sugar mixture must be precisely 250 °F / 120 °C before it is added to the egg whites.

The pine nut brittle is also not without its difficulty: if it is too light, the brittle may not have much flavor, but if it is too dark it can become bitter. Unfortunately, the outcome is not clear until the cream and meringue have been combined. Both should be very cold. All previous steps, however, can be carried out the previous day.

The strawberry sauce is made cold, so as to maximize its flavor. With other red fruits such as red currants or raspberries, it would be necessary to heat them briefly.

1. To make the brittle, melt the sugar and dextrose in a small pan. Reduce to the consistency of light caramel. Add the pine nuts and color in the caramel for 1 to 2 minutes, stirring constantly. Grease a baking tray and spread the brittle mixture on it. Allow to cool.

2. Make the meringue in two stages. Whip the cream until stiff, then refrigerate. In a pan heat the dextrose, sugar and honey to 250 °F / 120 °C. Once the mixture reaches this temperature, add it to the beaten egg whites and beat continuously until completely cooled.

with Heather Honey

3. Marinate the candied fruits in the Grand Marnier for 10 minutes, then chop and crumble the pine brittle. Combine the chilled whipped cream and the honey meringue. Line a cake pan with baking paper. Puree the strawberries in a blender and mix with the lemon juice. Pass through a fine sieve and refrigerate.

4. Mix the marinated fruit and the crushed brittle into the meringue and cream mixture. Pour everything into the cake pan (or individual molds) and freeze for 12 hours. To serve, cut into slices ¹/₂ in / 1 cm thick, arrange on plates and surround each slice with strawberry sauce.

Crêpe Pouches with Grand

Preparation time: 1 hour
Cooking time: 10 minutes
Cooling time: 1 hour
Difficulty: ★★★

Serves 4

For the ice cream soufflé:
6¹/₂ tbsp / 100 ml sugar syrup at 30 °Beaumé
8 egg yolks, beaten lightly
6¹/₂ tbsp / 100 ml Grand Marnier
2 cups / 500 ml cream
6 egg whites
1 cup / 250 g sugar
6¹/₂ tbsp / 100 ml water

For the crêpe batter:
1 cup / 125 g flour
2¹/₂ tbsp / 35 g sugar
2 eggs
a pinch of salt
1 cup / 250 ml milk
7 tsp / 35 g butter, melted
a dash of Grand Marnier
2 vanilla beans
sugar

To garnish:
blanched orange peel
oranges
orange sauce

For many decades, Grand Marnier has been indispensable to both master pastry chefs and gourmets. This exquisite liqueur, an invention of Louis-Alexandre Marnier-Lapostolles, has also left its mark on the training of several generations of chefs. Today Nicole Seitz is in charge of the quality of the brand: she is passionately devoted to the continuance and distribution of an entire assortment of first-class products. Our chef would like to acknowledge her services with this recipe. Refined with Grand Marnier, it becomes a showpiece dessert appropriate for celebrations.

Making the ice cream soufflé will not be all that easy for a beginner. It is especially important to proceed with the greatest of care when combining the various foamy mixtures (beaten egg whites, meringue, whipped cream).

The oranges should be split into large, fleshy segments, and they should definitely be free of seeds. The most obvious choice in this respect would be navel oranges, which derive their name from their recognizable "navel," a small notch-shaped growth on the underside of the fruit. Navel oranges are firm, quite large, and are easy to peel; they have relatively little juice, but produce a marvelous aroma. There are at least two varieties of navel oranges commonly available, the early-ripening naveline and the late-ripening navel. Both originate in Spain and are valued for their thin peel.

In the Far East, the orange is considered a fertility symbol. In Vietnam and China, brides and grooms are presented with oranges during their wedding ceremonies.

1. Begin the soufflé by pouring the boiling sugar syrup onto the lightly beaten egg yolks, stirring constantly. Heat to 175 °F / 80 °C, then whisk until cooled and add the Grand Marnier. Whip the cream until stiff. Make a meringue by bringing the sugar and water to 250 °F / 121 °C, then pouring the syrup over the stiffly whipped egg whites. Continue to beat until the mixture has cooled.

2. To make the crêpe batter, combine the flour, sugar, eggs, salt, and milk in a mixing bowl. Stir in the melted butter and Grand Marnier. Allow to rest. Prepare the crêpes.

Marnier Ice Cream Soufflé

3. Combine the meringue and egg yolk mixtures, and very carefully fold in the whipped cream. Add some chopped pieces of orange, pour the mixture into small molds, and freeze. For the garnish, blanch some orange peel and cut it into strips, and prepare orange segments.

4. Fold each crêpe to form a little pouch, fill it with a portion of ice cream soufflé and tie with a slit vanilla bean. Garnish the plate with orange segments and orange sauce, and sprinkle sugar on the crêpe pouches. Finally, flambé some marinated orange segments and garnish the dessert with the orange peel.

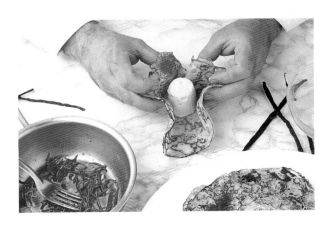

Delicate Apple Cake

Preparation time: 1 hour
Cooking time: 20 minutes
Difficulty: ★★

Serves 4

2 apples (e.g. Granny Smiths)
pieces of butter
superfine sugar

For the puff pastry (see basic recipes):
4 cups / 500 g flour
3 tsp / 15 g salt

1 cup / 250 ml water
2 cups / 500 g butter

For the tarragon sorbet:
1³/₄ cups / 100 g tarragon
3 cups / 750 ml milk
6¹/₂ tbsp / 100 g sugar
2¹/₂ tbsp / 60 g dextrose

Had a piece of nearby tarragon not accidentally fallen into a pan of cooking apples, our chef might never have had the idea to combine the two. After adding more tarragon (this time intentionally) and measuring it more precisely, one must admit that he has created an exquisitely light and refined dessert.

According to Jean Crotet, the most suitable apples for this dessert are Rennets, small yellow apples with red spots whose firm, crunchy flesh is sweet and aromatic. Alternatively, one could use the sour Granny Smiths, with light-green skins and white flesh. One should choose whichever variety one likes best and cut the apples into strips as thin as the cake base. This

results in an interesting contrast between the soft pieces of fruit and the crunchy pastry.

It is very unusual to use tarragon in a sorbet. For this purpose, it is recommended that one use only fresh leaves with a strong aniseed smell, which is brought out further by simmering in sweetened milk. It is advisable to prepare the sorbet a few hours ahead of time and serve it with the hot cake as soon as the latter has finished baking.

This sweet, invigorating dessert inevitably reminds one of that old English saying, "An apple a day keeps the doctor away."

1. Make the puff pastry according to the basic recipe, allowing the mixture of water, salt, and flour to stand for 1 hour. Fold the puff pastry six times. Roll out a dough ¹/₈ in / 2 mm thick. Trace and cut out a circle with a diameter of 9 in / 20 cm. Place on a baking sheet.

2. Peel and core the apples and cut into very thin slices.

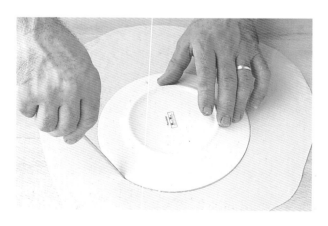

with Tarragon Sorbet

3. Arrange the apples on the dough base. Place some small pieces of butter on the apples and sprinkle with superfine sugar, which will caramelize the apples. Bake for about 15 minutes at 355 °F / 180 °C.

4. To make the sorbet, bring all the ingredients to a boil and add the washed and chopped fresh tarragon. Allow to seep for 1 hour. Pass through a pointed sieve and pour into a ice cream machine. Prepare the sorbet ahead of time so it can be served with the cake hot out of the oven.

Crunchy Turnovers

Preparation time: 1 hour
Cooking time: 10 minutes
Difficulty: ✴✴

Serves 4

For the semolina filling:
½ cup / 125 ml milk
½ cup / 125 ml cream
1½ tbsp / 25 g sugar
7 tbsp / 65 g semolina
¼ pineapple
½ banana
4 tsp / 20 g butter
1 tbsp acacia honey

For the fruit salad:
1 kiwi
¼ mango
8 strawberries
2 oranges
1 apple

For the fruit sauce:
14 oz / 400 g mango, pureed
6½ tbsp / 100 g sugar

For the ravioli dough (for 20):
2 cups / 250 g flour
2 egg yolks
2 eggs
1 tbsp olive oil
½ tsp salt

To garnish:
confectioners' sugar
sprigs of mint

If it were not for the spectacular walls surrounding the old town of Carcassone, Prosper Montagné, one of the city's famous sons, would perhaps be just as celebrated in travel guides as his birthplace. As it is, the outstanding chef is a little overshadowed by the medieval town, though he was responsible for the system that supplied provisions for the French forces during World War I. Nonetheless, a gastronomic prize that is awarded to important professional chefs each year is named after him. One potential candidate for it is undoubtedly Michel Del Burgo, who, though still young, has already won many awards; he proudly carries on the culinary arts of the Languedoc region.

His crunchy turnovers are prepared like ravioli and are filled with a mixture of the finest durum wheat semolina. The ravioli dough itself can be prepared the previous day, covered with plastic wrap, and kept in the refrigerator.

Our chef also recommends adding a dash of light vinegar to the dough. This prevents it from oxidizing and drying out too quickly. The vinegar also accentuates the slight sweetness of the dough, which is derived from the gentle aroma of the acacia or other flower honey.

The fruit salad with which the turnovers are served can also be made with different fruits. Michel Del Burgo prefers mangoes from Brazil, and these should certainly be part of the salad.

The Crusaders, who after their return from Jerusalem frequently stayed in the fortified town of Carcassone to gather their energy for new deeds, seem to have cast their shadow over this dessert. Jean-Michel Signoles, the owner of the local restaurant Barbacane, views himself as the heir to this tradition and works passionately for the public good.

1. To make the semolina filling, bring the milk, cream, and sugar to a boil. Remove from the heat and stir in the semolina. Allow to cool. Meanwhile, prepare the fruits for the fruit salad, cut into small pieces and combine.

2. Prepare and cut the pineapple and banana into small pieces, fry them in the butter and honey, then add to the semolina mixture. Put to one side.

à la Barbacane

3. To make the fruit sauce, use the sugar to make a caramel without using liquid. As soon as the caramel becomes light, deglaze it by slowly and gradually adding the pureed mangoes. Refrigerate. Make the ravioli dough using the ingredients listed above and allow it to rest for 3 to 4 hours.

4. Roll the dough out thinly and cut out circles with a diameter of $4^{1}/_{2}$ in / 10 cm. Place a teaspoonful of the semolina mixture on each round. Moisten the edges, fold into a triangle and deep-fry. Arrange some fruit salad in the center of each plate and cover it with mango sauce. Dust the turnovers with confectioners' sugar and arrange on the plates, garnishing with a sprig of mint.

Peach Soup

Preparation time: 30 minutes
Difficulty: ★

Serves 4

4 peaches

For the marinade:
4 cups / 1 l red wine
1¼ cups / 300 ml raspberry sauce
¼ cup / 60 g sugar
lemon juice

For the lemon verbena ice cream:
2 oz / 50 g fresh lemon verbena
1 cup / 250 ml cream
1 cup / 250 ml milk
6 egg yolks
¾ cup plus 1 tbsp / 200 g sugar
peel of 2 untreated limes

To garnish:
½ cup plus 2 tbsp / 100 g raspberries or
    wild strawberries
fresh almonds

Louis XIV had a royal passion for peaches, and his orchards were full of them – over 30 different varieties in the end. Peaches continue to be very popular and the flesh of these tender and juicy summer fruits is one of the great pleasures of summer. Peaches are one of the main products cultivated in the Languedoc-Roussillon region of France, and purists place great value on the quality of fruit from this area.

Our chef has chosen the yellow peach for its flesh, which is firmer and juicier than that of the white peach. Above all he recommends the peaches from the area around Carcassone, though these are not easy to come by. Due to the many vineyards around the medieval city, Michel Del Burgo need not worry about obtaining good quality wines; they flow, so to speak, right up to his doorstep.

The marinade used in this recipe has to be prepared with considerable care, for bruised raspberries should not be used even to prepare a sauce. If fresh raspberries of a suitable quality are not available, an alternative is to buy fruit pulp, which is frequently surprisingly good.

The same is true of the lemon verbena; preferably it should be fresh. But even in its dried form (as sold in herbal shops to make herbal tea) it can be used to produce an ice cream of amazing finesse, which is matched only by thyme and rosemary ice creams, if at all. And on the theme of possible variations, why not use flavorful, tender pears or red plums instead of peaches?

1. Mix the red wine, raspberry sauce, sugar, and lemon juice in a bowl without heating, to make the marinade for the peaches. To make the lemon verbena ice cream, use the ingredients listed above to produce a custard (see basic recipes) and then steep the lemon verbena in it. Glaze the lime peel and dice into small pieces. Add to the custard and thoroughly stir it in an ice cream machine.

2. Clean the peaches, peel them and cut them into eight pieces. Lay the pieces flat on a metal baking sheet.

with Red Wine

3. Pour the marinade over the peaches and allow to marinate for 2 hours. Peel the fresh almonds and cut them lengthwise.

4. Drain the peach segments, arrange them on a plate in a fan shape and place a ball of ice cream in the center. Pour some of the marinade around them, and garnish with wild strawberries or raspberries and the almonds. Serve cold.

Pear Gratin

Preparation time: 30 minutes
Cooking time: 10 minutes
Cooling time: 20 minutes
Difficulty: ★

Serves 4

For the pears marinated in wine:
6 pears
3 cups / 750 ml red wine
3/4 cup plus 1 tbsp / 200 g sugar
1 cinnamon stick
peel of 3 untreated oranges and 1 untreated
    lemon

For the gratin:
1/3 cup / 50 g confectioners' sugar
3 egg yolks
3/4 oz / 20 g licorice extract
1 cup / 250 ml cream, whipped

For the licorice ice cream:
1 cup / 250 ml milk
3 egg yolks
3 1/2 tbsp / 50 g sugar
3/4 oz / 20 g licorice powder

Nowadays, gratin is the accepted term for a tasty dish made of fruit or vegetables that is grilled in the oven, so that a soft filling is concealed beneath a crispy crust. Fruit gratins are an excellent and increasingly popular idea both for large-scale family gatherings and more intimate meals with friends.

This particular gratin is best prepared in an attractive earthenware dish that can be placed directly on the table. Alternatively, individual portions can be made in small pudding bowls or deep, ovenproof plates.

In this recipe Joseph Delphin recommends preparing the gratin a day ahead, but not putting it into the oven until the last minute. This will allow the pears to soak up the red wine more thoroughly.

One should use sour pears with a very fine flesh, which are well-suited to taking on the red color of the wine. To this sugary part of the dessert, which is made richer by the wine, one adds the sweet and bitter taste of licorice in the form of both a powder and an extract, which is likely to evoke childhood memories.

1. Bring the wine to a boil. Flambé the contents of the pan. Add some orange and lemon peel together with a cinnamon stick. Peel and halve the pears, core them and place them in the wine with the sugar. Poach for 10 to 12 minutes. Allow the pears to cool in the liquid.

2. To make the gratin, mix the confectioners' sugar with a scant tablespoon of water in a pan and then bring to a boil. Add the egg yolks, remove from heat, and stir thoroughly until completely cooled. Add the licorice extract with the whipped cream.

with Licorice

3. For the ice cream, bring the milk to a boil. In a bowl, beat the egg yolks and sugar and add the licorice powder. Mix well and pour the mixture into the boiling milk. Continue to heat while stirring constantly, but do not allow to boil again. Pour the mixture through a pointed sieve and place in an ice cream machine for about 20 minutes.

4. Cut the marinated pears into thin slices and arrange them attractively on serving plates, overlapping slightly. Pour the gratin mixture over the pears and bake for a few minutes. Immediately before serving, add a ball of ice cream to each plate.

Pancakes

Preparation time: 45 minutes
Cooking time: 25 minutes
Difficulty: ★

Serves 4

For the pancake batter:
(see basic recipes)
1 cup / 125 g flour
3¹/₂ tbsp / 55 g sugar
1 cup plus 2 tbsp / 280 ml milk
4 eggs
1 tbsp / 15 g butter
1 pinch of salt
2 tbsp / 30 ml water

For the orange sauce:
2 tbsp / 30 ml orange juice
2 cups / 500 ml water
³/₄ cup plus 1 tbsp / 200 g sugar
1¹/₂ tbsp / 20 ml Grand Marnier

For the crème Chiboust:
3 untreated oranges
sugar syrup at 30 °Beaumé
butter
¹/₄ cup / 60 ml lemon juice
2¹/₂ tbsp / 40 ml heavy cream
3 eggs
1¹/₂ tbsp / 20 g superfine sugar
2 tbsp / 15 g pudding mix powder
1 sheet of gelatin

No one knows for sure who Suzette was, but we know some of her professed inventors, including the great master chefs Escoffier and Charpentier. The latter professed to have invented this celebrated orange-flavored dessert in Monte Carlo in honor of the companion of the future King Edward VII of England, giving it her Christian name. The rapid rise of Charpentier, who worked for Queen Victoria and the Rockefellers, appears to confirm this version – assuming, of course, that the former heir to the British throne really did escort a young woman named Suzette.

Philippe Dorange prepares the dessert just as his parents, both experienced in gastronomy, taught him. The recipe retains all the basic elements of the classic suzette. Here the mandarin flavor is introduced by Grand Marnier, an orange liqueur based on cognac, which should be used sparingly as it can overpower the flavor of the pancakes if one adds even a few drops too many.

In order to both improve the taste of the pancake batter and make it firmer and smoother, one could add a little condensed milk. There should be a short break between preparing the mixture and making the pancakes to allow the flavors of the ingredients to blend more thoroughly.

The Chiboust cream, also called St. Honoré cream, reminds our Parisian chef of the 19th century, when a gifted pastry chef named Chiboust invented the classic St. Honoré gâteau and named it after the patron saint of pastry chefs; the cream was named after him. Its preparation requires a degree of care, especially when stirring the butter into the cream with a wooden spoon without causing the eggs to collapse. Once that has been done, half an hour in the refrigerator should give this special cream the desired consistency without further ado.

1. Prepare the pancake batter. Let it rest for a short time, and make small pancakes. Using a cookie cutter, cut out circles with a diameter of 3¹/₂ in / 8 cm.

2. For the orange sauce, make a caramel using water and sugar, then pour the orange juice into it. Add the Grand Marnier and simmer. Cut the peels of the oranges into thin strips and glaze them in the sugar syrup (30 °Beaumé). Add the butter. To make the Chiboust cream, mix the lemon juice with the juice of the 3 oranges, add the heavy cream and bring to a boil.

Suzette with Orange Sauce

3. Separate the eggs. Beat the egg yolks with the sugar, add the pudding powder, combine with the boiling cream in step 2 and finish like a pastry cream (see basic recipes). Remove from the heat, add the gelatin that has been soaked in cold water, and allow to cool. Beat the egg whites until stiff and fold into the cream.

4. Spread the Chiboust cream onto half of each of the pancakes, and then fold them together. Arrange on a deep plate and bake for 5 minutes at 355 °F / 180 °C. After removing from the oven, pour the orange sauce around the pancakes. Decorate with the glazed orange peel.

Sautéed

Preparation time: 30 minutes
Cooking time: 15 minutes
Difficulty: ★

Serves 4

1¹/₂ oz / 40 g puff pastry, baked
3 oz / 90 g each strawberries, raspberries,
     blackberries, cherries, peaches, apples,
     apricots, pears
3 tbsp / 40 g superfine sugar
6¹/₂ tbsp / 100 g butter
2¹/₂ tbsp / 40 ml lemon juice

For the red fruit sauce:
1 oz / 30 g each strawberries, raspberries
¹/₂ oz / 10 g red currants
3 tbsp / 40 g sugar
¹/₄ cup / 60 ml water

To garnish:
vanilla beans
8 sprigs of mint

After spending one's childhood in the Provence region of France, one cannot help being familiar with the taste of all the seasonal fruits, their myriad colors and varieties. Since they do not keep well, most fruit recipes can be prepared only shortly before serving them. With a little effort something truly exquisite can be conjured up: in this recipe, the crispy puff pastry plays with the sweet fruits, which have become meltingly tender in the pan and entice us with their fragrance.

The puff pastry should be flat, not puffed up into several layers. When it is placed on the fruit, it should look like the mortarboard worn by university professors in England. In order to add further refinement to the dessert, our chef suggests glazing the pieces of puff pastry under the hot grill, giving them a shining surface that reflects the fruit.

One cannot use the same fruit for this dish each time it is prepared, but only those that are actually in season at the time. One has to be extremely careful when using red berries because of their sensitivity: our chef suggests adding a little butter or a dash of vinegar before caramelizing them, so that they better withstand the heat. The sauce should be chosen to complement the fruit. Even dieters can savor this dessert, which contains little more than pure vitamins, with a clear conscience.

1. To make the sauce, press the red berries and liquidize in a blender. Pass through a sieve and mix with a syrup made from the sugar and water.

2. Wash the whole fruits and cut into small pieces without peeling. Sauté in a pan with the butter and the caramelized sugar.

Fruit Dessert

3. Pour a little water, the lemon juice and the red fruit sauce into the pan. Set the fruit and the sauce aside. From the glazed puff pastry, cut out rounds with a diameter of 3¹/₂ in / 7.5 cm.

4. Place the fruits mixed with the sauce on a plate, arrange a glazed slice of puff pastry on top and garnish with sprigs of mint and vanilla beans.

Mango Fans with

Preparation time: 30 minutes
Cooking time: 10 minutes
Difficulty: ✳

Serves 4

2 ripe mangoes
10 passion fruit
sugar

For the vanilla ice cream:
1 vanilla bean
³/₄ cup / 200 ml milk
3¹/₂ tbsp / 50 g sugar
2 egg yolks
1²/₃ cups / 400 ml crème fraîche

Slices of baked puff pastry
(see basic recipes)

To garnish:
4 sprigs of mint
confectioners' sugar

With this recipe, Claude Dupont is attempting to lure us into an imaginary "Garden of Earthly Delights." The fruit of the mango tree comes from India, though they can also be found in Africa and America. Passion fruit is grown mainly in Latin American (Brazil and Venezuela) and in the warmer regions of the United States (Florida and Hawaii).

There is nothing coincidental about the combination of mango and passion fruit: it is a successful balance of two fruits whose flavors complement without overpowering each other. However, both fruits should be at their very best. The mangoes must be just ripe and not too soft to the touch; it does not matter what color the skin is. Choose heavy fruits with a smooth skin. Avoid fruits with black spots on the skin, as these are signs of

overripe fruit with fibrous flesh. The mango has a large, flattened stone that is somewhat difficult to remove. One is left with about two-thirds of the fruit that can be used for the fans.

The passion fruit, with its brownish skin tinged with violet, makes a somewhat weatherworn impression. Its sour flesh is exceptionally well suited to making a fruit sauce, including all the fruit's little black seeds.

This tasty dessert is extremely rich in vitamins and, for that reason, need not deter those on a diet or watching their weight. Perhaps this recipe will inspire you to become creative and discover other ways to prepare and enjoy these two tropical fruits.

1. Peel the mangoes and remove the stones. To make the vanilla ice cream, pour the milk into a pan with the vanilla bean, bring to a boil and remove from the heat. In a mixing bowl, beat the sugar and egg yolks with a whisk, and pour the hot milk onto them. Combine thoroughly and allow to cool. Mix in the crème fraîche and stir in an ice cream machine until cold. Freeze.

2. Cut the four mango halves into thin segments, so that they can be arranged in a fan shape. Dust the mango fans with confectioners' sugar and heat slightly under a hot grill.

Vanilla Ice Cream

3. Halve the passion fruits and scoop out all the flesh. Puree in a blender and pass the resulting fruit sauce through a sieve, then add sugar to taste.

4. Place a mango fan on each plate. Pour some fruit sauce over each fan. Arrange two balls of vanilla ice cream on crispy slices of puff pastry. Garnish with a sprig of mint dusted with confectioners' sugar.

Raspberry Gratin with

Preparation time: 30 minutes
Cooking time: 15 minutes
Cooling time: 1 hour
Difficulty: ★

Serves 4

1 lb / 500 g raspberries

For the vanilla ice cream:
2 cups / 500 ml milk
1 vanilla bean
5 egg yolks
$1/2$ cup / 125 g sugar
$6^1/2$ tbsp / 100 ml crème fraîche

For the zabaglione:
4 egg yolks
$6^1/2$ tbsp / 100 g superfine sugar
1 glass of white wine
raspberry liqueur

To garnish:
sprigs of mint

Ice cream made with milk is not only a delicacy that we have appreciated since childhood, but, like most dairy products, it is also extremely nutritious. Here, the eggs and milk produce an ice cream with high protein and calcium content, which should help ease the conscience of committed ice cream fans. The gourmet Queen Marie de Médici introduced ice cream at the court of her husband, the merry Henry IV, who himself made fun of his stomach as a "Bastille tower in underwear."

Raspberries have always been a delicacy. In classical mythology we are told that Zeus himself loved to pick them from their thorny bushes. He did this because his foster mother had once brushed against a raspberry bush, and he had been scratched in the process. The raspberries permanently took on the color of

his blood, though a few raspberries managed to avoid the curse and thus remain yellow. Whatever stories are told about the raspberry, it is a delightful fruit that has certainly had plenty of admirers since classical times. Unfortunately, fresh raspberries are very sensitive and spoil easily if they are not frozen as a precaution. This method of storage has led to the raspberry being more widely used, even when not in season, something that is sure to please gourmets.

Nonetheless, a few tricks assure the success of this dessert: since it is composed mainly of ice cream, it is grilled briefly just before serving in order to glaze the zabaglione. This step must be executed with particular care and at the last minute, so as not to destroy the interesting hot-cold effect.

1. Place the milk, vanilla bean pulp and the empty bean into a pan. After boiling remove from the heat. Using a whisk, beat the egg yolks and sugar in a bowl in order to produce a thick cream. Remove the vanilla bean from the milk and gradually pour the hot milk onto the egg yolk mixture. Simmer and reduce over low heat.

2. Allow the mixture to cool, stir in the crème fraîche, mix and cool. Pour the ice cream into pudding molds and allow to set in the freezer for at least 1 hour. Place the carefully selected raspberries on top of each portion of ice cream.

a Light Zabaglione

3. Place the egg yolks, sugar, white wine and a few drops of raspberry liqueur into a pan. Mix everything thoroughly. Heat gently and beat with a whisk to produce the zabaglione.

4. Pour the hot zabaglione over the raspberries and glaze under a hot grill for about 20 seconds. Serve immediately, garnished with a sprig of mint.

Swabian Gugelhupf

Preparation time: 30 minutes
Cooling time: 12 hours
Difficulty: ★★

Serves 4

2 tbsp / 20 g raisins
3¹/₂ tbsp / 50 ml rum
3 egg yolks
4¹/₂ tbsp / 70 g sugar
grated peel of 1 untreated orange
2¹/₂ tbsp / 40 ml Grand Marnier

5 tsp / 25 ml cream
³/₄ oz / 20 g chocolate
1¹/₄ cups/300 ml cream, whipped

To garnish:
various fruits
mint leaves

There are almost as many varieties of gugelhupf as there are different ways of writing it in the German-speaking world: Kugelhopf, Kougelhof, Guggelhopf, etc. The Alsatians, old masters in this field, make it using yeast dough with raisins and almonds, and always bake it in the traditional gugelhupf tin with a large cylindrical opening in the middle. Lothar Eiermann, who comes from Swabia in Germany, swears by his regional black-and-white variation of the dessert. He has, however, added other gugelhupf variations to his repertoire over the years, including some savory ones with goose livers or salmon.

In this variation consisting entirely of ice cream, which is of course kept in the freezer, it is especially important to use the right quantity of sugar. Since the raisins also contains sugar, it might be necessary to reduce the amount slightly. One should also be careful with the egg yolks, which are rich in carbo-

hydrates. In the first stage of the work, the egg yolks and sugar must be beaten until they form an even, foamy mixture, for this is decisive in creating an ice cream cake with a light texture. It is obvious that everything needs to be prepared beforehand, as the ice cream needs at least 12 hours to set in the freezer.

Even after this period of time, it is possible that the mixture will still be soft and the ice cream will not be hard enough to turn out of the mold. This is usually the case when too much sugar has been added despite our chef's warning. If that should happen, do not say you were not warned ...

This excellent and very fresh dessert can be served with whipped cream, raisins, almond cookies or other dry cookies, according to taste.

1. Soak the raisins in the rum for 12 hours or longer. Beat the egg yolks and sugar until foamy, then add the drained raisins, orange peel and Grand Marnier.

2. Heat the cream and chocolate together and bring to a boil, then let cool. Combine one-third of the egg mixture with the chocolate sauce.

with Fruit

3. Fill a gugelhupf mold, or bundt pan, with alternating layers of the "white" and "black" mixtures.

4. Use a fork to create a marble effect, then freeze the gugelhupf for 12 hours. Decorate with fresh seasonal fruits and sprigs of mint and serve.

Quark Tart on Peach

Preparation time: 45 minutes
Cooking time: 5 minutes
Cooling time: 8 hours
Difficulty: ★★

Serves 4

For the quark tarts:
3 egg yolks
3¹/₂ tbsp / 50 g sugar
7 oz / 200 g quark (20 % fat)
6¹/₂ tbsp / 100 ml sour cream
³/₄ cup / 190 ml cream, whipped
2¹/₂ tbsp / 40 ml sugar syrup
3 sheets of gelatin

For the honey cookies:
1 tbsp / 7 g ground almonds
1¹/₂ tbsp / 10 g flour
3 tbsp / 30 g confectioners' sugar
1 tbsp / 12 g melted butter
1 tbsp / 15 g pine honey

For the peach sauce:
14 oz / 400 g peaches
²/₃ cup / 150 ml water
juice of ¹/₂ lemon
3¹/₂ tbsp / 50 ml sweet white wine
6 tbsp / 90 g sugar
¹/₂ vanilla bean

To garnish:
red berries, mint leaves

Not satisfied simply to excel at preparing poultry, fish, and game dishes, Lothar Eiermann is also eager to prove his talent for making desserts and here shows us one that is just as popular as his savory dishes. His guests tend to be well-informed and calorie-conscious, and as a result everything he prepares has been well thought out from a dietary point of view.

The same is true of this tart, which is light enough to pose no danger to anyone. Airy, delicious, foamy, flawless – there are no words adequate to describe this precisely balanced dessert, which does not leave you unpleasantly full.

The quark, which gives the mixture its consistency, should not contain more than 20 % fat, and its creaminess forms a welcome contrast to the crunchy pine honey cookie.

The dessert also does great credit to the exceedingly popular peach, whose Latin name, *Persica darna*, reminds us that it was introduced to the western world from Persia by Alexander the Great.

Decorating the dessert gives Lothar Eiermann tremendous pleasure, as it recalls many childhood memories of innocent little thefts from his father's garden and the subsequent pursuit.

1. To make the quark tarts, beat the egg yolks and sugar until creamy. Then fold in the other ingredients carefully. Pour into small molds and refrigerate for 7 to 8 hours.

2. For the cookie dough, knead all the ingredients together and allow to rest.

Sauce with Berries

3. Roll out the dough to a thickness of ¹/₈ in / 2 mm, cut out cookies with a diameter of 2 in / 4 cm, and bake for 5 minutes at 390 °F / 200 °C. To make the sauce, wash and stone the peaches, cut into pieces and boil with all the other ingredients. Let cool. Remove the vanilla bean, puree the peaches and pass through a pointed sieve.

4. Arrange a quark tart on the center of each plate, place a honey cookie on top, pour a little peach sauce over it and garnish with the red berries and mint leaves.

Fruit Gratin

Preparation time: 20 minutes
Cooking time: 3 minutes
Difficulty: ★★

Serves 4

2 mangoes
2 kiwis
12 strawberries

For the almond cream:
2 cups / 250 g finely ground almonds
1 cup / 250 g sugar
1 cup / 250 g butter
6¹/₂ tbsp / 100 ml rum
3 eggs

For the ice cream:
12 egg yolks
1¹/₄ cups / 300 g sugar
2 cups / 500 ml milk
2 cups / 500 ml almond milk
1 cup /250 ml cream

For the pastry cream:
(see basic recipes)
2 cups / 500 ml milk
6 egg yolks
¹/₂ cup / 125 g sugar
6¹/₂ tbsp / 50 g flour
1 vanilla bean

Do fruits such as kiwis, mangoes and strawberries actually go with an almond cream? It will be very difficult for gourmets to resist this enjoyable and tasty combination on their plates.

Once known only as an exotic fruit, the kiwi is now cultivated in more northern latitudes as well. Italy is the leading producer and exporter in Europe. Kiwis can be integrated into many dishes, and in addition to their high levels of vitamin C, they are also very low in calories. They also keep well, another point in favor of this fresh, invigorating fruit.

The fleshy, juicy mango was introduced to Europe by the Portuguese, who discovered it growing in Brazil. Both sweet and rich in vitamins, the mango traditionally has been used in the preparation of chutneys or spicy dishes such as Indian curries. Just like kiwi, the mango contains very few calories and is a favorite among dieters.

The almond cream derives its delicate flavor from the addition of powdered almonds, and is complemented by the almond milk in the ice cream.

1. To make the almond cream, mix the ground almonds, sugar, and softened butter in a mixing bowl. Add the eggs and rum and beat thoroughly with a whisk.

2. To make the ice cream, beat the egg yolks and sugar until foamy. Bring the milk to a boil and carefully mix with the egg yolk and sugar mixture. Add the almond milk and cream. Pour everything into the ice cream machine. Peel the kiwis and mangoes and cut into thin slices. Also slice the strawberries.

with Almonds

3. Make the pastry cream according to the basic recipe, and combine it with the prepared almond cream.

4. Spread some almond cream onto the center of each plate and decoratively arrange the fruit on it. Place under a hot grill for a few minutes and serve with a scoop of ice cream.

Blancmange with

Preparation time: 1 hour
Cooking time: 20 minutes
Cooling time: 30 minutes
Difficulty: ★★

Serves 4

5¼ oz / 150 g white chocolate

For the almond mousse:
½ cup / 80 g confectioners' sugar
1 cup / 250 ml milk
3½ tbsp / 50 g sugar
3 egg yolks
3 sheets of gelatin
1 cup / 250 ml cream, whipped
½ cup / 50 g ground almonds

2 bitter almonds, ground
bitter almond extract

For the almond sponge cake:
1 egg yolk
1 egg
6 tbsp / 60 g confectioners' sugar
½ cup / 60 g ground almonds
7 tbsp / 50 g flour
2½ tbsp / 40 g sugar
2 egg whites

For the kirsch syrup:
2½ tbsp / 40 ml kirsch
6½ tbsp / 100 ml sugar syrup (60 °Beaumé)
2½ tbsp / 40 ml mineral water

Blancmange was originally completely white. It was made using almond milk and thickened with jelly, which was occasionally flavored. Constant Fonk has enriched his modern version of blancmange with a gold leaf decoration, quite in the style of the Venetians, whose merchant ships brought spices and silks from the Far East to Europe in the 15th century. The Dutch, so history tells us, were keen to emulate them and in the following century founded the Dutch colonial empire. This led to the incorporation of herbs and a range of spices in Dutch gastronomy from an early stage.

The almonds in this recipe have to be ground extremely finely so that the ingredients combine completely and form a light, airy mousse. The bitter almonds and bitter almond extract have to be measured carefully, as they otherwise might spoil the flavor of the entire dish. But it is precisely this combination of the two most important types of almond that make it a classic in haute cuisine.

It is unusual that one's very first attempt to make a complete chocolate ruffle is successful. Even the majority of professional chefs admit that their own efforts only led to failure at first. So you must have a little patience! One more tip about the white chocolate ruffles: briefly placing the baking sheet in the refrigerator will give the chocolate a firmer consistency and make it easier to form complete ruffles.

When making the kirsch syrup, please do not experiment or use inexpensive substitute ingredients: use only genuine kirsch.

1. For the almond mousse, mix the ground almonds and confectioners' sugar. Bring the milk to a boil with half of the sugar. Beat the egg yolks and the remaining sugar until foamy. Pour the boiling milk onto the eggs. Cook like a custard (see basic recipes), then add the soaked gelatin. Pour over the almond mixture and allow to cool. Add the stiffly whipped cream and blend carefully.

2. Pour a thin layer of melted white chocolate onto a warmed baking tray. As soon as it is firm, use a metal spatula to create chocolate ruffles.

White Chocolate Ruffle

3. To make the sponge cake, combine the egg yolk and whole egg with the confectioners' sugar. Add the ground almonds and flour. Finally, fold in the egg whites, which have been whipped until stiff with the sugar. Pour the mixture onto a baking sheet lined with baking paper and bake for about 10 minutes at 355 °F / 180 °C. Cool, then cut with a cookie cutter.

4. Prepare a mold with a diameter of 8 in / 18 cm and height of 1³/₄ in / 3.5 cm or 4 individual molds with a diameter of 2³/₄ in / 6 cm and height of 2 in / 4 cm. Line the bottom with almond sponge cake and soak with the kirsch syrup. Fill each mold with almond mousse right to the top and allow to set in the refrigerator. Turn out onto a dessert plate and decorate with the chocolate ruffles. If desired, garnish with gold leaf.

Three Winter Sorbets

Preparation time: 30 minutes
Cooking time: 30 minutes
Cooling time   1 hour
Difficulty: ★★

Serves 4

For the chocolate sorbet:
6$\frac{1}{2}$ oz / 180 g cocoa paste
$\frac{1}{2}$ cup plus 1 tbsp / 200 g acacia honey
1$\frac{1}{4}$ cups / 300 ml mineral water

For the quark sorbet:
9 oz / 250 g quark, 40 % fat
1 cup / 250 ml whole milk

$\frac{1}{2}$ cup / 175 g honey
the peel of 1 untreated lemon

For the sweet chestnut sorbet:
2 egg yolks
2$\frac{1}{2}$ tbsp / 40 g sugar
1 cup / 250 ml whole milk
5$\frac{1}{4}$ oz / 150 g pureed chestnuts, flavored with vanilla

For the hot chocolate:
1 cup / 250 ml whole milk
$\frac{1}{4}$ cup / 60 ml cream
$\frac{1}{2}$ cup / 50 g cocoa powder
1$\frac{3}{4}$ oz / 50 g milk chocolate

Is it a contradiction in terms to serve a sorbet in winter? Not as far as our chef is concerned, and in order to support his theory he presents us with a dessert that is prepared like an ice cream without sugar. "Please in order to give satisfaction," is the motto of this very exacting chef who, like the first violinist before a concert, is an expert at precisely tuning the instruments used to tickle our taste buds.

Clearly, the chocolate sorbet depends entirely on the quality of the cocoa paste, which is produced by grating roasted cocoa beans. As this sorbet contains about 50 % cocoa paste, the result is a dessert that should satisfy even the most discriminating palate. In addition, it is a wonderful tribute to the Dutch seafarers who introduced cocoa from America to all of Europe.

It is important to pay particular attention to the aroma and consistency of the hot chocolate, which in this instance echoes the sorbets. Its temperature and liquidity should combine with the similar-tasting sorbet to create a harmonic contrast, especially when both melt in the mouth at the same time.

The quark sorbet is prepared using a quark that is high in fat, which is especially pleasant in winter. The use of honey instead of sugar makes the sorbet both lighter and more flavorful.

Finally, the sweet chestnut puree complements the other two sorbets well, with its high levels of roughage and vitamin B. This fruit is mixed with sugar, as it is not dry like walnuts or hazelnuts.

1. To make the chocolate sorbet, melt the cocoa paste and remove from the heat. Without heat, make a syrup from the honey and mineral water. Mix everything together thoroughly. Freeze at 10 °F / −12 °C.

2. For the quark sorbet, blanch the grated lemon peel. Combine all the ingredients in a mixing bowl. Stir with a mixer and freeze at 15 °F / −8 °C.

with Hot Chocolate

3. To make the sweet chestnut sorbet, beat the egg yolks and sugar until foamy. Bring the milk to a boil and pour onto the egg yolks. Continue as for a custard (see basic recipes) and add the chestnut puree that has been flavored with vanilla. Allow to cool. Stir thoroughly with a mixer and freeze at 15 °F / −8 °C.

4. To make the hot chocolate, bring the milk to a boil in a pan, add the cocoa powder and milk chocolate, and finally stir in the cream. Arrange the sorbets in three miniature ice buckets and serve with a small cup of hot chocolate.

"Chocolat-Café"

Preparation time: 2 hours
Cooking time: 20 minutes
Difficulty: ★★★

Serves 4

1 cup / 100 g shelled walnuts
¹/₂ cup / 50 g cocoa powder

For the chocolate sponge cake:
6 eggs
¹/₂ cup plus 2 tbsp / 150 g superfine sugar
¹/₄ cup / 30 g cocoa
³/₄ cup plus 1 tbsp / 100 g flour

For the praline mixture:
6 oz / 175 g bittersweet chocolate coating

³/₄ cup / 200 ml cream
7 tsp / 35 g butter

For the pastry cream with coffee
pastry cream (see basic recipes)
a little instant coffee
³/₄ cup / 200 ml cream, whipped

For the coffee custard (see basic recipes):
2 cups / 500 ml milk
6 egg yolks
1¹/₂ oz / 40 g coffee beans
6¹/₂ tbsp / 100 g sugar

chocolate coating, melted

Opinions are divided as to when exactly cocoa was introduced to France from America. Some think it was Queen Anna of Austria, daughter of the Spanish king, who introduced it at court in 1615. Others believe it was Alphonse de Richelieu, archbishop of Lyon and brother of the priest, who used the cocoa bean after 1661 to "calm the humors of his spleen" at the advice of a Spanish monk. Once condemned by theologians, frequently made out to be the root of all evil, chocolate is now a much-revered candy of the very best quality and the object of devotion.

This dessert, in which chocolate and coffee are combined, can only be made using products of an exceptional quality. A dark bittersweet chocolate with a pure cocoa content of at least 60 to 70 % should be used. The best coffee is surely that from

Colombia, which is both milder and more acidic, and this is particularly true of the Supreme variety. It is frequently used as an instant coffee, as its dry essence does not alter the consistency of the cream. For a lighter pastry cream, a little whipped cream can be added to the ingredients.

The walnuts give this dessert a delightfully crunchy touch. After shelling, they are chopped and refrigerated. Varieties with nuts that are easy to remove from the shell are particularly suitable.

This exceptional dessert sweetens the days in Drouant, where members of the Academie Goncourt have been received since 1914, and some of them positively lust for chocolate ...

1. To make the chocolate sponge cake, beat the eggs and sugar with an electric mixer in a double boiler for 7 to 8 minutes in order to produce an even batter. Mix in the cocoa and flour using a skimmer. Pour onto a baking sheet lined with baking paper and bake for 8 to 10 minutes at 355 °F / 180 °C.

2. For the praline mixture, cut up the chocolate coating, add the boiling cream, stir with a spatula, add the butter and reduce, stirring occasionally, until thick.

with Walnuts

3. Prepare the pastry cream and, towards the end of the cooking process, add the instant coffee. Allow to cool and blend in the very stiffly whipped cream. To make the coffee custard, boil the crushed coffee beans in the milk, allow to steep for 10 minutes, then continue as described in the basic recipe. Pass through a sieve and refrigerate.

4. Cut the sponge cake using round cookie cutters with a diameter of 3¹/₂ in / 7 cm and a height of 2 in / 4 cm. Spread the praline mixture on the sides and then alternate layers of pastry cream and walnuts. Finish with a piece of sponge cake. Cover with chocolate coating and arrange on a plate with the custard.

Honey Ice Cream

Preparation time: 45 minutes
Cooking time: 10 minutes
Difficulty: ★

Serves 4

For the ice cream:
4 cups / 1 l whole milk
³/₄ cup / 250 g acacia honey
12 egg yolks
2¹/₂ tbsp / 40 ml Suze (gentian liqueur)

For the tulips:
3 egg whites
1 cup / 150 g confectioners' sugar
1 cup / 120 g flour
5 tbsp / 70 g butter, melted
7 tbsp / 50 g chopped almonds
7 tbsp / 50 g chopped hazelnuts
7 tbsp / 50 g chopped pistachios

To garnish:
honey
mint leaves

In classical times, honey's delicacy led to its designation as the food of the gods, and the bees on Mount Hymettus produced many different varieties. It is said that they sat on the lips of the great Plato and made his words gentler. During the Middle Ages, honey was an extremely valuable source of nutrition; it was also used extensively as a medical remedy. Nowadays it is widely used in desserts and is one of the most important ingredients in fine ice cream.

In this unusual dessert, the honey both blends and contrasts with the Suze, the popular French liqueur made from the gentian plant. Its bitter taste has been tempting the nation since 1899, when Fernard Moureaux invented the technique of infusing the root of the great yellow gentian in alcohol and twice distilling the resulting liquid.

This very original combination requires a light, well-balanced honey that is liquid and flavorful. Acacia honey meets these requirements, and is preferable to other sorts with more intense flavors, such as lavender and pine honey. Honey is best stored in glass jars with tight-fitting lids, as the tight seal preserves its flavor.

Following this recipe is fairly straightforward, with the exception of the custard, which should under no circumstances be allowed to boil. Forming the dough into tulip shapes between two deep plates requires some dexterity, but that is simply a matter of practice. If you are unsure of your tulip-forming talents, they can be made ahead of time and kept in the refrigerator for up to 48 hours.

1. For the ice cream, bring the milk and honey to a boil. Pour a third of the hot milk onto the egg yolks and beat thoroughly with a whisk, then add the remaining milk and cook for about 3 minutes at 188 °F / 87 °C. Allow to rest for 12 hours. Stir the mixture in the ice cream maker and allow to harden. Add the Suze halfway through the process.

2. Prepare the tulip dough. Combine the egg whites, confectioners' sugar, flour, and bubbling hot butter in a bowl. Allow to cool for an hour.

with Gentian

3. Using a spatula, spread six circles of dough (7 in / 15 cm diameter) onto a non-stick tray. Sprinkle the mixture of chopped pistachios, almonds and hazelnuts onto the circles. Bake in the oven at 355 °F / 180 °C until they are slightly colored.

4. Remove from the oven and immediately place each circle onto a deep plate with another plate on top, in order to create tulip shapes. Then place the tulips onto the serving dishes. Using tablespoons, scoop three generous balls of ice cream and arrange them in the form of a star in each tulip. Pour some honey over the ice cream and garnish with mint leaves.

Dessert with Licorice

Preparation time: 35 minutes
Cooking time: 3 hours
Cooling time: 2 hours
Difficulty: *

Serves 4

6 egg yolks
$^1/_3$ cup / 50 g confectioners' sugar
$1^1/_4$ cups / 300 ml cream
1 oz / 25 g agar (from natural foods stores)
1 oz / 30 g licorice powder
$1^1/_4$ cups / 250 g sugar cubes

$^2/_3$ cup / 150 ml cream, whipped
3 apples (e.g. Golden Delicious)
4 tsp / 20 g butter
2 tbsp / 30 g sugar
1 tbsp / 15 ml Calvados

To garnish:
1 tsp instant coffee
licorice powder
2 pieces of licorice root

Baked apples and licorice capture some of the magic of childhood. This recipe has an air of nostalgia about it and, for our chef, awakens memories of chewing little pieces of licorice root on his way home from school, and its dry taste that lingered in one's mouth for hours.

Nowadays, licorice is often used in a powdered form in the kitchen, a development that allows one to add just the right amount when cooking. If one adds an entire piece of licorice, it is impossible to control precisely the intensity of the flavor, and an excess of licorice can destroy the balance of flavors in a dessert.

When making this dessert, it is important to use precisely the given quantities so that its consistency does not become too tough. One should use molds that are not too large and can be easily removed.

Several varieties of apples are well suited to making this dessert, but Golden Delicious apples are highly recommended because they are firm enough to hold up during even long cooking times. The apple is the most popular and widely eaten fruit in all of the western world. It is indeed *the* fruit, for the French word for the apple, *pomme*, is derived from the Latin word for fruit, *pomum*.

The caramel sugar, whose color blends nicely with the licorice, and the other ingredients used in this recipe provide the discriminating palette with a fascinating array of tastes and sensory experiences that arises from the combination of bitter coffee, dry licorice, and sweet caramel sugar. One would have to be very virtuous indeed to be able to resist such a delicacy and leave it for the children.

1. Beat the egg yolks and confectioners' sugar with a whisk and set aside until later. Mix the cream, agar and licorice powder and warm over a low heat for 3 minutes.

2. Use the sugar cubes, without adding water, to make a dry caramel. Carefully pour it onto the lukewarm licorice cream and stir to combine. Pour this onto the whisked egg yolks, stirring constantly, and then fold in the whipped cream.

and Caramelized Apples

3. Peel the apples and cut into thick round slices. Caramelize them in a pan with the sugar and butter, then flambé with the Calvados. Fill the individual molds with alternating layers of caramel mixture and apples, and refrigerate for at least 2 hours.

4. Reserve some of the liquid caramel and allow it to harden, then break it into small pieces. Arrange the dessert on serving plates, decorate with a little caramel, and sprinkle on the coffee and licorice powders. Garnish the dessert with the licorice root sticks.

Bittersweet

Preparation time: 40 minutes
Cooking time: 15 minutes
Cooling time: 2 hours
Difficulty: ★★

Serves 4

5¼ oz / 150 g bittersweet chocolate
2 tsp / 10 g butter
¼ cup / 60 g superfine sugar
4 tsp / 20 ml water
¼ oz / 10 g agar
5 eggs

¾ cup / 200 ml crème fraîche
to taste amarena cherries, stoned

To garnish:
2 bananas
4 tsp / 20 g butter
4 tsp / 20 ml rum
6 tbsp / 40 g cocoa powder
12 amarena cherries (in their own juice)
4 candied mandarin oranges
8 mint leaves

The restoration of the Louvre in Paris has drawn great attention to pyramids. In this recipe our chef combines some of the rules of geometry with the elements of a traditional chocolate dessert to create a confection incoporating rum, bananas, and amarena cherries.

As far as chocolate is concerned, Philipp Groult prefers products from Central America, which have a cocoa content of almost 70 %, and he confesses to having a particular weakness for the refined and mellow aroma of Venezuelan chocolate.

The cacao tree, *Theobroma* ("food of the gods") *cacao*, is native to the Americas. Its oval fruits are called cocoa pods, and contain the cocoa beans from which cocoa powder is made. Cocoa powder, and all chocolate products, should be kept in a dark and damp place.

While making this dessert, it is important that the melted chocolate is not allowed to cool: curdled chocolate that is reheated to make it fluid again is simply indigestible. Agar, a thickening agent made from algae, is used instead of the unflavored gelatin called for in many recipes, because agar leaves no aftertaste at all.

The three-dimensional, almost sculptural appearance of the pyramid gives expression to the refined blend of sour and sweet flavors that make this dessert so unique.

1. Melt the chocolate with the butter in a double boiler. Boil the sugar and water for 2 minutes, then add the agar. Whisk the eggs and add the sugar syrup. In a separate bowl, stir the crème fraîche until creamy. Add the melted chocolate to the eggs, then add the crème fraîche together with the cherries, which have been cut in half.

2. Peel the bananas and halve them lengthways, then cut the long pieces in half. Heat the butter in a pan, fry the banana pieces for 1 minute and then flambé with the rum.

Chocolate Pyramids

3. Pour the chocolate filling into the prepared pyramid molds and form a base using the cooled bananas. Refrigerate for 2 hours, then turn out of the molds.

4. Place a pyramid on each plate. Dust with cocoa powder and pour some cherry juice around the base. Decorate with a candied mandarin with mint leaves, some cherries, and slices of banana.

Peach

Preparation time: 1 hour
Cooking time: 20 minutes
Cooling time: 2 hours
Difficulty: ★★

Serves 4

4 cups / 1 l water
2 cups / 500 g sugar
4 peaches
2 vanilla beans

For the pistachio ice cream:
2 cups / 500 ml milk
2 cups / 500 ml cream

1 vanilla bean
1 cup / 250 g sugar
10 egg yolks
bitter almond extract
2 cups / 250 g pistachios, shelled and crushed

For the champagne zabaglione:
8 egg yolks
1 cup / 250 g sugar
1²/₃ cups / 400 ml champagne
6¹/₂ tbsp / 100 ml cream

To garnish:
whipped cream

From June until September, the peach is the quintessential summer fruit. Its tender, juicy flesh can be enjoyed in a number of ways: as it is, with or without the downy skin that adds so much to the charm of the peach. Originally from China, where it is a symbol of both fertility and immortality, the peach reached the western world via Persia. That is also the source of the Latin name, *persicum* or *persica*. Whether yellow or white (the latter is famed for its aroma), peaches should be peeled at the last minute because they oxidize very quickly, and they should be handled carefully, as they bruise easily.

Great care and attention is needed in preparing the zabaglione: the mixture must be beaten continuously with a whisk while it

is being heated and cooled. This produces a thick consistency, even though the final effect of this cream, which is whipped with champagne, is very light.

Our chef recommends serving a flavorful ice cream with vanilla, bitter almonds, and pistachios with this dessert. Bitter almond extract is usually so concentrated that just a few drops are enough. The high fat and sugar content of the pistachios ensures an intense flavor. In order to achieve the optimal flavor, as Marc Haeberlin does, use pistachios from the Mediterranean region. The dessert should be served very cold with a glass of champagne or Gewürztraminer wine (a very sweet wine from Alsace).

1. To make the ice cream, boil the milk and cream with the vanilla bean and half of the sugar. Beat the egg yolks with the remaining sugar and pour the hot milk over them. Return to the stove and simmer over a low heat. Remove from the heat and add a few drops of bitter almond extract. Stir in the ice cream maker and add the shelled, crushed pistachios at the last minute.

2. To prepare the peaches, bring the water and sugar to a boil with the vanilla beans. Wash the peaches and place in the syrup without peeling. Poach at a low temperature for 15 to 20 minutes. Test with the tip of a knife to check their tenderness. Allow to cool in the syrup.

"Haeberlin"

3. To make the zabaglione, beat the egg yolks and sugar until foamy. Add the champagne and the cream. Whisk at a low temperature in a double boiler until the mixture thickens. Remove the frothy wine cream from the heat.

4. Place the hot pan in a bowl with ice cubes and continue to beat with the whisk until cool. Peel the cooled peaches. Arrange a peach and a ball of pistachio ice cream in a large deep plate. Cover with zabaglione and garnish with whipped cream.

Preparation time: 20 minutes
Cooking time: 30 minutes
Cooling time: overnight
Difficulty: ☆

Serves 4

For the chocolate mousse:
5 egg yolks
$^1/_2$ cup / 125 g sugar
$3^1/_2$ oz / 100 g bittersweet chocolate
$3^1/_2$ tbsp / 50 g butter
1 sheet of gelatin
$1^1/_2$ cups / 350 ml heavy cream
2 egg whites
7 tbsp / 50 g chopped walnuts
7 tbsp / 50 g chopped hazelnuts

For the green coffee sauce:
2 cups / 500 ml milk
$^1/_3$ cup / 50 g green coffee beans
4 egg yolks
$6^1/_2$ tbsp / 100 g sugar

For the chocolate crêpes:
6 tbsp / 40 g cocoa powder
1 cup / 250 ml milk
2 eggs
$^3/_4$ cup / 100 g flour
1 pinch each of salt and sugar

To garnish:
grated chocolate

It is already unusual to make crêpes out of a chocolate dough. But the most uncommon aspect of this exquisite and simple recipe is that the crêpes are folded into cannelloni shapes, filled with a creamy chocolate mousse and served with an exceptional sauce made with green coffee. This sauce's finesse guarantees that the dessert will be a success. All it requires is a little planning and organizational skills.

The mousse should be prepared using quality chocolate with a high cocoa content. Since there is no arguing with personal preferences, milk or white chocolate could be used instead of bittersweet, always assuming that the chocolate is fresh and shiny and has a good consistency. The chocolate must melt in the mouth and form a thick, creamy mass when heated.

If you are decidedly passionate about chocolate, you might wish to join one of the discriminating and elite clubs of chocolate-tasters, whose festive gatherings are evidently an outstanding cure for every type of stress. And to think that not all too long ago cocoa was quite unfairly accused of causing a plethora of bad side effects ...

Green coffee consists of shelled, sorted beans that have not been roasted, and which produce an unusually intense aroma. They are not so readily available, but turn the coffee sauce into something that even experts will find unforgettable, and your guests are also sure to enjoy. If you wash and freeze the green coffee beans after using them for the infusion, you will be able to use them again.

1. To make the mousse, whisk three egg yolks and the sugar to produce a glistening, foamy mixture in a double boiler. Melt the chocolate and butter in another double boiler. Add 2 egg yolks and the soaked gelatin to the chocolate. Combine the two mixtures. Fold in the heavy cream, the stiffly beaten egg whites and half of the chopped nuts. Refrigerate overnight.

2. Infuse the milk with the green coffee beans for 20 minutes. Beat the egg yolks and sugar until foamy and add the boiling hot milk. Beat over low heat until the sauce starts to thicken. Pour through a pointed sieve and allow to cool for 1 hour.

Mousse Cannelloni

3. Prepare the crêpe dough using the given ingredients and allow to rest for a short time. Make the crêpes one after the other in a very hot pan, frying each side for 2 minutes. Place on a plate and let cool for 1 hour.

4. Fill the crêpes with the chocolate mousse, sprinkle them with the remaining chopped nuts, and roll them up. Before serving refrigerate for 3 to 4 hours. Arrange two "cannelloni" on each plate in a V-shape. Pour the coffee sauce in between the crêpes and sprinkle them with dark and white chocolate flakes.

Cake with

Preparation time: 20 minutes (excluding puff pastry)
Cooking time: 20 minutes
Difficulty: ★★

Serves 4

4 apples (e.g. Golden Delicious)
1 lb / 500 g puff pastry (see basic recipes)
1 cup / 250 g sugar
4 tsp / 20 g butter

For the custard:
1 cup / 250 g superfine sugar
a pinch of salt
8 egg yolks
2 cups / 500 ml milk
a pinch of cinnamon

For the caramel:
$3/4$ cup / 200 g sugar
$2/3$ cup / 150 ml water

To garnish:
strawberries
coarse sugar

The apple is the oldest fruit there is. Can we really blame Adam and Eve for not being able to withstand the temptation to try it? Apple trees galore flower all over Europe and North America, and the different varieties that have been developed over the course of centuries stagger the imagination.

For this recipe, Michel Haquin prefers to use Golden Delicious apples, which were first bred in America about 1912. This preference is not surprising, as Belgium is the leading producer of Golden Delicious apples in Europe. It is a variety that is available year round. It contains vitamin C, iron, and potassium, and does not fall apart even if baked for a long time.

The puff pastry gains its body by being turned six times rather than four, as is sometimes called for. For the layman, this means that after resting the prepared dough has to be rolled out and folded in thirds six times, preferably on a cold marble slab. Ideally, the pastry should rest for two hours between each turn. It is therefore recommended that the puff pastry be prepared a day ahead of time.

Ingredients full of character are used for the custard: in this case cinnamon has been used, but a little vanilla or leftover apples would be equally suitable, though for this purpose, the latter would have to be passed through a fine sieve. Two varieties of cinnamon are commonly available: canel and cassia. Our chef recommends canel, which comes from Sri Lanka, but the Chinese cassia can also be used. Whatever the case, though, one should not add more than a pinch, as too much is likely to impair the flavor of the dessert.

1. Make the puff pastry and cut out four circles with a diameter of 8 in / 18 cm. Peel the apples and cut into slices. Sprinkle the apples with sugar and add a little butter. Arrange the apples on the dough.

2. Fold over the edge of the dough. For the custard, bring the milk to a boil and add the cinnamon. In another bowl, mix the sugar, salt, and egg yolks. As soon as the mixture has a creamy consistency, slowly add the hot milk. Return to the heat and simmer until thickened without allowing it to boil.

Caramelized Apples

3. To make the caramel, dissolve the sugar in the water and cook until golden brown. Bake the cakes for 15 minutes at 275–320 °F / 140–160 °C. After baking, spread a little caramel on the dough in order to increase its sheen.

4. Pass the custard through a fine sieve and keep warm. Pour a little custard onto each plate. Arrange an apple cake in the center and scatter with some coarse sugar crystals. Place a small strawberry, cut into slices, in the center. Serve very hot.

Almond Waffles

Preparation time: *1 hour*
Cooking time: *20 minutes*
Difficulty: ★

Serves 4

30 small strawberries

For the waffle dough:
1 cup / 250 g sugar
6¹/₂ tbsp / 100 ml water
7 tbsp / 50 g flaked almonds

For the caramelized almonds:
15 blanched whole almonds
¹/₃ cup / 50 g confectioners' sugar
olive oil
confectioners' sugar to garnish

For the almond cream:
³/₄ cup / 190 ml cream, whipped
a little almond oil
sugar to taste

For the strawberry sauce:
9 oz / 250 g strawberries
6¹/₂ tbsp / 100 g sugar

This crunchy delight for the tastebuds, which looks pretty and is simple to prepare, requires only a little patience and above all small, ripe strawberries. It is important that they are small and rounded in flavor. Supposedly, strawberries were so fashionable in 18th-century France that even baths were decorated with them, which is less surprising if one considers that the French word for strawberry, *fraise*, is derived from the Latin word *fragrare*, which means "to smell good."

Fresh strawberries must be red and shiny, not soft to the touch, and have a firm stem. It is best to remove the stems after the fruits have been washed so they do not fill with water.

The waffles are ready to be removed from the oven when they start to vibrate gently. The almond mixture for the waffles can be prepared the previous day and kept in the refrigerator overnight. This gives one more time to attend to the final preparations without distraction, and perhaps even devote a little time to the life and achievements of Marshall Plessis-Praslin (1598–1675), who was an ardent defender of royal power during the Fronde revolts and was victorious at Turenne Rethel (1650). Roasted almonds are supposed to have been invented in his kitchens, and in French they are called *praline*, a term derived from his name. They are the original form of the sweets that we now know as pralines.

These waffles can, of course, be prepared with other flavors: instead of using strawberries and almonds, one might, for example, use raspberries and hazelnuts, oranges and pistachios or other similar combinations.

1. To make the waffle dough, boil the sugar and water until they take on a golden color, then allow to become hard. Once the caramel is firm, combine it and the blanched almonds in a blender and blend to produce a fine powder. Store in an airtight container in the freezer until needed.

2. To caramelize the almonds, pour olive oil into a hot pan and sprinkle in the confectioners' sugar. Once the mixture is well browned, sauté the whole almonds until they are coated with caramel. Then roll them in additional confectioners' sugar. Set aside. Add the almond extract to the cream and beat until stiff. Add sugar to taste. Set aside.

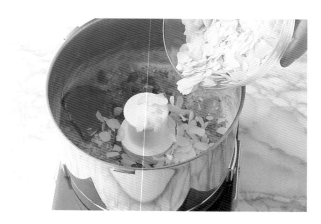

with Strawberries

3. Place molds with a 4½ in / 10 cm diameter on a non-stick baking tray and sprinkle in a layer of the caramel powder. Remove the molds and bake the waffles in the oven for approximately 2 minutes. Allow to cool until they are only lukewarm, remove from the baking tray and allow to rest on a plate. One needs three waffles per serving.

4. To make the strawberry sauce, boil the strawberries and sugar with a little water for 8 minutes, and then pass through a pointed sieve. Pour a little sauce onto the plate, then use a pastry bag to alternate mounds of almond cream and strawberries around the edge of four of the waffles. Place waffles on top of the cream and strawberries and repeat. Garnish with the caramelized almonds.

Banana Soufflé with

Preparation time: 1 hour 15 minutes
Cooking time: 10 minutes
Difficulty: ★★

Serves 6

For the butter caramel sauce:
$^1/_2$ cup / 120 g superfine brown sugar
1 cup / 240 ml apple syrup
$^1/_4$ cup / 60 g butter
$^1/_2$ cup / 120 ml cream

For the honey ice cream:
3 tbsp / 60 g honey
5 egg yolks
$^1/_2$ cup / 130 ml crème fraîche
$1^1/_4$ cups / 290 ml milk

2 tbsp / 30 g sugar
a little vanilla pulp

For the tulip dough (see basic recipes):
$^1/_2$ cup / 125 g butter
$1^1/_2$ cups / 225 g confectioners' sugar
1 cup plus 2 tbsp / 140 g flour
5 egg whites

To garnish:
2 bananas
$^2/_3$ cup / 100 g confectioners' sugar
a little oil

For the banana soufflé:
8 oz / 225 g bananas
juice of 1 lemon
3 tbsp / 20 g cornstarch
4 egg whites
$^1/_3$ cup / 50 g confectioners' sugar

The influence of India on British gastronomy is still clearly evident, particularly in regard to the way English chefs use certain exotic products. They combine ingredients, sauces, herbs, and dishes with an unsurpassed skill, in order to present impressive, well-balanced creations full of finesse and character.

Preparing the soufflé is generally simpler than the final stages of its production, though the addition of the relatively heavy bananas requires some care. Though indigenous only to tropical and subtropical climates like South and Central America, their many virtues have long since made bananas a year-round staple in Westerners' diets. Portable, conveniently packaged, and extremely nutritious, they are a wonderful source of potassium and vitamin C. The most widely available sort in Europe and the United States, the yellow Cavendish banana, is well suited to this dessert, assuming of course that it is thoroughly ripened.

All that remains is to praise the countless virtues of honey, which is used to make the ice cream and contributes to the impressive taste of this dessert. Incorporating honey into the caramel sauce, which should be sampled while cooking to check its flavor, adds just the right dose of sugar and vitamins to be universally appreciated.

1. To make the butter caramel sauce, melt the sugar, apple syrup, and butter in a saucepan, add the cream and bring to a boil. Allow to simmer until the mixture is golden brown. Prepare the honey ice cream by stirring all the ingredients together thoroughly, then allow it to harden in an ice cream maker.

2. Prepare the tulip dough according to the basic recipe, but using the amounts given above. Refrigerate the dough for 30 minutes, then roll it out and cut out circles with a diameter of $6^1/_2$ in / 15 cm. Bake for 10 minutes at 320 °F / 160 °C, then quickly shape into tulips using a form or draping them over a small cup. For the garnish, slice the bananas and brown them in the sugar and a little oil. Set aside.

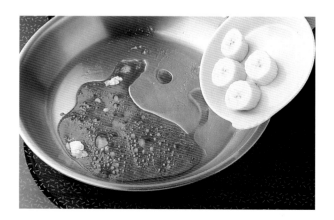

Honey Ice Cream

3. For the soufflé, place the sliced bananas in a saucepan, add just enough water to cover them and a little lemon juice, and cook over low heat. Pass through a sieve. Put a third of the puree to one side; mix the rest with the cornstarch and a little water.

4. Whisk the egg whites with the confectioners' sugar and the remaining lemon juice until stiff, mix with the retained banana puree, then gently fold in the remaining puree mixture. Grease six ovenproof dishes and sprinkle with sugar, fill with the soufflé mixture, and bake in a moderate oven for 8 to 10 minutes. Serve the soufflés with ice cream in a pastry tulip garnished with three slices of banana and some caramel sauce.

Cloudberries with

Preparation time: 30 minutes
Cooking time: 4 minutes
Difficulty: ✶

Serves 4

14 oz / 400 g cloudberries
²/₃ cup / 150 ml cream
6¹/₂ tbsp / 100 g superfine sugar

For the blini dough:
1¹/₂ cups / 200 g flour
1 cup / 250 ml milk
1 oz / 25 g yeast
2 egg yolks

3 egg whites, beaten
a pinch of salt

For the sauce:
3¹/₂ oz / 100 g cloudberries
6¹/₂ tbsp / 100 g superfine sugar
6¹/₂ tbsp / 100 ml Lakka (schnapps made with cloudberries)
juice of 1 lemon

To caramelize the blini:
6¹/₂ tbsp / 100 g sugar
6¹/₂ tbsp / 100 g butter

The forests of the Scandanavian countries on the Arctic circle are full of fantastic creatures: goblins and trolls – the stuff of countless legends. The forests are also bountiful, home to many kinds of mushrooms and wild berries. In addition to the various well-known red berries, there is a very unique fruit, the cloudberry, also known as the yellow berry or mountain berry. It is so tart that it is impossible to eat without adding sugar, which is why a relatively large amount of sugar is needed in this recipe. If red raspberries are substituted, the sugar should be reduced accordingly. The cream also mellows the wild character of this fruit.

It is not difficult to layer the blini. Our chef recommends using wheat flour to make them, as it makes them tastier and softer.

There are, of course, also variations using other types of flour. Here the blini are caramelized, browned thoroughly in sugar and butter. Be careful not to let them become too dark.

In addition to the cloudberries cooked with the blini, some are also used to create the sauce. A good dash of rosemary is added to the berry syrup, which underlines the fruit's flavor without robbing it of its individual character. The Lakka, a liqueur made from cloudberries and very popular amongst the Saami in winter, is also a prominent flavor. If this is not available, another complementary fruit liqueur can be substituted.

Hot tea, black coffee or a glass of aquavit would go very well with this exquisite dessert.

1. Prepare the blini dough by combining all the ingredients except the egg whites, stirring thoroughly and adding the beaten egg whites at the end. Make three blini per serving, dropping a few berries onto each before turning over and cooking the second side.

2. For the sauce, mix the cloudberries with the superfine sugar. Add the liqueur and lemon juice. Puree, then pass everything through a pointed sieve.

Caramelized Blini

3. Caramelize the blini by melting the butter and sugar in a pan, then rapidly fry the blini in this mixture until they take on a light golden color. Keep warm. Beat the cream with the remaining sugar until stiff.

4. Layer the blini on a warm plate. Start with a blini, pipe a ring of whipped cream onto it, add a few cloudberries, repeat and finish with a third blini. Garnish with a strip of cloudberry sauce and some reserved cloudberries.

Rhubarb

Preparation time: 20 minutes
Cooking time: 30 minutes
Difficulty: ★

Serves 4
2 lb 3 oz / 1 kg fresh rhubarb
1 cup / 250 g sugar
1¼ cups / 300 ml water
9 oz / 250 g strawberries
3½ oz / 100 g wild strawberries
2 vanilla beans
1 tbsp cornstarch

For the vanilla ice cream (see basic recipes):
2 cups / 500 ml milk
6 egg yolks
6½ tbsp / 100 g sugar
2 vanilla beans

This rhubarb-based dessert combines tradition, freshness, and lightness with a somewhat unusual ingredient. The rhubarb plant consists mainly of decorative leaves, and has fibrous red and green stems that are used in numerous desserts, cakes, and compotes. Rhubarb is also known as a plant with medical and astringent properties.

The main problem in using rhubarb is its sourness, which can be reduced by marinating it in sugar for several hours or blanching it briefly in boiling water. Whichever method one chooses, one should use firm, thick stems with intense coloring, and check for an intense aroma when sliced. In this recipe, the rhubarb is cooked together with strawberries for about half an hour.

Unfortunately, wild strawberries do not keep very long and there is nothing one can do to alter this. Our chef claims to have found a variety that is still fresh the day after being picked, but they are not widely available. One should use the freshest berries possible.

Eyvind Hellstrøm feels that the soup is perfect without any other additions, and does not require spices such as cinnamon and ginger such as the English, for example, like to add. It can be prepared at any time of year, served cold in summer and hot in winter.

1. Coarsely dice 1 lb 12 oz / 800 g of the rhubarb and simmer with the sugar, water, and strawberries for 20 to 30 minutes. Pass through a pointed sieve.

2. Bring the resulting liquid to a boil again, spoon off the foam and add the vanilla beans. Reduce slightly and add the cornstarch.

Soup "Bagatelle"

3. Dice the remaining 7 oz / 200 g rhubarb finely. Prepare the vanilla ice cream according to the basic recipe.

4. Briefly brown the diced rhubarb in a pan with some additional sugar, and then add to the rhubarb soup. Pour a little rhubarb soup into each bowl, place a spoon of vanilla ice cream in the middle and arrange the wild strawberries around it. Serve either cold or hot, according to the time of year.

Orange Jelly with

Preparation time: 15 minutes
Cooking time: 30 minutes
Cooling time: 1 hour
Difficulty: ✸

Serves 4

3 untreated lemons
juice of 2 oranges
2¼ cups / 550 g sugar
2 sheets of gelatin

This very simple and heavenly light dessert, shining with the light of the Mediterranean sun, is a worthy conclusion to a special meal. It can be prepared effortlessly at any time of year, keeps well, and seduces the diner with its freshness and finesse, which are combined with an exceptionally high vitamin content. Oranges contain not only vitamin C, but are also very high in calcium and magnesium, and contribute to one's well-being in many different ways. Originally grown in Southeast Asia, Liguria in Italy is the first place this fruit was cultivated in Europe. Today the United States is the world's leading producer of oranges.

For this dessert, the first step is to squeeze orange juice using juicy fruits of a very high quality. The navel orange, given that name by the British because it has a "navel," the Valencia orange or the blood orange with its red flesh would all be sure to make this dessert a success. The oranges should not be squeezed until the last minute, so that the utmost flavor is retained and any oxidization is minimized.

Since the Middle Ages, lemons have also been cultivated in Italy. As this recipe uses only lemon peel, one should choose untreated fruits that are sufficiently large and firm. In addition, it is recommended to wash them in warm water and brush the peels thoroughly before grating.

This delicious, refreshing citrus fruit jelly, in which the fruits can be cut according to one's own imagination (giving the dish a personal decorative touch), is also easy to digest. Try serving it with a glass of Grand Marnier – its amber color and superb taste provide a masterly finishing touch.

1. Peel and thinly slice the lemon rinds. Wash the lemon peel in 2 cups / 500 ml cold water. Repeat five or six times. Bring 2 cups / 500 ml water to a boil with 2 cups / 500 g of the sugar and the lemon rind, and simmer for an hour over low heat.

2. Meanwhile, in another pan, carefully reduce the orange juice with the remaining sugar and ⅔ cup / 150 ml water for half an hour.

Marinated Lemon Peel

3. Dissolve the sheets of gelatin in cold water, then add them to the reduced and slightly cooled fruit juice. Pour into a dish and refrigerate.

4. Cut various shapes out of the set jelly. Place on serving plates and garnish with the reduced lemon peel.

Eggplant Pastry

Preparation time: 45 minutes
Cooking time: 35 minutes
Difficulty: ✷✷

Serves 4

5¼ oz / 150 g ricotta cheese
⅓ cup / 50 g confectioners' sugar
9 oz / 250 g bittersweet chocolate coating
⅓ cup / 60 g candied fruit
1 eggplant
1 tbsp / 15 ml Marsala

For the cake mixture:
4 eggs
½ cup / 125 g sugar
1 cup / 125 g flour

In case there are still skeptics who find it difficult to imagine the eggplant as an ingredient for a dessert, this extraordinary creation will convert them. A member of the nightshade family, which includes potatoes and tomatoes, eggplant is actually a fruit. Our chef Alfonso Iaccarino comes from Naples, in the heart of the eggplant-growing region in Italy, and in this recipe he combines it with chocolate and candied fruit.

In the Middle Ages, the eggplant was brought to Italy from India, and has been a native of the Mediterranean area ever since. In the ensuing centuries, countless recipes have been developed. For this dessert young, medium-sized eggplants with few seeds are needed. They are skinned and cut into thin strips, which are steamed until tender so they do not lose their

taste and color. The next surprising ingredient is the ricotta, a fresh cheese that is made from sheep's milk in Italy, instead of cow's milk as in the United States. In this instance it is mixed with candied fruit. Although ricotta traditionally comes from Tuscany and Sardinia, this dessert is a specialty from Naples, where many other sweets use these ingredients. The finished dessert is covered with chocolate sauce and Marsala, the Sicilian dessert wine that is used for both savory and sweet dishes. Alternatively, one can use port.

The recipe was derived from a dish using eggplants au gratin, *la parmigiana de melanzana*, which is traditionally served on August 15, the feast day of the Assumption.

1. Mix the ricotta cheese and confectioners' sugar. Add 7 oz / 200 g of the chopped chocolate coating and the candied fruit. Peel the eggplant and cut it into long, thin strips. Steam the eggplant for 5 minutes.

2. Once the eggplants are tender, place two strips of eggplant into each of four individual dishes in a cross shape as shown below.

with Chocolate

3. For the cake dough, combine the eggs and sugar. Whisk them in a double boiler until a creamy consistency has been achieved. Carefully blend in the sifted flour. Pour the batter into a pan and bake for 30 minutes at 355 °F / 180 °C. Cut the baked dough into little cubes measuring $1^1/_2$ x $1^1/_2$ in / 3 x 3 cm and sprinkle on the eggplant slices.

4. Cover the small cake cubes with enough ricotta mixture to fill the dishes, then fold over the protruding ends of the eggplant strips to cover it. Invert the molds onto serving plates. Melt the remaining chocolate coating with a little Marsala, and pour over the dessert. Decorate with mint leaves.

Mocha Charlotte with

Preparation time: 2 hours
Cooking time: 20 minutes
Cooling time: 30 minutes
Difficulty: ★★★

Serves 4

For the sponge cake dough:
3 eggs
5 tsp / 25 ml water
2 tbsp / 15 g cocoa
1/2 cup / 130 g sugar
1 cup / 130 g flour
1 tsp / 3 g baking powder
coffee liqueur (Kahlua)

For the mocha cream:
5 tbsp / 70 ml pastry cream (see basic recipes)

1/2 tsp / 2 g gelatin
2 tbsp / 30 ml strong coffee (espresso)
3/4 cup / 200 ml crème fraîche
bittersweet chocolate

For the light chocolate sauce:
9 oz / 250 g white chocolate coating
1/2 cup / 125 ml heavy cream
4 tsp / 20 ml water

For the dark chocolate sauce:
9 oz / 250 g bittersweet chocolate coating
1/2 cup / 125 ml heavy cream
4 tsp / 20 ml water

For the caramelized nuts:
almonds, cashews, pistachios, sugar, oil

For the peppermint ice cream:
vanilla ice cream (see basic recipes)
a little melted chocolate
3/4 cup / 200 ml peppermint liqueur

This outstanding dessert originally derived its name from Queen Charlotte, the wife of King George III of England. Ever since, the charlotte has been enjoyed in countless permutations of cake-lined, cream-filled delicacies according to country and era, and charlotte russe is still one of the favorite versions. It is best to prepare the charlotte early and refrigerate it until it is served; this gives it a firmer consistency and lets the sponge cake gradually absorb the flavor of the filling. As sponge cake can absorb an enormous quantity of liquid, the charlotte should be covered while it is in the refrigerator so that it does not pick up any other flavors.

Mocha is a type of coffee with a very mild aroma, which produces an extremely oily drink. For that reason it is best suited to making espresso, which is used to make the cream filling for the charlotte. The flavour is enhanced by the coffee liqueur

(Kahlua) with which the sponge cake is drenched. Mocha beans first appeared in Yemen in the 6th century, and their name is derived from the Yemen port of Mokka.

In this recipe our chef has created an imaginative combination of two ingredients that are extremely well-suited to each other: coffee and chocolate. Chocolate appears in various nuances of flavor in the sponge cake and sauces, which contrast and yet complement each other. The two sauces must have the same consistency and must not be allowed to simmer when heated, as this would cause them to lose their sheen. The sauces should not be poured onto the plates until immediately before serving the dessert, as they might otherwise set and detract from the quality of the presentation. This dessert will be an absolute success and is guaranteed to be irresistible accompanied by a glass of dessert wine.

1. To make the sponge cake, beat the eggs, water, sugar, flour and baking powder until fluffy. Separate the mixture into two halves and mix the cocoa into one half. Line a baking tray with baking paper. Using two pastry bags, pipe alternating strips of the two mixtures. Bake at 430 °F / 220 °C.

2. Line the sides and bottoms of individual molds with the sponge cake. Soak the sponge cake with coffee liqueur. Beat the pastry cream. Dissolve the gelatin in cold water, pour into the espresso and mix with the pastry cream. Stir the crème fraîche until creamy, then carefully fold it into the mocha coffee cream.

Ice Cream and Nuts

3. Caramelize the nuts in sugar and place on an oiled plate. Prepare the light chocolate sauce by heating the heavy cream and water, adding the chopped chocolate coating, and stirring over low heat until a smooth sauce is produced. Make the dark chocolate sauce in the same way. Fill the charlottes completely with mocha coffee cream and smooth off the excess. Refrigerate.

4. Prepare the vanilla ice cream and divide into two bowls. To make the peppermint ice cream, add the peppermint liqueur to one bowl of ice cream; stir until cold in an ice cream maker and, shortly before finishing, add a thin stream of liquid chocolate. Pour the two sauces onto the dessert plates, place a charlotte in the center of each, and arrange the ice cream and caramelized nuts decoratively around them.

Pastry Leaves with

Preparation time: 30 minutes
Cooking time: 35 minutes
Cooling time: 10 minutes
Difficulty: ☆

Serves 4

8 sheets of wonton dough (from Asian stores)
10½ oz / 300 g strawberries
3½ tbsp / 50 ml crème fraîche
¼ cup / 60 g sugar
grated peel of 1 untreated orange
6½ tbsp / 100 g butter

oil for deep-frying
ground cinnamon
confectioners' sugar

For the ice cream with rice:
4 cups / 1 l milk
2 vanilla beans
⅔ cup / 120 g short grain rice
¾ cup / 200 g sugar
2 tsp / 10 g candied fruit
grated peel of 1 untreated lemon and
    1 untreated orange

The nuances of the strawberry's flavors are almost limitless: it was already highly valued in Roman times and was called *fraga* ("the scented"), a name that is still reflected in the Latin name of its genus, *fragaria*. Depending on availability or preference, raspberries can also be used for this recipe. Treat these extremely sensitive fruits very carefully; they should not be immersed in water or exposed to high temperatures. The fruit sauce for this dessert involves heating – but not boiling – the berries, creating a pleasing contrast of warm and cold.

Rice "à l'Impératrice" was the favorite dessert of Empress Eugénie, the wife of Napoleon III. Evidently this was a sort of compromise between a creamy rice pudding and blancmange, which was served in a dome shape and covered with finely diced candied fruit. The original cream has been transformed into an ice cream here, though still containing suitable quantities of the typical ingredients, rice and candied fruit. Using rice in a dessert is an excellent opportunity to use this widely known and cultivated foodstuff (more than 8,000 varieties are known!) in a different way. The great popularity of this grain has, however, led many an amateur to produce truly disgraceful gastronomic faux pas in the name of rice pudding. Fortunately, sophisticated cooks such as André Jaeger are endeavouring to uphold and nurture the long tradition of this dessert.

Wonton is the Asian version of phyllo dough, consisting of flour, eggs, and oil. When deep-fried, it becomes crunchy, and here forms an elegant casing in which to serve the ice cream.

1. Bring the milk to a boil with the vanilla beans and the grated lemon and orange peel. Add the rice and simmer for 20 minutes over a low heat. Stir in the sugar. After cooking pour through a sieve, retaining the liquid. Stir the sieved cooked rice and candied fruit into the liquid. Place in the freezer for 10 minutes.

2. Wash and clean the strawberries. Cut one-third of the berries into slices and puree the remainder in a blender. Heat the crème fraîche in a pan, then add the sugar and grated orange peel.

Rice "à l'Impératrice"

3. Add the strawberry puree to the crème fraîche mixture and heat slowly without boiling. Remove from the heat and add the butter in small pieces. Cut out round pieces of wonton pastry and deep-fry in hot oil.

4. Dust the pastry slices with confectioners' sugar and a little cinnamon. For each serving pour some of the warm sauce into a deep plate, then add sliced strawberries and finish with a ball of ice cream between two pastry cases.

Ice Cream with Prunes and

Preparation time: 30 minutes
Cooking time: 10 minutes
Difficulty: ★★

Serves 4

10¹/₂ oz / 300 g prunes
2¹/₂ cups / 600 ml red wine
¹/₂ cup plus 1 tbsp / 200 g raspberry jam
1 cinnamon stick
1 untreated orange
1 untreated lemon

For the ice cream:
12 egg yolks
³/₄ cup / 200 g sugar
2 cups / 500 ml milk
2 cups / 500 ml cream
4¹/₂ tbsp / 100 g plum jam
3¹/₂ tbsp / 50 ml cognac

For the zabaglione:
2 egg yolks
3¹/₂ tbsp / 50 ml white wine
3 tbsp / 40 g sugar
3¹/₂ tbsp / 50 ml Grand Marnier

We now turn to the desserts produced by Paul Bocuse's restaurant, which are called "delicacies and treats for the taste buds" on the menu. Cakes, sponge cakes, creams, ice creams, and sorbets – all these dainties compete with each other in countless interesting flavors, aromas, and colors. One should not miss Roger Jaloux' creation, which is presented here.

The choice of prunes is made according to specific criteria: flavorful, not too soft, and with a slight coating, i.e., the fruits should be a little waxy. Despite their juiciness, the fruits should not give when pressed. Though there are many different sorts of plums, those best suited to becoming prunes have a skin capable of containing the fruit's juices during cooking. Such plums are cultivated in the southeast of France, for example, and are derived from the damson plums introduced by the

Knights Templar returning from the Crusades, which long had the reputation of being "devil's fruit." But how could one possibly resist these plums in the marketplace of Villeneuve-sur-Lot, where they are dried over a wood fire, as their gentle aroma combines with the smoke to create an incomparable fragrance?

Enough poetry. It is time to turn to the zabaglione, which must be prepared in an extremely clean pan. Nothing should be allowed to interfere with its preparation, which must be carried out in an even rhythm. The Grand Marnier is added at the last minute so that the rich bouquet of this high-quality liqueur does not evaporate. To enjoy the full impact of this unusual dessert, try to have a little zabaglione, ice cream, and prune in each mouthful.

1. The day before serving, marinate the prunes in the red wine with the raspberry jam, cinnamon stick, and the peel of the orange and lemon. To make the ice cream, whisk the egg yolks with the sugar until foamy, then add the heated milk and cream. Heat everything together and then allow to cool. Add the plum jam and cognac, and stir in an ice cream maker.

2. Bring the prunes that have been marinating in the red wine, raspberry jam, cinnamon and citrus peel to a boil (in the marinade).

Grand Marnier Zabaglione

3. Cut the peeled orange and lemon into round slices. As soon as the prunes are soft, add the orange and lemon slices to the liquid. Allow to cool.

4. To make the zabaglione, whisk the egg yolks, white wine and sugar in a double boiler. Add the Grand Marnier. To serve, arrange four or five prunes on each plate and add a little of the cooking juices. Place a ball of ice cream in the middle and cover with the zabaglione.

Crispy Leaves

Preparation time: 20 minutes
Cooking time: 8 minutes
Difficulty: ★★

Serves 4

8 sheets of phyllo dough
13 tbsp / 200 g clarified butter
1⅓ cups / 200 g confectioners' sugar
¾ cup / 200 ml pastry cream (see basic
 recipes)

1 untreated lemon
⅔ cup / 150 ml cream, whipped
2 cups of raspberries
1 cup of blackberries or blueberries
2 passion fruit
some red berries (e.g. wild strawberries,
 red currants)
6½ tbsp / 100 g sugar

The aesthetics of cakes were neglected for a long time: bakers were perfectly content to produce simple cake mixtures using flour and water, which were enriched with honey, grains or spices, or better quality bread doughs. Not until the 19th century was importance increasingly attached to the external appearance of cakes. The creation depicted here, consisting of delicate sheets of dough layered with pastry cream, is now a classic and in addition a real treat for the eyes.

For this recipe, our chef uses a very fine dough that can dry out even at room temperature, and burns easily. But it is not only because of the dough that one has to be very careful when preparing this dessert; the red berries also require sensitive treat-ment. Red currants, for example, which are available mainly in July, are very sensitive to touch and like all red berries should be used as quickly as possible. Raspberries, which are also available in a yellow variety, are a real summer fruit. It is advisable not to let them come into contact with water for too long, as they very rapidly lose their flavor in water.

This composition is dominated by red berries, with the trans-parent yellow flesh of the passion fruit providing contrast. However, this is not merely a question of color: the sour taste of the passion fruit is very noticeable alongside the sweetness of the berries, so it needs to be used with care.

1. On a board, roll out two slices of phyllo dough and brush them with clarified butter. Sprinkle on some confectioners' sugar, then place another layer of dough on top and once again cover with butter and confectioners' sugar. Continue until all the phyllo dough has been used.

2. Cut out 12 circles from the dough and bake them for 5 minutes at 355 °F / 180 °C. Once they are glazed, take them out of the oven and allow to cool on a tray. Prepare the pastry cream and combine this carefully with the grated lemon peel.

with Raspberries

3. Combine the pastry cream and lemon peel with the stiffly whipped cream. Place a spoonful of the cream and a few sugared fruits on each plate.

4. Place a piece of glazed pastry on the fruits, then make two additional layers, finishing with a piece of phyllo dough. Pour a little raspberry sauce (made from strained raspberries) around it, and add the juice and seeds of the passion fruits. Decorate with red berries that have been rolled in confectioners' sugar.

Apple Tarts

Preparation time: *1 hour*
Cooking time: *25 minutes*
Difficulty: ★★

Serves 4

1 lb / 500 g apples (Granny Smiths)
3 tbsp / 40 g sugar
$^1/_4$ cup / 50 g raisins
1 tsp ground cinnamon
juice of $^1/_2$ lemon
4 prunes, marinated in red wine
a few large strawberries
$4^1/_2$ tbsp / 100 g red currant jelly

For the streusel topping:
3 tbsp / 25 g flour
4 tsp / 25 g sugar
8 tsp / 40 g butter
3 tbsp / 25 g finely ground almonds
$^1/_2$ tsp cinnamon

For the sponge cake:
4 egg whites
$^1/_2$ cup plus 1 tbsp / 140 g superfine sugar
3 tbsp / 20 g flour
$^3/_4$ cup / 90 g finely ground almonds

Custard (see basic recipes):
1 cup / 250 ml

The term "streusel" is derived from the German verb *streuen*, "to scatter." This particular streusel topping is a sweet dough with ground almonds and cinnamon, which is scattered on individual apple cakes. It should be prepared a day in advance with soft butter, then warmed again just before serving on top of the apple filling.

Human history has been shaped by the apple and the countless ways in which it can be prepared. It is now the most commonly eaten fruit in Europe and North America, with new varieties constantly being developed. The Granny Smith, which Émile Jung recommends here, was introduced to Europe from Australia in the 1950s. Both juicy and acidic, it is very suitable for cooking, and even the stewed pieces used in this recipe will still be firm when eaten. This variety of apple ripens relatively late, is then shining green and is harvested in October or November. When selecting apples, it is important to make sure that the skins are as smooth and perfect as possible.

For truly superior flavor, nothing can compare to homemade red currant jelly. Émile Jung is an expert in this and recommends using a mixture of both red currants and black currants. The strawberries and prunes that are soaked in it will be even tastier if the prunes have been marinated in red wine.

Nonetheless, there should be some unity to this "lively streusel sonata" – if music-lovers will allow this little word play. And although our chef suggests variations using pears, pineapple or peaches, one should make sure not to overdo the mixture of ingredients.

1. A day in advance, make the streusel topping using the flour, sugar, butter, ground almonds, and cinnamon. Form a ball of dough and grate it. Refrigerate the dough. To make the sponge cake, beat the egg whites until stiff, beat in the sugar, then fold in the flour and ground almonds. Bake at 340 °F / 170 °C for 15 minutes. Set aside.

2. Peel the apples and core them. Dice into 1 in / 2 cm cubes. Combine the apples with the sugar, raisins, cinnamon, and lemon juice, and cook for about 10 minutes over a low heat. Then remove the pieces of apple from the liquid.

with Streusel

3. Bake the streusel mixture on a baking tray at 340 °F / 170 °C for 5 minutes. Allow to cool, then crumble it up. Add the prunes and strawberries to the red currant jelly and allow them to soak in it.

4. Line four round molds with a diameter of 3 in / 7.5 cm and a height of 1¹/₂ in / 4 cm with the sponge cake and cover with stewed apples. Sprinkle the streusel topping over the apples. Heat in the oven until lukewarm and dust with confectioners' sugar. Pour some custard onto serving plates and arrange an apple tart in the middle of each plate, and decorate with the prunes and strawberries.

Printen

Preparation time: 45 minutes
Cooling time: 2 hours
Difficulty: ★★

Serves 4

3 egg yolks
3¹/₂ tbsp / 50 g sugar
1 cup / 250 ml cream
1³/₄ oz / 50 g printen or other spiced cookies, chopped
3¹/₂ tbsp / 50 ml rum

For the spiced oranges:
3 large oranges
3¹/₂ tbsp / 50 g sugar
6¹/₂ tbsp / 100 ml orange juice
1 whole clove
cinnamon, vanilla, star anise, cardamom

For the caramel:
2 tbsp dextrose
¹/₂ cup / 120 g sugar
3 tbsp / 40 ml water

"Good Christmas printen are baked at Easter," states our chef like a shot, eager to revive this old gourmet tradition. Printen, a variation of the cookies spiced with cinnamon and cloves that are beloved throughout northern Europe, derive their name from *printen*, "to press," because they are made with specially carved rolling pins that literally press the dough into various shapes.

This parfait, which has a firmer consistency than usual that suits the oranges well, is a true symphony of spices and astonishing tastes. The ingredients should be chosen carefully.

Star anise should not be confused with aniseed, which is used in many other desserts and dry cakes. The fruit of this bush,

native to Vietnam, contains an intensely aromatic extract that has a soothing effect on the digestive system. Cardamom is the name given to fruits and brown seeds derived from several Indian plants that have a distinctive, peppery flavor. In India these are combined to make a spice that is used in many curries and rice dishes. In European recipes cardamom is mainly used for baking, especially spiced bread. Due to its intense flavor, it should be added carefully.

Cinnamon is the dried inner bark of the cinnamon tree. It can be obtained as a whole piece of curled bark (cinnamon stick) or in a ground form. Here, too, it is important to be careful with the quantity, as too much can destroy the flavor of the dessert.

1. Whisk the egg yolks in a double boiler with the sugar. Allow to cool, stirring constantly, and add the liquid cream. Add the chopped printen cookies and the rum, pour into a bowl, and place in the freezer.

2. For the spiced oranges, peel the oranges and divide them into segments. Use the sugar to make a dry caramel, then carefully and gradually add the orange juice to it. Add the spices and orange segments. Bring to a boil and allow to cool in an uncovered bowl.

Parfait

3. In a small pan, make a brown caramel out of the sugar, dextrose, and water. Coat the outside of a ladle with oil and pour fine strands of the caramel over it to form a cage. Allow to cool and remove from the ladle. Repeat, making one caramel cage per serving.

4. Remove the parfait from the freezer and divide into portions. Place a slice of the parfait onto the center of each plate, cover with a caramel cage and arrange some spiced oranges around it.

Preparation time: 2 hours 30 minutes
Cooking time: 15 minutes
Difficulty: ★★★

Serves 4

For the parfait:
¹/₂ cup / 120 g sugar
juice of 1 pineapple
5 egg yolks
2 cups / 500 ml cream, whipped
2 tbsp / 30 ml Grand Marnier

For the ice cream:
1 pineapple
10 sugar cubes
3 egg yolks

1 cup / 250 ml cream
a dash of Grand Marnier

For the glazed pineapple:
1 pineapple
3¹/₂ tbsp / 50 g sugar
a little cornstarch

Pancakes (see basic recipes)

For the zabaglione:
juice of ¹/₂ pineapple
1 egg
1 egg yolk
3¹/₂ tbsp / 50 ml white wine
2 tsp / 10 g sugar

"You never stop learning," Dieter Kaufmann confides in our test kitchen while preparing this recipe. "I am always open to new ideas, especially when they come from the youngest members of my own team." This recipe using pineapple is an excellent example of this principle.

Dieter Kaufmann discovered the small pineapples cultivated on the island of Réunion in Paris – exquisite, juicy fruit that, due to its consistency, can easily be made into parfaits or ice cream. This is not to say that fruit from other countries, Martinique and Australia in particular, would not be equally good.

In order to flavor the parfait, it is best to use Grand Marnier with a red ribbon, which is made from orange peel that has been marinated in brandy instead of cognac. This makes it less

penetrating, so that it does not dominate the dessert. The flavor of both the parfait and the ice cream are enriched with the liqueur, and the addition of sugar softens the natural acidity of the pineapple.

In order to do justice to these manifold flavors, the frothy wine cream has to be very light and neutral in taste. Thus, it is primarily the consistency of the zabaglione that completes the dessert. Zabaglione could even be combined with a dessert based on beer. In fact, Dieter Kaufmann once rounded off a very special meal created for members of Gault & Millau, who were on a journey through Germany, with a bier soufflé with spicy plums and a wine zabaglione that those present will never forget.

1. To make the parfait, caramelize the sugar slightly, gradually add the pineapple juice and reduce by a third. Whisk the egg yolks in a double boiler until foamy. Remove from the double boiler and continue beating until cooled. Add the reduced juice and carefully fold in the whipped cream. Flavor with Grand Marnier and freeze in a bowl for 3 hours.

2. For the ice cream, dice the pineapple into small cubes. Retain the juice, heat carefully, and dissolve the sugar in it. Stir the egg yolks into the juice until it is hot. Add the slightly heated cream and beat until the mixture has an even consistency. Add the diced pineapple and a little Grand Marnier. Allow to harden in an ice cream maker.

3. To make the glazed fruit, quarter the pineapple, select the two nicest quarters, halve them lengthwise and refrigerate. Chop the fruit of the remaining quarters and caramelize in the sugar, binding them with a little cornstarch if necessary. Prepare a pancake batter according to the basic recipe, make small pancakes and fill them with the caramelized pineapple pieces.

4. Shortly before serving, prepare a classic zabaglione using the ingredients listed above. Arrange the three pineapple variations attractively on large plates. The zabaglione can be served as a sauce or separately.

Fresh Cheese Cake

Preparation time: 1 hour
Cooking time: 1 hour 15 minutes
Difficulty: ★★★

Serves 4

¹/₂ tbsp rennin
1 tbsp water
12³/₄ cups / 3 l whole milk
7 tbsp / 50 g flour
7 tbsp / 50 g blanched almonds

2 eggs
³/₄ cup / 200 ml crème fraîche
¹/₃ cup / 50 g confectioners' sugar
butter for the molds

As accompaniments:
cloudberry jam
whipped cream

Even a country with a rough, harsh climate, such as Sweden, is capable of producing sweet delicacies. The multitude of delicious cakes and baked goods that are prepared there proves this and reveals a tireless culinary creativity. Småland, our chef's home in the south of Sweden, is no exception. An example is the Swedish apple cake (*svensk äppelkaka*), in which the cook used to hide an almond; it was said that whoever bit the nut would soon be married.

This cake made with fresh cheese has similar traditions. It was served during celebrations that lasted several days, and every guest would try it and praise its perfection. Originally prepared with old cow's milk (even sour old cow's milk), it is now refined by adding rennin, an enzyme used to make cheese that is available in larger grocery stores.

The almonds are chopped before being added to the filling. North Americans have the luxury of being able to find reasonably fresh almonds easily; sweet almonds are so unknown in Sweden that our chef has to import his supply from Greece. However, he has access to a local specialty very difficult to find: the cloudberry (or yellow berry), which produces a particularly tasty jam. Since these berries grow almost exclusively in the wild in cold climates like Scandanavia, Maine, and Canada, few ever find their way to a grocery store. If you cannot locate cloudberry jam, replace it with blueberry, cherry or raspberry jam.

1. Combine the rennin and water. Mix a little milk with the flour. Heat the rest of the milk to 90 °F / 35 °C, then remove from the heat and add the two mixtures to the lukewarm milk while stirring constantly. Cover and let stand for 30 to 40 minutes.

2. Using a knife, prick the mixture several times so that liquid can drain off. Pass the cheese through a sieve and allow to drain. Chop the almonds coarsely.

from Småland

3. Whisk the eggs, then mix the creme fraîche and confectioners' sugar with the almonds. Combine everything with the fresh cheese mixture.

4. Grease the cake pans with butter, pour in the batter and bake for an hour. Cover the cake with aluminum foil at the beginning of the baking period so the cake does not become too dark. Important: do not move the pan while the cake is baking! Serve lukewarm with cloudberry jam and whipped cream.

Pears with Cranberries

Preparation time: 1 hour
Cooking time: 40 minutes
Difficulty: ★★

Serves 4

1 lb / 500 g cranberries
6¹/₂ tbsp / 100 ml water
1¹/₃ cups / 200 g confectioners' sugar
1 cinnamon stick
5 pears (with stems)

For the vanilla sauce:
³/₄ cup / 200 ml milk
6¹/₂ tbsp / 100 ml cream
1 vanilla bean
1 egg yolk
2 tbsp confectioners' sugar

Örjan Klein, who presents us here with a Swedish dessert, is very enthusiastic about traditional dishes using the produce of his native country. This dish is a further example of his culinary skill, and it calls to mind two memories for Örjan Klein: the orchard full of pear trees around his country house in Nølgarder, and the cranberries from Småland, where he was born. This delight for the taste buds used to be served on Sundays, and he had many opportunities to enjoy it as a child.

The pears should be very flavorful and cook well. Of the numerous varieties available, several will be suitable for this recipe. They need only be peeled shortly before adding them to the stewed cranberries, whose sour taste will permeate the pears.

The small, red cranberries are often served as an accompaniment to game, which in Sweden includes reindeer and elk, and feature in a whole variety of recipes. Whole berries keep for an astonishingly long time. In this recipe, their sour taste combines with the gentle flavor of vanilla, which moderates the acidity of the berries somewhat. Cranberries grow not only in North America, but throughout Sweden as well, which certainly contributes to their popularity in that country. It would be difficult to replace them in this recipe, except perhaps with a red wine syrup flavored with cinnamon.

1. Reserve some of the cranberries for garnishing. Puree the rest in a blender. Cook the puree in a saucepan for 15 minutes with the water, sugar, and cinnamon.

2. Peel the pears without removing their stems, set them into the saucepan with the puree mixture and continue to simmer for 20 minutes.

and Vanilla Sauce

3. Remove the pears and place them in a deep bowl. Pass the puree through a sieve and pour the resulting liquid over the pears. Refrigerate for a few days.

4. To make the vanilla sauce, mix the milk and cream and bring them to a boil with the opened vanilla bean. Whisk the egg yolk and sugar, then pour onto the vanilla milk, stirring continuously until slightly thickened. Pass the sauce through a pointed sieve and allow to cool. Pour the sauce onto plates, place a pear on each one, and garnish with cranberries.

Caramelized

Preparation time: 45 minutes
Cooking time: 5 minutes
Difficulty: ★

Serves 4

For the sorbet:
black tea
2 cups / 500 ml water
1 cup / 250 g sugar
4 tsp / 25 g dextrose
1/4 cup / 45 g candied ginger
1/2 cup / 125 ml milk

For the caramelized bananas:
5 bananas
3 1/2 tbsp / 50 g brown sugar
a pinch of ground cinnamon
a pinch of ground ginger
5 thin slices of phyllo pastry
6 1/2 tbsp / 100 g butter

Bananas originally came from Asia, but today are imported mainly from the Antilles and South America. Of the approximately 350 different varieties, the most widely available is undoubtedly the Cavendish with its smooth yellow, though occasionally striped, skin. Americans and Europeans consider the banana to be exclusively a sweet fruit; the chefs of other regions and continents integrate it more often in savory dishes.

Bananas taste best when they are an even light or dark yellow. However, because fully ripe bananas very quickly turn black and then spoil, the fruits are picked while green and transported to their destinations while still unripe. Once arrived, they are ripened in warehouses that are specially designed for that purpose. Unfortunately, that means that the quality of these fruits varies. The purpose of our recipe is to retain the distinctive qualities of the banana as far as possible. Most of

the elements can be prepared ahead of time, but the bananas should be baked immediately before serving.

Whatever tea you use for the accompanying sorbet, make sure it is fresh and do not allow it to steep too long. Use five to eight not-too-large teaspoons of tea per liter of water and allow it to steep for five minutes to produce a nicely flavored infusion. Darjeeling tea is especially recommended.

The imaginative cook can take this recipe as the starting point for myriad variations: the croquettes could be made with apples or pears; the sorbet with lemon, mango or passion fruit. The choice of ingredients is virtually unlimited. However, our chef's version of the sorbet using tea and ginger is a very special delight.

1. To make the sorbet, prepare the black tea and allow it to steep for 5 minutes. Add the sugar and dextrose and allow to cool. Chop the candied ginger very finely and stir into the tea. Pour the milk into the tea. Stir until cold in a ice cream maker.

2. Peel the bananas and cut into pieces 2 1/2 in / 5 cm in length. Mix the brown sugar, ground cinnamon, and ground ginger. Coat the bananas in the mixture; reserve the rest.

Banana Croquettes

3. Brush melted butter onto the phyllo dough, and cut each slice in half.

4. Wrap the coated bananas in the phyllo dough, roll the croquettes in the remaining brown sugar mixture, and bake for 5 minutes at 390 °F / 200 °C. Arrange two banana croquettes and a ball of tea sorbet on each plate.

Passion Fruit in Eggcups

Preparation time: 20 minutes
Cooking time: 20 minutes
Cooling time: 20 minutes
Difficulty: ✶

Serves 4

12 passion fruit
5¼ oz / 150 g bittersweet chocolate coating
6½ tbsp / 100 g sugar
1 cup / 250 ml cream
½ cup / 80 g confectioners' sugar

Our chef found his inspiration for this refreshing dessert in the relationship between eggs and passion fruit. A very special fruit, also known as a maypop, the passion fruit is hidden inside a brown, wrinkled skin; it has a jelly-like flesh with an extremely acidic flavor that contains vitamins A and C. It is the fruit of a tropical shrub that is mainly cultivated in America and Africa.

There are many interpretations of the passion fruit's name, but it is generally thought that its form reminded Spanish missionaries of different elements of Christ's Passion. Slices of passion fruit are compared with the crown of thorns, its stems with the nails on the cross, and the stamens to the hammers with which they were driven into the cross. Passion fruit come in several varieties and sizes (including the *Passiflora edulis*,

which can weigh up to 1 lb / 500 g); but the largest are not necessarily the best.

The passion fruit is valued both for its crunchiness and its decorative uses, and particularly because of the small black seeds in its flesh. In this recipe the seeds are mixed into the cream, which moderates their intense flavor without concealing it. The pectin contained in these fruits gives the cream a firm consistency.

Étienne Krebs recommends serving the cream with chocolate sticks made from chocolate that has a very high cocoa content. The chocolate should be carefully shaved into rolls using a spatula in order to produce the thin, elegant sticks.

1. Slice the tops off six passion fruit and carefully remove the flesh. Halve the other six fruits and remove the flesh from them, as well. Retain the hollowed out shells, together with 10 teaspoons of the flesh, for garnishing. Combine the remaining flesh and the sugar over a medium heat and cook until the mixture has a thick consistency. Allow to cool for 10 minutes.

2. Whip the cream and confectioners' sugar until stiff, add the sweetened passion fruit pulp, and then fill a pastry bag with the mixture.

with Chocolate Sticks

3. Pipe the passion fruit cream into all the hollow shells, then cover with the remaining fruit flesh.

4. To make the chocolate sticks, melt the chocolate coating at about 85 °F / 30 °C and, using a spatula, spread it onto a marble slab to a thickness of $\frac{1}{8}$ in / 1 or 2 mm. Allow to set, then draw the spatula across the chocolate in order to roll up little sticks. Allow to harden for 10 minutes in the refrigerator, and serve with the passion fruit.

Elderberry Apples

Preparation time: 30 minutes
Cooking time: 10 minutes
Refrigeration time: 12 hours
Difficulty: ★★

Serves 4

4 apples (Gala or Golden Delicious)
juice of 1 lemon
3 tbsp / 40 g sugar
a little chocolate, melted

Vanilla ice cream (see basic recipes)

For the syrup:
2 cups / 500 ml water
1 cup / 250 g sugar
$6^{1}/_{2}$ tbsp / 100 ml elderberry sauce

For the parfait:
2 eggs
3 egg yolks
$6^{1}/_{2}$ tbsp / 100 g sugar
$1^{1}/_{4}$ cups / 300 ml cream, whipped
$3^{1}/_{2}$ tbsp / 50 ml pine bud syrup

In Switzerland, the apple has been the object of a genuine cult ever since William Tell aimed his crossbow at an apple placed on his own son's head at the command of the tyrannical Austrian governor Gessler. The legend of this famous shot, which was handed down in the 13th century by Saxo Grammaticus of Norway or Denmark, is seen as a symbol of Swiss independence.

In keeping with tradition, Étienne Krebs suggests a special way of serving apples – filled with an apple puree. The most suitable variety for this creation are the crunchy, sweet Gala apples, and firm, juicy ones should be chosen. One can also use Golden Delicious, which are equally suitable for cooking. To ensure the best results, one should carefully cut off the tops of

the fruits and hollow the apples out to a thickness of $^{1}/_{4}$ in / 0.5 cm.

Other ingredients used in this recipe are elderberry and pine buds, which are designed to give the humble apple a dash of wildness. The little elderberries, which ripen in the summer, are turned into a sauce that is thinned with sugar syrup. Ideally, the syrup-drenched apples should made up to a week in advance and stored in the refrigerator to allow the various ingredients to combine.

Alternatively, pears and red currants could also be used to prepare this dessert – the delicious pine bud syrup is, however, a must!

1. Prepare the syrup and set it aside. Peel the apples, carefully slice off their tops and completely hollow them out. Retain both the lids and the removed fruit. Make vanilla ice cream according to the basic recipe. This can be served in a pastry tulip.

2. Poach the apples in the syrup for 4 to 5 minutes at a low temperature. Add a little cold water to the cooking liquid and allow the apples to marinate in it overnight, so that they take on the elderberry color.

with Pine Bud Parfait

3. To make the parfait, whisk the whole eggs, egg yolks, and sugar until foamy in a double boiler. Remove from heat but continue to beat until cooled. Finally, add the whipped cream and pine bud syrup. Taste and add more syrup if necessary. Refrigerate for 12 hours.

4. Using the scooped out fruit, sugar, and lemon juice, make a compote. Add it to the frozen pine bud parfait, then fill the drained apples with the resulting mixture. Reduce the elderberry syrup to a jelly. Pour the melted chocolate into a pastry bag and use it to trace the outline of an apple on each plate. Fill this outline with thickened elderberry syrup and place the filled apples, with the lids, in it. Serve with ice cream.

Grapefruit Gratin with

Preparation time: *30 minutes*
Cooking time: *5 minutes*
Difficulty: ✱

Serves 4

2 grapefruit
some almonds, colored pink and roasted
2¹/₂ tbsp / 40 ml cream

For the zabaglione:
6 egg yolks
¹/₂ cup / 125 ml sugar syrup at 30 °Beaumé
3¹/₂ tbsp / 50 ml grapefruit juice
¹/₂ cup / 125 ml cream

The brilliant 17th-century French military leader, Marshall César de Plessis-Praslin, surely could not have guessed that three hundred years after his death his name would become synonymous with exquisite sweets. It was actually one of his cooks, rather than Plessis-Praslin himself, who had the idea to make roasted almonds (*praline* in French).

Almonds can be bought flavored or colored. For example, pink ones are popular in the Auvergne or Bourbonnais for decorating brioches, giving them a bit of color and taste. They can always be found at fairs, and are sometimes even replaced by peanuts, which is a less expensive, though much less tasty option.

The tart or even slightly bitter taste of grapefruit, with its yellow, pink or red flesh, provides a strong contrast to the almonds. Pink grapefruit would be attractive in this dessert because of the complementary colors. The grapefruit is a descendant of the sweet orange, which is called *pompelmoes* in Dutch, and is very rich in vitamins A and C. It should be prepared at the last minute in order to retain its freshness and vitamins. That is true for the segments, which are arranged on the serving plates, and the juice, which is used in the zabaglione.

The zabaglione, the only part of this recipe that can be a little difficult to create, is prepared at a temperature no greater than 160 °F / 70 °C. One starts with low heat and increases it slightly once the zabaglione starts to thicken. The whipped cream is not added until the mixture has cooled, as the heat would otherwise make it collapse. A sorbet made of passion fruit, or grapefruit if one uses a different fruit for the gratin, would be an excellent accompaniment to this dessert.

1. To make the zabaglione, mix the slightly beaten egg yolks with the syrup. Stir in the grapefruit juice, heat until it thickens slightly, and then allow to cool.

2. Peel the grapefruit and remove the skin. Remove the seeds, together with any small pieces of skin that could leave a bitter taste.

Roasted Almonds

3. Whip the cream until stiff and combine with the cooled zabaglione, stirring carefully.

4. Pour some zabaglione onto each plate and arrange grapefruit segments on it in the form of a rosette. Sprinkle on the crushed pink almonds, then place under a hot grill for a few minutes. Serve with a passion fruit sorbet.

Sour Cherries with

Preparation time: 20 minutes
Cooking time: 10 minutes
Cooling time: 30 minutes
Difficulty: ✭

Serves 4

40 sour cherries
10 slices of phyllo pastry
a little confectioners' sugar
clarifed butter

For the ganache filling:
6¹/₂ tbsp / 100 ml cream
3¹/₂ oz / 100 g chocolate coating

4 tsp / 20 g butter
1 tbsp / 20 g dextrose
1 egg

For the syrup at 15 °Beaumé:
2 cups/500 ml water
2³/₄ cups/700 g sugar

For the orange marmalade:
2 oranges
a dash of Grand Marnier
a dash of orange juice

A light dessert can be satisfying both for those who are watching their figures and for gourmets. This dessert, composed of fruits full of character such as cherries and oranges, the former in a light pastry and the latter as a marmalade, is an excellent example.

The sour cherry, with its firm, lightly sweet flesh, is harvested in July and August. It is frequently sold in stores in the form of preserves, syrup or fruit schnapps. Of course, cherries can also be eaten raw, but keep in mind that they keep for only a few days. In order to help sweet tooths control their natural appetite for sweet morsels – who can withstand a bowl full of cherries? – Jacques Lameloise has prepared these little pastries, in which the sour cherries are strictly counted out, nestled in a chocolate filling and wrapped in a crisp pastry. There should be a balance between the flavors of the fruit and the chocolate, so that neither detracts from the individual taste of the other.

The chocolate filling must be quite thick. If it is prepared a day in advance, it will have a more even consistency and be easier to work with. The origin of the name *ganache* (French for "fool") for this tasty combination of chocolate and cream – a term normally reserved for the old fools in slapstick farces – remains mysterious.

Oranges, in this case used to make a marmalade, are always well received when combined with chocolate. Oranges with a thin peel should be used, and their flavor is enhanced by the Grand Marnier, which is produced using orange peel marinated in cognac.

1. For the chocolate filling, bring the cream to a boil. Immediately add the chocolate coating and let it melt. Then add the butter, dextrose, and egg, and thoroughly mix everything over a low heat.

2. For the orange marmalade, cut the oranges into slices and cook them for about 10 minutes in the sugar syrup at 15 °Beaumé. Strain. Use a hand blender or food processor to chop them, then add orange juice that has been enriched with a dash of Grand Marnier until the marmalade has the desired consistency.

Chocolate and Oranges

3. Cut the slices of phyllo dough in strips 2 in / 4 cm wide. Using a pastry brush, brush on a little clarified butter, so that the dough becomes saturated with it.

4. Place a little chocolate filling in the center of each strip of dough, then top with two sour cherries. Wrap the dough around the filling like candy wrappers and bake in a 390 °F / 200 °C oven for 5 minutes. Sprinkle the pastries with a little confectioners' sugar and serve with the orange marmalade, adding a little chocolate ice cream if desired.

Rote Grütze

Preparation time: 30 minutes
Cooking time: 25 minutes
Difficulty: ★

Serves 4

3 cups / 750 ml water
1 lb 10 oz / 750 g berries (1 lb 5 oz / 600 g red currants, 2¹/₂ oz / 75 g raspberries, 2¹/₂ oz / 75 g black currants)
1 vanilla bean

³/₄ cup / 180 g sugar
7 tbsp / 50 g cornstarch
7 tbsp / 50 g flaked almonds

To garnish:
7 tbsp / 50 g chopped almonds
whipped cream

Our chef, Erwin Lauterbach, admits that he prepared this delicious dessert in order to round off his contribution to Eurodélices, and that it is more of a family tradition than a gastronomic specialty. Indeed, *rote grütze*, a kind of thickened fruit soup or pudding, is a beloved dessert in many northern European countries. Our chef recalls that it was a great favorite of his and his grandmother often served it to him in bed before he went to sleep.

Countless variations of *rote grütze* exist, all of them delicious, and virtually any combination of ripe red fruits can be used. This recipe calls for a typical summer mixture. As always, the berries should be ripe, fresh, and carefully selected so that no spoiled or bruised fruits are used.

Instead of incorporating other flavors into this dessert, which already has an intense taste, our chef has decided to add only vanilla and chopped almonds, but he readily admits that even this is not necessary if the berries are ripe and flavorful enough. However, it is still customary to decorate all traditional Danish desserts with whipped cream.

The addition of black cherries to this dessert would provide a good opportunity to discover the Danish Cherry Heering, an excellent liqueur that is frequently served with pancakes, but also goes very well with *rote grütze*.

1. Combine the water and berries in a saucepan and bring to a boil. Pass through a pointed sieve into another pan, bring the sauce to a boil again and then simmer carefully.

2. Scrape the pulp out of the vanilla bean and add both the pulp and husk of the bean to the fruit sauce. Add sugar to taste. Let cool.

with Almonds

3. Pour ³/₄ cup / 200 ml of the cooled fruit puree into a pan and add the cornstarch. Mix thoroughly with the remaining puree, bring to a boil again and add the flaked almonds.

4. Quickly cool the red jelly by placing the pan in cold water and covering it with a lid. Pour the cold jelly into a serving bowl and garnish with the chopped almonds if desired. Serve with whipped cream.

Ice Soufflé with

Preparation time: 20 minutes
Cooking time: 10 minutes
Cooling time: 6 hours
Difficulty: ✳✳

Serves 4

8 dried figs
6½ tbsp / 100 ml Armagnac
5 egg yolks
⅔ cup / 150 ml water
5 tbsp / 75 g superfine sugar
1 oz / 30 g chocolate coating
1 cup / 250 ml crème fraîche

For the almond cookies:
(see basic recipes)

For the custard:
(see basic recipes)
8 egg yolks
3 cups / 750 ml milk
1 vanilla bean
1 ⅔ cups / 250 g confectioners' sugar
a little coffee extract

Figs were already used for countless purposes in classical times. For example, it is known that the Romans used them to fatten geese. Whether fresh or dried, the fig is one of the most important fruits grown in the Mediterranean region.

Dried figs are available all year round. However, they are at their best from September to November, when they are prepared using very ripe and large fruits, which explains their specially high quality. In this recipe the figs are marinated in Armagnac, whose intensive fragrance evokes dreams of the south, to regain their size and juiciness. If necessary, the figs could be replaced by prunes.

When preparing this dessert, one has to be very careful about the temperature of the egg yolks. If they are overheated they will become hard, which is not reversible. Our chef recommends removing them from the heat and stirring them vigorously while pouring on the boiling syrup. For a pronounced chocolate flavor, use a chocolate coating with a very high cocoa content (70% or higher) and follow the recipe precisely.

The almond cookies are shaped after being removed from the oven. Because they are so thin, they unfortunately cool very quickly, so one has to work swiftly.

1. Cut the figs into pieces. Allow them to marinate in the Armagnac for 2 to 3 hours. Prepare the dough for the almond cookies according to the basic recipe. After allowing the dough to rest for 30 minutes, roll it out, cut out cookie shapes and place on a greased, floured baking tray. Bake for 2 to 4 minutes at 390 °F / 200 °C. Remove from the oven, form into desired shapes, and allow to cool completely.

2. Mix the sugar and water. Bring to a boil, and pour the resulting syrup onto the egg yolks while beating rapidly. Remove from the heat and whisk carefully. Place to one side.

Figs and Armagnac

3. Melt the chocolate coating in a double boiler. Combine the lukewarm egg yolk mixture with the figs and melted chocolate coating. Allow to cool, then fold in the crème fraîche.

4. Place the fig mixture in the freezer for 5 to 6 hours. Prepare the custard. Remove the set fig soufflés from the molds and arrange on plates. Serve garnished with the custard, decorated with a few drops of coffee extract, and two or three almond cookies.

Grandmother's Egg

Preparation time: 30 minutes
Cooking time: 10 minutes
Difficulty: ★★

Serves 4

4 cups / 1 l whole milk
1 cup / 240 g superfine sugar
2 vanilla beans
8 eggs
1 tsp cornstarch

What would family cooking be without grandmothers? Full of good advice and wisdom based on experiences gathered over the course of decades, every grandmother has her special culinary delights that her family associates with trust and tenderness. Léa Linster also has lovely memories like this and honors her grandmother with a dessert that is a masterly combination of feeling and expertise.

Before she started, our chef's grandmother always "borrowed" the things she needed from her husband, who was a baker. She whipped the egg whites in a copper bowl, using a primitive whisk with a wooden handle and a conical head. It is still best to whip the eggs by hand for this recipe, and it is essential to use only very fresh eggs. They must be whipped until they are very stiff, so that they do not lose their shape while cooking.

Most people will already be familiar with low-quality desserts made with beaten egg whites. This is partly due to the use of electric mixers, and is also a sign that the beaten egg whites were not used quickly enough. They should, therefore, be whisked at the very last minute and the egg white dumplings poached as soon as they have the right consistency.

It is important to add a small spoonful of cornstarch to the custard in order for it to thicken. If the mixture seems too thick when it is finished, one can always add a little cold cream and stir it again. In keeping with tradition, only real vanilla should be used, rather than artificial flavors.

1. Put the milk and 6¹/₂ tbsp / 100 g of the sugar and the halved vanilla beans into a pan and bring to a boil. Separate the eggs and beat the egg whites, preferably by hand, with 3¹/₂ tbsp / 50 g of sugar in a copper bowl until stiff.

2. Using two tablespoons, shape the stiffly beaten egg whites into dumplings and carefully poach them in the hot milk for 3 minutes on each side. Make sure that the milk does not boil again. Drain the dumplings.

White Dumplings

3. Whisk the egg yolks with the remaining sugar and add a teaspoon of cornstarch. Pass the milk through a pointed sieve, pour onto the egg yolks and prepare like a custard (see basic recipes). Allow to cool.

4. Pour a ladle of the custard into small dessert bowls and place two egg white dumplings on top. Serve immediately.

Preparation time: *1 hour 30 minutes*
Cooking time: *30 minutes*
Difficulty: ✶✶

Serves 4

4 cups / 1 l milk
$^1/_2$ cup / 100 g fine durum wheat semolina
1 vanilla bean
6$^1/_2$ tbsp / 100 g superfine sugar
$^1/_4$ cup / 30 g dried milk
2 tbsp cream, lightly whipped

1 tbsp heavy cream
3 eggs, beaten

For the yeast dough:
1 oz / 30 g yeast
4 cups / 500 g flour
3 eggs
13 tbsp / 200 g butter, softened
$^1/_3$ cup / 80 g sugar
2 tsp / 10 g salt

The abundance of tea-rooms in Luxembourg and the Grand Duchy in general explains the proliferation of flan and cake recipes available from caterers in the area. Among the lightest and simplest of them is Léa Linster's semolina flan, an old favorite of her family's. Since her father died before he could pass on his culinary secrets and her mother was unable to remember the quantities, our chef has recreated this dessert, much beloved in her childhood.

If the recipe's instructions are followed precisely, success is almost guaranteed. The semolina cake requires a fine durum wheat semolina, which results in a delicate, easily digestible cake. For a light, creamy dessert, whip the cream lightly before adding it to the cake mixture. Beat the eggs until foamy, as well.

A wide range of variations is possible. Flavor the cake with vanilla, cinnamon, and caramel, for instance, or add raisins marinated in liqueur or brandy.

The semolina flan may be served lukewarm or cold, depending on the occasion. Present it as a classic dessert, or serve with a cup of coffee or tea. And, in the unlikely event that any is left over, it makes for a fine breakfast.

1. To make the yeast dough, dissolve the yeast in a little water and then combine with a little flour. Allow to rise. Add the eggs, softened butter, sugar, salt, and remaining flour. Knead thoroughly and allow to stand at room temperature for 1 hour. Bring the milk to a boil, then add the semolina, vanilla bean, and sugar. Simmer for 4 to 5 minutes, stirring occasionally.

2. Add the dried milk, lightly whipped cream, heavy cream and the beaten eggs. Pour into a metal or copper bowl and allow to cool.

Semolina Flan

3. Roll out the dough to a thickness of ¼ in / 0.5 cm and use it to line a greased pie pan with a diameter of 9 in / 20 cm. Allow to rest for 15 minutes.

4. Pour the semolina mixture into the pastry shell and bake for about 30 minutes at 340 °F / 170 °C. Remove from the oven and allow to cool completely. Cut into pieces and serve with tea, hot chocolate or coffee.

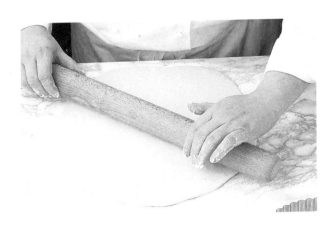

Preparation time: 1 hour
Cooking time: 45 minutes
Difficulty: ★★

Serves 8

For the short pastry:
10 tbsp / 150 g soft butter
$^2/_3$ cup / 100 g confectioners' sugar
$^1/_2$ tsp vanilla extract
$^1/_4$ cup / 30 g finely ground almonds
2 cups / 250 g flour
2 eggs

For the vanilla ice cream with ginger:
4 cups / 1 l milk
1 vanilla bean

2 tbsp / 25 g fresh ginger, finely grated
12 egg yolks
1 cup / 250 g sugar

For the caramel sauce:
$6^1/_2$ tbsp / 100 g sugar
$^2/_3$ cup / 150 ml cream
$6^1/_2$ tbsp / 100 ml water

For the filling:
$10^1/_2$ oz / 300 g sweet chestnut puree
$3^1/_2$ tbsp / 50 g butter
$1^1/_4$ cup / 310 g sugar
$6^1/_2$ tbsp / 100 ml rum
5 egg yolks
2 eggs
1 cup / 250 g sugar

In gastronomy, sweet chestnut refers not to the fruit of the chestnut tree that often grows in public places, but to an improved, domesticated form of the chestnut tree that yields a nut in every shell. Wild chestnuts produce nuts of varying sizes, which are more difficult to use.

Chestnut trees have always been very important in areas where grains do not grow well; they are even called "bread trees" by farmers on Sardinia, Corsica, and in the Massif Central region of France. The nutritional value of sweet chestnuts was recognized very early. They contain phosphorus and vitamin B, both of which stimulate the nervous system. These increasingly

widespread trees must be at least eight years old, however, before they start to produce nuts that are large enough to eat.

There is no particular difficulty involved in producing the tart shell. It may be easiest to prepare the dough the previous day and refrigerate it, then remove it half an hour before rolling it out as thinly as possible. Preparing the filling is a little more tricky, in particular blending in the chestnut puree; achieving a foamy consistency is very important. Adventurous cooks may like to try a somewhat more original variation of this cake, for example with lentil puree, which will certainly produce an amazing effect.

1. For the short pastry, combine the butter with the confectioners' sugar, then add the vanilla extract, almonds, flour, and eggs. Refrigerate the pastry for one hour, then roll it out evenly. Line a pie pan with the pastry and bake blind at 390 °F / 200 °C.

2. Bring the milk for the ice cream to a boil with the vanilla bean and ginger and allow to steep. Whisk the egg yolks and sugar until foamy and then heat gently. Add the hot vanilla milk and allow to simmer. Pass through a pointed sieve, stir thoroughly and allow to harden in an ice cream maker. To make the caramel sauce, caramelize the sugar and water. Add the cream and set aside.

Chestnut Tart

3. For the filling, stir the sweet chestnut puree with the butter, ¼ cup / 60 g sugar and the rum until soft. Using the egg yolks, whole eggs, and the remaining sugar, prepare a cold cream. Once this has taken on a firmer consistency, carefully combine it with the chestnut mixture.

4. Pour the sweet chestnut cream onto the pre-baked tart shell. Bake for about 15 minutes in a preheated 390 °F / 200 °C oven. Check frequently to be sure the cake does not become too dry. Serve the tart cold or lukewarm with the vanilla ice cream and caramel sauce.

Savoy

Preparation time: 15 minutes
Cooking time: 45 minutes
Difficulty: ★★

Serves 6

4 eggs
¹/₂ cup plus 3 tbsp / 175 g sugar
grated peel of 1 untreated lime
³/₄ cup/100 g flour

¹/₄ cup/30 g cornstarch
5 tsp / 25 g butter
5 tsp / 25 g sugar
salt
vinegar

This sponge cake, undoubtedly one of the *pièces de résistance* of Savoy cuisine, is said to have been created in 1348 by Master Chiquart, the chef of Duke Amadeus VI of Savoy. Guy Martin, himself from Savoy and proud of his origins, bakes it only in the cast iron baking pan that was presented to him by his friends from Albertville on the occasion of his departure from Château Divonne-les-Bain. This turns the Savoy sponge cake made at the Grand Véfour into an extraordinary cake worthy of the same enthusiasm and devotion with which it was made.

The sponge cake is simple to prepare and stays fresh for several days. It tastes best eaten in thin slices.

The light dough has to be prepared carefully. The beaten egg whites must be folded in from bottom to top, and it is best to use a metal spatula for this. If desired, the dough can be refined with a spice such as ginger or nutmeg, though this flavoring should remain discreet. The sponge cake should not, by the way, be confused with Savoy gâteau, which is made in a completely different way.

A further tip from Guy Martin: so that the sponge cake bakes evenly all around, it is worth turning the pan several times in the oven while baking. When finished, turn the sponge cake out onto a cooling rack to cool; allowing it to stand in the oven would dry it out. Do not cut for several hours.

1. Separate the eggs. Beat the egg yolks with 6¹/₂ tbsp / 100 g of the sugar until the mixture is foamy and almost white.

2. Stir the grated lime peel, 7 tbsp / 50 g of the flour and half of the cornstarch into the egg yolks. Grease a Bundt pan and sprinkle it with sugar.

Sponge Cake

3. Rinse a stainless steel bowl with salt and vinegar, then rinse with clear water; beat the 4 egg whites in it until stiff and then stir in the remaining sugar.

4. Fold half of the beaten egg whites into the egg yolk and flour mixture, then mix in the remaining flour and cornstarch. Finally, fold in the remaining egg whites. Turn the dough into the pan and bake at 355 °F / 180 °C for 45 minutes. After baking, carefully invert the sponge cake onto a cooling rack.

Quark Dessert

Preparation time: 20 minutes
Cooking time: 10 minutes
Difficulty: ★

Serves 8

For the quark:
1¼ cups / 300 g quark
6 tbsp / 95 g sugar
2 sheets of gelatin
½ cup / 130 ml cream, whipped

For the sweet pastry:
½ cup / 60 g flour
3½ tbsp / 50 g slightly salted butter

1 egg yolk
3 tbsp / 40 g sugar
a pinch of salt
⅕ oz / 5 g dried yeast
15 almonds, finely ground

For the raspberry sauce:
2 cups / 500 ml raspberry puree
½ cup / 125 ml sugar syrup at 30 °Beaumé
confectioners' sugar

1 lb / 500 g raspberries

In this simple, light, and enticing dessert, which can be prepared at any time of year, quark is harmoniously combined with red berries, which are rich in vitamin C. Quark is a very mild, smooth, unripened cheese popular in several European countries, which has a consistency something like sour cream.

The natural fat content of quark makes it an ideal companion for fruits, as it moderates their acidity. Served with a dry cake, such as these cookies made from sweet pastry, the result is a delicious contrast of soft quark and crunchy dough. All this contributes to the perfect balance of this composition.

The red berry sauce, which can be made using red currants, blackberries or a combination of berries instead of raspberries, is passed through a sieve in order to remove the small seeds, hairs, and stems that one could not otherwise neatly remove from the berries. If desired, this dessert can be prepared using figs or quinces, and a sauce made with apples would be marvelous with them.

1. Mix the quark with the sugar and beat until foamy. Add the dissolved gelatin, then fold in the whipped cream.

2. Line the molds with a spoonful of the quark mixture. Place three raspberries in each mold, then fill them with quark. Refrigerate.

with Raspberries

3. For the cookie dough, combine the flour and butter. Mix the remaining ingredients together, than add the flour and butter mixture. Roll out the dough and cut out cookies in the shape of glasses, then make eye-shaped holes in half of the cookies. Bake for 10 minutes at 355 °F / 180 °C. Place cookies with eye-shaped holes on top of plain cookies and dust with confectioners' sugar.

4. Using the raspberry puree and sugar syrup, make the raspberry sauce. Arrange the raspberries in the shape of a bunch of grapes on the plates, and pour the sauce onto the bottom of the plate. Decorate with some thinned quark. Turn the quark balls out of the molds onto the plates. Pour a little red sauce into the holes in the cookies.

"Madonna"

Preparation time: 45 minutes
Cooking time: 45 minutes
Difficulty: ✳

Serves 6

1 cup / 250 g sugar
6 eggs, separated
2 cups / 250 g crushed walnuts
1 tsp breadcrumbs

For the egg cream:
10 egg yolks
6¹/₂ tbsp / 100 g sugar
1 cinnamon stick
6¹/₂ tbsp / 100 ml water

For the roasted walnuts:
6¹/₂ tbsp / 100 g sugar
a little lemon juice
7 tbsp / 40 g shelled walnuts

For the sweetened whipped cream:
2 cups / 500 ml cream
¹/₃ cup / 80 g superfine sugar

In order to avert the sin of gluttony, Portuguese desserts implore religion, saints, and the almighty divinity for aid with dishes such as "nuns' stomachs," "heavenly bacon," or, as in this case, "Madonna" walnut tree. Throughout Portugal there are 200 different terms of this sort. This tradition is not so very astonishing in a country densely populated with abbeys and monasteries, which played a major role in the development of agriculture and livestock breeding until the 17th century.

In this quite unusual recipe, two very monastic products are contrasted: the egg (which can be prepared in thousands of ways, both sweet and savory) and the walnut from Cascais, close to Lisbon. As usual, whole walnuts do not betray the

quality of the nut they conceal. They must be shelled to ascertain whether they are rancid or too dry. Caution is advised when selecting the nuts, as a single bad nut can destroy the entire dessert.

Cinnamon is used for the egg cream in this cake, though it should be added in moderation. This element we owe to the Portuguese seafarer Vasco da Gama, the courageous discoverer of far-off places, who brought substances back to Europe that had never been seen before.

There is a large spectrum of Portuguese delicacies, all of which in principal should be preceded by a prayer ...

1. To make the egg cream, pass the egg yolks through a fine sieve. In a pan, make a syrup from the sugar, cinnamon stick, and water. Allow to cool. Remove the cinnamon stick. Add the egg yolks. Rapidly whisk over low heat with a wooden spatula or spoon so that the eggs become creamy. Do not boil!

2. Grease a cake pan with a diameter of 10 in / 22 cm and a height of 2 ³/₄ in / 6 cm, and line it with greased baking paper. Prepare the cake. In a mixing bowl, stir the egg yolks and sugar until creamy, then add the crushed nuts and breadcrumbs. Whisk the egg whites and add. Fill the pan and bake for 30 minutes at 320 °F / 160 °C.

Walnut Tree

3. For the roasted nuts, cook the sugar and several drops of lemon juice in a pan and add the shelled walnuts. Once the caramel is brown, pour the mixture into an oiled bowl. Allow to cool, and divide it into two halves. Crush one portion with a rolling pin, and grind the other half in a blender.

4. Take the cake out of the oven and turn it out of the pan. Allow to cool on a rack and then cut through once horizontally. Mix the crushed, roasted nuts with the egg cream, and spread this on the bottom layer of the cake. Replace the top half and cover the top and sides with the cream that has been whipped until stiff with the sugar. Sprinkle the cake with the ground nuts.

Exotic White

Preparation time: 2 hours
Cooling time: 2 hours
Difficulty: ★★★

Serves 4

For the white chocolate mousse:
3 sheets of gelatin
3¹/₂ oz / 100 g white chocolate coating
1 egg
2 egg yolks
4 tsp / 20 ml white rum
1 cup / 250 ml cream, whipped

For the passion fruit mousse:
1¹/₄ cups / 300 g passion fruit flesh
2¹/₂ tbsp / 40 ml Cointreau
4 sheets of gelatin

2 egg whites
1 cup / 250 g sugar
1¹/₃ cups / 330 ml cream, whipped

For the moscato jelly:
1¹/₂ cups / 350 ml moscato or muscatel wine
3¹/₂ tbsp / 50 g sugar
3 sheets of gelatin

For the Cointreau ice cream:
4 cups / 1 l milk
4 cups / 1 l cream
1 vanilla bean
20 egg yolks
1¹/₂ cups plus 2 tbsp / 400 g sugar
1¹/₃ cups / 300 ml Cointreau

To garnish:
1 baby pineapple
mint, bittersweet chocolate

Thanks to Dieter Müller, white chocolate has become better known in Germany and this recipe promises to make further converts: in an exotically colored dessert, the sweet melting sensation of chocolate is combined with the tart taste of passion fruit. One can accurately speak of a passion when it comes to our chef's innovative use of first-class produce from distant countries to conjure up repeatedly new color and taste combinations.

As the combination of white chocolate and passion fruit mousse does not produce any particularly great contrast in color, our delicate Charlotte is served in a fine dark chocolate cage, which serves as a kind of lace border. It would be unforgivable to do without the baby pineapple – a product of the island of Réunion: a few slices of it, cut wafer-thin and arranged on the plates in fan shapes, round off the decoration

of the dessert. Connoisseurs value this little pineapple above all for its concentrated flavor, which lends this recipe a considerable part of its effect. However, a large pineapple can be used if the smaller ones are not available.

According to our chef, a key element for the success of this dessert is the correct consistency of the chocolate mousse, which is prepared entirely without sugar; before freezing it must be almost liquid. In the end it will have a soft consistency that harmonizes marvellously with the creamy Cointreau ice cream with which it is served. The orange liqueur, which is produced using a combination of bitter oranges from the Antilles and mild oranges from the Mediterranean, is shown off to advantage here. Its alcohol content of 40% adds a welcome flavor to the charlotte.

1. Melt the bittersweet chocolate in a double boiler. Using a pastry bag, pipe a net of diagonal lines onto strips of waxed paper. Allow to harden, then carefully peel off the paper. For the white chocolate mousse, dissolve the gelatin in cold water. Melt the white chocolate in a double boiler. Add the egg, egg yolks, gelatin, rum, and cream and combine well. Pour the mousse into individual molds with a diameter of 3¹/₂ in / 8 cm to a depth of 1 in / 2 cm and freeze.

2. Heat part of the passion fruit flesh, then add the Cointreau and gelatin that has been dissolved in the liqueur. Combine everything with the remaining passion fruit flesh. Make a meringue: whisk the egg whites until very stiff, add the melted sugar and allow to cool. Combine with the fruit mixture and whipped cream. Pour 1 in / 2 cm of the passion fruit mousse onto the chocolate mousse in the molds and freeze.

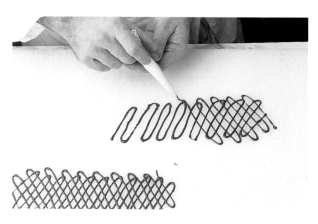

Chocolate Charlotte

3. To make the jelly, heat the moscato, then remove it from the heat and add the sugar and dissolved gelatin. Allow to cool. Cover the top of the charlottes with the jelly. For the Cointreau ice cream, bring the milk, cream, and pulp of the vanilla bean to a boil. Whisk the egg yolks and sugar, then add the hot milk mixture and reduce while stirring. Allow the ice cream to cool, stir in the Cointreau, and let it harden in an ice cream maker.

4. Arrange thin slices of pineapple on four plates. Place a charlotte in the center of each and surround with a chocolate cage. Garnish with finely chopped mint leaves. Serve with a ball of Cointreau ice cream and a chocolate stick made of rolled up bittersweet chocolate.

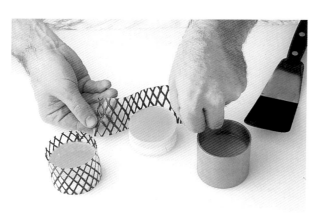

Banana Soufflé with Cocoa

Preparation time: *2 hours*
Cooking time: *15 minutes*
Difficulty: ★★

Serves 4

¹/₄ cup / 60 g butter
¹/₄ cup / 60 g sugar
2 eggs, separated
2 bananas
juice of ¹/₂ lemon
2¹/₂ tbsp / 25 g roasted almonds
¹/₄ cup / 20 g grated chocolate
1 tbsp / 10 g wheat starch
butter and sugar for the molds

For the cocoa zabaglione:
1 tbsp cocoa powder
3 egg yolks

3 tbsp / 40 g sugar
¹/₄ cup / 60 ml milk
4 tsp / 20 ml crème de cacao

For the citrus fruits:
1 tsp orange marmalade
4 tsp / 20 ml Grand Marnier
3 untreated oranges
2 untreated pink grapefruit
4 kumquats
sugar syrup

To garnish:
a little cocoa powder and confectioners' sugar
8 basil leaves

Dieter Müller seems to invite us to consider cooking a party game in which the ingredients are the playing pieces with his presentation of this soufflé. He was inspired by a blancmange he was once served for breakfast in the United States, which was arranged on a checkerboard pattern.

In this game, the soufflé itself is the main attraction and is prepared using only bananas of the highest quality. This tropic fruit, most widely cultivated in the Antilles and South America, is available all year round, though the quality differs considerably. Bananas are transported in an unripe condition and ripened at their destinations, which unfortunately means that their incomparable aroma does not always develop its full intensity. Therefore, the bananas should be selected particu-

larly carefully to ensure the complete success of the soufflé in this delicious dessert creation.

The citrus fruits are a vital part of this dessert. Oranges are used in two different ways in this recipe, as a marmalade and in the form of individual fruit segments. The small exotic variety of oranges known as kumquats are not dissimilar to limes. They are cut in halves to expose their interior, which has many seeds, little flesh, and a distinctive flavor.

Other members of the citrus family that are not mentioned in this recipe can, of course, also be used: mandarins, tangerines ...

1. Mix the butter, one-third of the sugar and the egg yolks. Peel the bananas and mash them with the lemon juice. Add the bananas to the butter mixture, together with the roasted almonds, grated chocolate, and wheat starch. Beat the egg whites with the remaining sugar and fold in.

2. Put all the ingredients for the cocoa zabaglione into a bowl and stir until creamy in a double boiler. Prepare a marinade for the citrus fruits by carefully heating the orange marmalade until runny, then adding the Grand Marnier.

Zabaglione and Citrus Fruits

3. Grease four soufflé dishes, sprinkle them with sugar and fill with the soufflé mixture. Place the filled dishes in a pan of water in the oven and bake for 12 minutes at 340 °F / 170 °C. Peel the oranges and the grapefruit and divide them into segments. Halve the kumquats and cook all the citrus fruits for 3 minutes in sugar syrup.

4. Using a stencil, make a checkerboard pattern with the cocoa powder and confectioners' sugar on one side of the plates. Arrange some fruits decoratively on the other side. Pour some marinade over the fruit, garnish with a basil leaf and pour some cocoa zabaglione next to them. Finally, turn the soufflés out of the dishes and arrange on the checkerboards.

Quince Sorbet with

Preparation time: 40 minutes
Cooking time: 25 minutes
Difficulty: ★★

Serves 4

1 lb / 500 g quinces
a sprig of rosemary
sugar
1 untreated lemon
10¹/₂ oz / 300 g rhubarb
1 glass quince liqueur
sugar syrup

For the fruit sauce:
7 oz / 200 g black currants or blueberries
1 tsp cassis (black currant liqueur)

For the spice cookies (see basic recipes)

To garnish:
sprigs of rosemary
several whole berries

This recipe would not exist if it were not for the fertile quince tree in Jean-Louis Neichel's garden. The quince, a curious little yellow fruit (*Cydonia vulgaris* in Latin), has more to offer than its unassuming appearance might lead one to suspect at first sight. Quinces cannot be eaten raw; they have to be turned into jelly, pastries or syrup. Some methods of preparation have justifiably gained a certain degree of fame, such as the quince preserves from Orléans, a jam made using quinces and bitter orange, which was highly regarded by Louis XIV and remains popular throughout the world.

Quinces are categorized according to their shape either as apple quinces, with a tart flavor, or as milder pear quinces. In some Jewish communities whole cloves are stuck into quinces on New Year's Day. They are passed around during prayer so that they can fill the room with their pleasant fragrance.

Quinces have to be cooked carefully, and much longer than apples; this is best done in a pot with a closed lid so that the cooking juices do not evaporate. This yields a delicious amber-colored compote that can easily be turned into a sorbet.

Our chef loves rhubarb mainly because of its connections with Alsace; in central Europe (Germany and Switzerland), it is very highly valued. It is harvested twice a year, and because of its digestibility is suitable for many recipes.

1. Peel the quinces, cut them into pieces and cover with water. Cook for 15 minutes at a low temperature with a sprig of rosemary, some sugar, the lemon peel, and some of the lemon juice. Cut the fruit into small pieces in the liquid.

2. Peel the rhubarb and cut it into small pieces. Cook it in a little water until it is reduced to the consistency of a compote, adding sugar to taste.

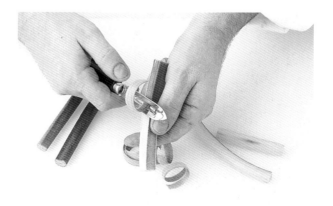

Rhubarb Compote

3. Cook the black currants or blueberries briefly with a little sugar. Mix and pass through a pointed sieve. Add a few drops of cassis and a little lemon juice to the sauce. Put the quince puree and the glass of quince liqueur into an ice cream maker. Add a little sugar syrup and mix everything thoroughly, then put in the freezer.

4. Prepare the cookie dough, spread it on a baking sheet in very thin circles and sprinkle on spices. Bake for a few minutes. In deep plates, arrange some of the rhubarb compote on one side and a scoop of the quince sorbet on the other. Pour a little fruit sauce in the center and garnish the dessert with some whole berries and a sprig of rosemary.

Cake with Fresh Figs

Preparation time: 30 minutes
Cooking time: 25 minutes
Difficulty: ★

Serves 4

10$^{1}/_{2}$ oz / 300 g violet figs
7 oz / 200 g puff pastry
6$^{1}/_{2}$ tbsp / 100 g butter
3$^{1}/_{2}$ tbsp / 50 ml hazelnut liqueur
6$^{1}/_{2}$ tbsp / 50 g flaked almonds
$^{3}/_{4}$ cup / 200 ml cream, whipped with cinnamon

For the pastry cream with kirsch:
1 vanilla bean
1 cup / 250 ml milk
3$^{1}/_{2}$ tbsp / 50 g sugar
2 egg yolks
3 tbsp / 20 g cornstarch
3$^{1}/_{2}$ tbsp / 50 ml kirsch

Salvador Dalí was one of the numerous artists who painted in Catalonia (others included Picasso, Casals and Gaudí). The town of Figueras is proud that Dalí was born there, and has named its only museum after him. This famous son almost causes one to forget that Figueras is also renowned for its particularly good figs. Jean-Louis Neichel is certainly an art lover, but he is also able to appreciate culinary uniqueness, such as the merits of this small, juicy fruit full of seeds, whose elastic peel conceals an intensely colorful and flavorful flesh.

Due to its tender peel, our chef has chosen the violet fig for this cake; it is known as the poor man's caviar. In the past Jean-Louis Neichel has frequently used figs for meat dishes, but here he uses them to create a delicious dessert. The whipped cream that accompanies the fig cake is flavored with a little cinnamon – it tastes truly spectacular with a dash of hazelnut liqueur, as well.

The figs must be ripe, but still firm enough to be cut into attractive slices. The slices are then lightly browned in butter before being arranged on the cake base.

The recipe is derived from an apple cake recipe by Alain Chapel, and is well suited to being made in individual cakes. The individual molds, or a round pie pan, are lined with the puff pastry and baked for about 20 minutes at 430 °F / 220 °C.

1. To make the pastry cream, add the vanilla to the milk and bring to a boil. In a separate pan, mix the other ingredients except for the kirsch. Pour the hot milk onto the egg mixture and combine well. Return the pan to the heat and, stirring constantly, bring the mixture to a boil briefly. Remove from the heat. Remove the vanilla bean and add the kirsch. Spread the cream on the pre-baked puff pastry. Allow to cool.

2. Wash the figs and carefully slice the fruits into rounds. Set the most attractive slices aside.

and Cinnamon Cream

3. Brown the fig slices in a pan in the melted butter. Roast the almond flakes under a grill.

4. Arrange the fig slices on the pastry cream in the form of a rosette. Sprinkle on the roasted almond flakes. Serve with the whipped cream, which has been enhanced with cinnamon and hazelnut liqueur.

Ice Cream

Preparation time: 20 minutes
Cooking time: 10 minutes
Difficulty: ★

Serves 4

4 apples (Golden Delicious)
4 tbsp / 60 ml butter
4 tbsp / 60 ml superfine sugar
2 tbsp / 30 ml brown rum

For the vanilla ice cream:
2 cups/500 ml milk
6 egg yolks
$^1/_2$ cup/125 g sugar
1 Bourbon vanilla bean

The apple is probably the oldest and most widespread poma-ceous fruit. Though most people are familiar only with the thirty-odd kinds that are widely available in grocery stores, there are in reality more than a thousand different variations of this quintessential fruit, and still others have unfortunately dis-appeared. Just reciting their names stimulates the imagination with their echoes of country life: Ontario, Clochard, McIntosh, Winesap, Rome Beauty ...

The Golden Delicious apple is a relative newcomer: it was first discovered in the USA in 1912. The color of this apple, which is available all year round, varies from an even green to yellow depending on its ripeness. It has a fine, juicy sweet flesh, which achieves a melting consistency when cooked. For this recipe one should use large, thoroughly ripe and intensely flavored fruits. By the way, the peel contains a large part of the apple's vitamin C, so it should not generally be removed.

The caramel is made with equal parts of butter and sugar and should be light; a dark caramel would taste bitter. But the most outstanding element of this dessert is the harmonious combina-tion of softly cooked apples and vanilla. The origins of vanilla date back to the pre-Columbian Aztec civilizations. The beans of this tropical orchid plant should be soft and fleshy and have a very intense fragrance. The fame of vanilla led to its being very desirable for a long time, so that a variety of alternatives were invented. For our recipe, however, only Bourbon vanilla is good enough. Our chef, Pierre Orsi, has named the dessert after his wife as a small token of his esteem for her.

1. Peel and core the apples, then cut them into slices $^1/_4$ in / 0.5 cm thick. For the ice cream, bring the milk to a boil. Whisk the egg yolks with the sugar until foamy. Scrape out the vanilla pulp and add to the milk. Pour the vanilla milk onto the frothy eggs and stir in. Simmer for 3 minutes at 195 °F / 90 °C, then cool and allow to harden in an ice cream maker.

2. Heat the butter and the sugar in a non-stick pan and cook until the mixture forms a light caramel.

"Geneviève"

3. Add the apple slices to the pan with the caramel, and brown evenly all around over a high heat.

4. Once the apples are soft, add the rum, flambé them and remove from the heat. Put a large ball of vanilla ice cream into each dessert bowl. Arrange the apples around the edges and serve immediately.

Raspberries and

Preparation time: 1 hour
Cooking time: 5 minutes
Difficulty: ★

Serves 4

10¹/₂ oz / 300 g strawberries
10¹/₂ oz / 300g raspberries
4 tsp Grand Marnier
3¹/₂ tbsp / 50 g superfine sugar

For the vanilla ice cream:
2 cups / 500 ml milk
6 egg yolks
¹/₂ cup / 125 g sugar
1 vanilla bean

The name of this recipe might lead one to think it comes from Russia, since Romanov is the name of the last dynasty of czars that ruled over the mighty empire for four hundred years until the fateful year 1917. But this is mistaken: this dessert was very popular in the USA in the 1960s, and that is where our chef discovered it.

Tradition demands that this particular dessert be prepared in the dining room by the head waiter. The mashed raspberries and strawberries are mixed with brown sugar and a thick cream laced with vodka (this might explain the reference to the Romanovs). As one can see, Pierre Orsi has altered this tradition in a quite delightful manner.

Above all, he recommends using only the best berries, ideally the small, deep red strawberries that are available from specialty markets between April and October. Very large strawberries tend to have a milder flavor, so the petite ones are preferable. The same is true for raspberries, which contain more minerals and vitamins than one might think. The growing season for raspberries is very short, but nowadays very good deep-frozen raspberries are available, which make it possible to prepare this dessert all year round. In France they say that eating red berries makes one happy. The French even have a song that could easily accompany this dessert: "Oh! Strawberries and raspberries! And the good wine we have drunk ..."

1. Remove the stems from the strawberries, then cut them into slices and place in a cooled bowl. Add the raspberries. Pour the Grand Marnier over the berries.

2. Add the sugar to the berries and mix well so that the sugar dissolves. Refrigerate.

Strawberries Romanov

3. To make the ice cream, bring the milk to a boil. Meanwhile, whisk the egg yolks with the sugar until the mixture has a creamy consistency. Add the pulp of the vanilla bean to the milk and then add the hot milk to the egg mixture while stirring. Pour everything back into the pan and simmer for 3 minutes at 195 °F / 90 °C, then cool and freeze in an ice cream maker.

4. In a mixer, puree the raspberries and strawberries. Pass through a sieve and refrigerate the sauce. Place a ball of vanilla ice cream in thoroughly cooled dessert bowls. Arrange some whole berries around the ice cream and pour berry sauce over it.

Sweet Chestnut Dessert

Preparation time: 45 minutes
Cooking time: 15 minutes
Difficulty: ★

Serves 4

9 oz / 250 g chestnut puree, unsweetened
3/4 cup / 120 g confectioners' sugar
9 oz / 250 g bittersweet chocolate coating
5 tbsp / 70 g butter

For the hazelnut custard:
(see basic recipes)
4 eggs
1/4 cup / 40 g confectioners' sugar
1 cup / 250 ml milk
2/3 cup / 100 g hazelnuts, shelled and finely
   chopped
2 1/2 tbsp / 50 g pureed almonds

The sweet chestnut (not to be confused with the inedible horse chestnut) was for a long time an essential source of nourishment for poor people in the Mediterranean countries. Whether served as a soup or puree, chestnuts are an extremely good source of energy. Unshelled nuts, which can be gathered during October and November, should have a smooth, shiny, round shell.

Underneath the shell one finds a fibrous skin, which is easily removed if the chestnuts are briefly dipped into boiling water. To make a puree, the chestnuts are cooked in milk at a low temperature for about 40 minutes, without adding sugar. If the puree will be kept for a few days, one should avoid oxidization by adding a slice of lemon before mashing them, and refrigerate the mixture in an airtight container. Unsweetened chestnut puree is also available in grocery stores.

The hazel tree produces oval-shaped nuts in a very hard shell. Our ancestors thought they had magical and medicinal properties. Nowadays, crunchy hazelnuts are valued mainly for their abundance of roughage and fats, and their fine taste adds a pleasant flavor to the custard. The third nut flavor is also added to the custard, in the form of almond butter or pureed almonds, not to be confused with almond paste, available at natural foods stores.

1. Mix the chestnut puree with the confectioners' sugar. Melt the chocolate coating in a double boiler and stir in the butter.

2. Combine the chestnut puree and the melted chocolate. In order to produce a soft, light mixture, beat thoroughly with a whisk.

with Hazelnut Sauce

3. Pour the mixture into a rectangular pan and freeze for 48 hours. Using the eggs and sugar, prepare a custard according to the basic recipe. Then add the milk, to which the shelled and finely chopped hazelnuts have previously been added, and cook over low heat until thick.

4. After preparing the custard, dissolve the almond puree in it. Before serving, turn out the dessert and cut into slices like a cake. Serve with the hazelnut custard.

Orange Terrine

Preparation time: 1 hour
Cooking time: 10 minutes
Cooling time: 24 hours
Difficulty: ✶

Serves 4

6 kiwis
12 oranges
1¹⁄₂ cups / 180 g superfine sugar
8 sheets of gelatin
mint leaves

Sun-ripened oranges used to be a luxurious and symbolic present that was frequently given in the season leading to Christmas. They were also wrapped in silver foil and used as a table decoration on important occasions, such as Christmas dinner.

There are more than a thousand different varieties of orange. The best known are the navel, valencia, and blood oranges.

As this terrine needs to be refrigerated for a long time, it is best to prepare it a day ahead of time, using seedless oranges so that the overall result is not impaired. Oranges have peak flavor in autumn and winter. Grapefruit would also be an interesting alternative in this recipe. Though pineapples might seem to be another delicious variation, their acidity interferes with the setting of gelatin, and thus cannot be recommended.

The first layer of the terrine consists of jellied orange juice, which holds the whole dessert together. One then alternates layers of orange pieces and juice, covering the oranges with juice each time so that each layer is firm.

Kiwis are also called Chinese gooseberries, though they originated in New Zealand. They are mainly cultivated in California and New Zealand, though increasingly also in Europe, and are available all year round, making them far less exotic than they used to be. Large, juicy kiwis are most suited to this dish, for they yield an outstanding sauce. The very high vitamin C content of both the fruits used makes this dessert extremely invigorating.

1. Peel and quarter the kiwis. Puree in a blender or food processor with 2 tbsp / 30 g sugar.

2. Squeeze the juice from 2 oranges. Peel the remaining oranges and cut them into segments. Retain the resulting juice and add to the juice of the squeezed oranges. Heat the juice with the remaining sugar.

with Kiwi Sauce

3. Pour the warm orange juice onto the gelatin, which has been soaked in water, and bring to a boil.

4. Fill a terrine with alternating layers of orange segments and jellied juice. Allow each layer to set in the refrigerator for 12 minutes. Finally, refrigerate the entire terrine for 24 hours. Serve with the kiwi sauce and garnish with mint leaves.

Puff Pastries

Preparation time: 2 hours
Cooking time: 15 minutes
Difficulty: ★★

Serves 4

9 oz / 250 g strawberries
sugar

For the puff pastry (see basic recipes):
4 cups / 500 g flour
2¹/₂ tsp / 13 g salt
³/₄ cup / 200 ml water
³/₄ cup / 185 g butter, melted (use one-third for folding the dough)

confectioners' sugar
mixed spices (pepper, nutmeg, cloves, ginger)

For the Chiboust cream:
1 egg yolk
4 tsp / 20 g sugar
1 tbsp cornstarch
4¹/₂ tbsp / 65 ml milk
¹/₂ sheet of gelatin
kirsch
for the meringue:
1 egg white
3¹/₂ tbsp / 50 g sugar

Puff pastry was invented in the 19th century and remains extremely popular today. Since it can be used in almost limitless variations, new recipes are created daily, each better than the last. Our puff pastry flower is but one example, and one should feel free to vary both the filling and the shape of the petals.

The Chiboust cream is part of a French *gâteau* using choux and puff pastry called "Saint-Honoré." It is a type of pastry cream that is made especially light by the addition of whipped egg white. Its texture depends, of course, on the success of the meringue. In this recipe, Paul Pauvert uses kirsch to flavor the cream, though one could also use Grand Marnier.

There are about one hundred different varieties of strawberries, and their main season is in spring and summer. Our chef's

favorite variety is the Gariguette, grown in the French *département* of Lot-et-Garonne; it is an early-ripening berry with an ideal balance of sweetness and acidity. It is not surprising that the strawberry is highly regarded worldwide, for it is juicy and fragrant, soft on the inside and firm on the outside, full of vitamin A and virtually tastes of summer sunshine.

The pitfall of this dessert is that the puff pastry will soak up liquid if it comes into contact with the other ingredients, thus losing its crispness. To prevent this, the individual components of the dessert should be stored separately and not combined until immediately before serving. For the same reason, the dessert cannot be kept – though it is highly unlikely that any will be left over.

1. Prepare the puff pastry and allow it to rest for about 2 hours. Form the paste into thin rolls with a diameter of about ¹/₂ in / 1 cm and allow to harden in the refrigerator. Cut small pieces from the rolls of pastry and roll them out as thinly as possible in a mixture of confectioners' sugar and mixed spices. Bake the puff pastry between two layers of baking paper at 390 °F / 200 °C for 5 to 10 minutes.

2. For the Chiboust cream, whisk the egg yolk and sugar until pale yellow, then add the cornstarch and stir to combine. Bring the milk to a boil, add to the egg yolk, and mix in the sheet of gelatin (previously soaked in cold water) as well as a dash of kirsch. Bring this mixture to a boil.

with Strawberries

3. To make the meringue, beat the egg white until stiff. Heat the sugar to 250 °F / 120 °C and add it to the egg white and continue beating until the mixture has completely cooled. Fold the meringue into the cream. Cut the strawberries to be used for the filling into thin slices.

4. Arrange the pieces of pastry, cream, and finely sliced strawberries in alternate layers on top of each other and arrange on the serving plates. Bring a little sugar to a boil in water and caramelize. Dip the strawberries into the caramel and arrange between the filled pieces of pastry. Serve lukewarm.

Melon Sorbet

Preparation time: 1 hour
Difficulty: ✱

Serves 4

2 melons, each 2 lb 3 oz / 1 kg
1 ²/₃ cups / 250 g confectioners' sugar
juice of ¹/₂ lemon
1 lb / 500 g strawberries

For the sauce:
9 oz / 250 g strawberries
3 tbsp / 30 g confectioners' sugar
juice of 1 lemon
1 glass vodka

To garnish:
peppermint leaves

One fine day the Chinese discovered that a mixture of milk, water, and fruit gained a very special consistency when it was frozen. Frozen desserts and sorbets have been a success ever since. It is recommended that a sorbet be prepared at the last minute and that an alcoholic flavoring that complements the fruit be poured over the sorbet after it is frozen. In this case, a muscatel would be the ideal finishing touch for the melon. However, it is not necessary to add alcohol. In this recipe, only the strawberry sauce contains alcohol in the form of vodka.

As is the case with all summer fruits, melons used in a dessert should always be ripe and aromatic. There are a number of varieties, and cantaloupe melons in particular have a very delicate flesh. For our chef, it is impossible to talk about melons without thinking of the small Provençal town of Cavaillon in France, where they are cultivated. In summer, the air there is thick with the scent of melons.

The strawberry sauce requires very ripe berries, whose stems are easily removed, to produce the most intense color and flavor. The strawberries used for garnishing, in contrast, should be firmer and a little less ripe, so that they are easier to cut. Strawberries do not keep for long, so they cannot be bought in large quantities or ahead of time.

For the finishing touch, Paul Pauvert recommends decorating the two-fruit composition with peppermint leaves, whose refined flavor lends a slightly piquant contrast to the sweetness of the melon sorbet.

1. Quarter one melon, remove the seeds and cut the flesh into cubes. Puree in a blender. Combine the melon puree with the confectioners' sugar and lemon juice. Prepare the sorbet in an ice cream maker.

2. Halve the second melon. Remove the seeds and scoop large balls out of the flesh.

with Strawberries

3. Carefully wash the strawberries with the stems on. Halve them and arrange on the serving plates with the cut side facing upwards, alternating with balls of melon.

4. To make the sauce, wash the strawberries and pass them through a sieve. Add the sifted confectioners' sugar, lemon juice, and vodka. Pour the sauce onto the plates and arrange a ball of sorbet in the center.

Flan with White

Preparation time: 45 minutes
Cooking time: 45 minutes
Difficulty: ★★

Serves 4

For the buttermilk ice cream:
1 cup / 250 ml buttermilk
1 cup / 250 g plain yoghurt
1/2 cup / 120 g sugar
6 marinated mint leaves
grated peel and juice of 1 untreated orange
  and lemon

For the flan:
3 1/2 oz / 100 g brioche
1/4 cup / 60 g sugar

6 1/2 tbsp / 100 g butter
2 vanilla beans
1 2/3 cups / 400 ml milk
3 eggs

For the peach compote:
4 ripe white peaches
4 cups / 1 l water
1/2 cup plus 1 tbsp / 140 g sugar
2 cinnamon sticks
2 whole cloves
grated peel and juice of 1 untreated lemon

To garnish:
a few fresh mint leaves

According to etymology, the French word *flan* is derived from the Franconian word *flado*, used to describe flat objects. A flan was originally a sweet or savory tart covered with a topping made of eggs and flour. Today, a flan more commonly denotes a custard that is either turned out of the mold or served in it, and which can be prepared in a variety of ways with the most diverse flavors. The refined taste of juicy peaches gives this dessert its special flavor.

In China, from whence the peach originates, it is a symbol of marriage and fertility. The various varieties of peaches often bear women's names – Alexandra, Benedictine, Mireille – and they are generally available from May through September. This dessert can be prepared with a wide range of peach varieties. The peach compote is prepared on a sugar base with the addition of cinnamon and other spices.

The flan is sure to be a success if one uses very fresh produce and keeps strictly to the given temperatures and cooking times. The custard is baked in molds placed in a pan of water for at most 25 minutes in an oven that has been preheated to between 265 °F / 130 °C and 300 °F / 150 °C (Important: do not go above the maximum temperature!). It is suggested that one checks the flan frequently during baking to make sure the pudding does not boil over.

The ice cream recommended by our chef is both light and delicious, and one can enjoy it without having to worry about committing too great a sin. Buttermilk is the liquid produced during the butter-making process, and it contains very little fat. Alternatively, this pudding, delicious cool or lukewarm, can be served with vanilla ice cream or a fruit sorbet.

1. To make the buttermilk ice cream, mix all the ingredients without heat and beat. Pour into an ice cream maker and allow to harden. Begin the flan by cutting the brioche into cubes. Caramelize them in a pan with the sugar and butter, stirring continuously. Set aside to cool.

2. Cut open the vanilla beans. Scoop out the pulp and place it and the vanilla husks in the milk. Bring to a boil. Remove the husks and pour the hot milk onto the eggs, which have been beaten until foamy with a little sugar, and combine carefully.

Peach Compote

3. Preheat the molds and fill them half-full with the browned brioche cubes. Pour the custard into the molds and bake for 25 minutes in a water bath in an oven preheated to 265 °F / 130 °C. Wash the peaches, halve them and remove the stones. To make the compote, place all the ingredients except the peaches into a saucepan. Bring to a boil.

4. Add the peach halves and let them steep for 15 minutes over low heat. Remove the cinnamon sticks and cloves, then skin the peaches. Chop half of the peaches in a blender and then pass them through a pointed sieve. Divide the compote between the plates, then place a flan crowned with a peach half on each. Serve with the ice cream and garnish with fresh mint.

Quark Soufflé with

Preparation time: 30 minutes
Cooking time: 12 minutes
Difficulty: ★★

Serves 4

4 eggs
4 tbsp confectioners' sugar
1 vanilla bean
4 tbsp low fat quark

For the sauce:
1 lb / 500 g wild strawberries
6¹/₂ tbsp / 100 ml sugar syrup at 28 °Beaumé
white rum

A soufflé should ideally be served immediately after baking, when it is still hot and fully risen. The version presented here is lighter than a traditional soufflé, as the butter has been replaced by low fat quark. Switzerland could be considered the inventor of quark, since curdled milk was already being processed on the shores of Lake Neuchâtel 5,000 years ago.

Preparation of the soufflé is simplified by using very cold eggs. The egg whites are whipped with a pinch of salt until very stiff, and carefully folded into the quark mixture. Individual soufflé dishes, which have been greased and sprinkled with sugar, are then filled two-thirds full. They should be refrigerated for 20 minutes, but no longer.

Because the soufflé rises very rapidly, one has to be very vigilant. The oven should be preheated to 430 °F / 220 °C, but during the baking process itself, which takes 12 to 14 minutes at most, the oven temperature should be between 355 °F / 180 °C and 390 °F / 200 °C. It is best to place the individual dishes in a pan of water inside the oven. During baking, do not open the oven door! Such disturbance can easily take the air out of a soufflé.

Any fruits that are in season at the time one is making this soufflé can accompany it. The bottoms of the individual soufflé dishes could even be lined with very ripe raspberries, in which case the soufflé would best be served in the mold and accompanied by a sauce made with the same type of fruit.

1. Using a metal bowl, separate the eggs. Beat the egg yolks with the sifted confectioners' sugar and vanilla bean pulp until foamy. Mix in the drained quark.

2. Beat the cold egg whites until very stiff and carefully fold them into the quark mixture. Grease the soufflé dishes and sprinkle them with sugar. Examine the fruit and halve half of the wild strawberries, placing them to one side. Puree the remaining fruit in a blender with the syrup to make a sauce. Pass through a pointed sieve and flavor with rum. Refrigerate.

Wild Strawberries

3. Preheat the soufflé dishes. Fill each form completely with the soufflé mixture. Place the dishes in a pan of water inside the preheated oven and bake for 10 to 12 minutes. While they are baking, decorate the plates.

4. Pour some strawberry sauce onto each plate. Surround it with the strawberry halves. Take the soufflés out of the dishes and place in the center. Serve immediately.

Fruit Stew with

Preparation time: 30 minutes
Cooking time: 30 minutes
Difficulty: ☆

Serves 4

4 vineyard peaches
1 untreated lemon
7 tbsp / 50 g blanched pistachios
7 tbsp / 50 g blanched almonds
large grapes, white and black
$^1/_3$ cup / 80 g sugar

6$^1/_2$ tbsp / 100 ml peach schnapps
2$^1/_2$ tbsp / 40 ml marc brandy
3$^1/_2$ tbsp / 50 g butter

Apart from the name and their common history, vineyard peaches have nothing in common with grapes. Rather, the term is used to describe late-ripening, extremely delicious peaches that are cultivated in unprotected sites that are open to the winds, in contrast to the more ordinary peaches that have been trained on a trellis. These lose some of the wild taste of the original fruit due to constant exposure to strong sunshine. Vineyard peach trees used to be grown in vineyards in the gaps between the vines, hence their name. Another connection to wine is the lovely, dark, wine-red color of this peach, and the dark juice found in varieties such as the Alberge and Sanguine peaches. Unfortunately, these varieties are only very rarely found in most grocery stores.

It would thus seem very fitting to reunite the peaches in this delicious fruit stew with a perfectly suited grape, preferably large grapes, either a black one such as the Alphonse-Lavallé, or white ones like the Italia and Ideal grapes. While it is certain that the peach came to the western world via Persia, extremely little is known about the origins of the grape. However, its symbolic importance was written about in the Bible (where it is said in Jeremiah that "the fathers have eaten a sour grape, and the children's teeth are set on edge") and Aesop's fables.

A suggested refinement for the combination of fruits recommended here is old marc brandy, which is produced using what remains after grapes have been pressed, mainly the stems, skins, and seeds.

1. Briefly submerge the peaches in a pan of boiling water, then quickly cool them and remove their skin. Remove the stones and cut each of the peaches into six slices.

2. For the garnish, peel the lemon rind very thinly and cut into the thinnest possible strips. Chop the pistachios and almonds; squeeze the lemon to obtain the juice.

Peaches and Grapes

3. Carefully skin the grapes and remove the seeds without bruising the flesh.

4. Make a dark caramel with the sugar, then carefully deglaze it with the peach schnapps. Add the lemon juice and marc brandy. Stir in the butter and heat everything again. Bring to a boil once, remove from the heat, add the peach slices and grapes and warm gently over a low heat. Serve the warm fruit in small pans decorated with chopped pistachios and almonds.

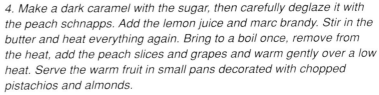

Rosemary Apples with Semolina

Preparation time: 1 hour
Cooking time: 20 minutes
Difficulty: ★★

Serves 4

3 apples (Golden Delicious)
a little butter
¹/₄ cup / 60 g sugar
a sprig of rosemary

For the semolina sponge cake:
¹/₂ cup / 120 ml milk
3 tbsp / 35 g semolina
2 eggs, separated
8 tsp / 40 g butter
3 tbsp / 40 g sugar

For the cocoa sorbet:
3 cups / 750 ml water
1¹/₃ cups plus 1 tbsp / 350 g sugar
1¹/₄ cups / 135 g cocoa powder

Why not surprise guests or loved ones by using rosemary in a dessert – an herb that at first glance appears to go better with meat. Its slightly bitter flavor is also an excellent accompaniment to apples, which are thought to have had a more pungent taste in their original form. Prehistoric people must have shared this opinion, for they strung pieces of apple up on threads to dry in the sun.

Adam, William Tell, Newton: the apple stimulates human curiosity, makes demands on our physical dexterity and nimbleness of mind. Where flavor is concerned, hybridization has given rise to thousands of varieties, and the ingenuity of great chefs has made its own contribution. There are infinite variations of desserts in which the sweetness of apples is combined with

alcohol or other ingredients. Here, one needs flavorful fruits suitable for stewing with the rosemary, and Golden Delicious apples are ideal. This is a relatively recently discovered variety that is naturally sweet, and almost caramelizes by itself in the pan.

The sponge cake dough is not difficult to prepare. Do be careful not to put too much dough into the molds, for it rises a great deal during baking. Turn out of the molds immediately after baking and serve lukewarm. The sprig of rosemary used as a garnish is not merely decorative; the warmth of the apples causes it to exude the aroma that earned it the name "sea-dew," thus providing a foretaste of this hot and cold dessert.

1. To make the sponge cake, bring the milk to a boil, add the semolina and simmer briefly until thickened. Remove from the heat and stir in the egg yolks and butter. Meanwhile, beat the egg whites with a whisk until stiff, then add the sugar.

2. Carefully combine the egg whites with the semolina mixture. Turn the sponge cake dough into greased pans and bake at 355 °F / 180 °C. After baking, turn out of the pans and allow to cool until lukewarm.

Sponge Cake and Cocoa Sorbet

3. To make the cocoa sorbet, bring the water and sugar to a boil to produce a syrup. Add the cocoa, stir thoroughly, and allow to cool. Mix thoroughly in the ice cream maker and freeze. Peel and core the apples and cut them into very small cubes.

4. In a pan, heat the butter and sugar to make a caramel. Add the apples and rosemary leaves. Allow to cook until the mixture gains some color. Spread some apple pieces on each plate, topped with sponge cakes and a scoop of sorbet. Garnish with a sprig of rosemary.

Orange Jelly with Puff

Preparation time: 1 hour 30 minutes
Cooking time: 10 minutes
Cooling time: 4 hours
Difficulty: ★★

Serves 4

For the ice cream:
6¼ cups / 1½ l milk
6½ tbsp / 100 g superfine sugar
½ cup / 55 g powdered milk

For the orange jelly:
7 oranges
2 sheets of gelatin
2½ tbsp / 35 g sugar
Grand Marnier

To garnish:
5 oz / 135 g puff pastry (see basic recipes)
confectioners' sugar
mint leaves

Originally oranges were used only for decorative purposes in Europe. Orange trees planted in containers lined the avenues of French gardens. They were kept in orangeries over winter, and particularly fine examples of this type of building still exist in the Tuileries and Versailles. Later it was discovered that oranges were edible and contained high levels of vitamins. Whether consumed fresh, as juice, or in another form, they retain their stimulating effect and their flavor.

Oranges can still be found sold in square pieces of silky paper, which children used to love to collect. Nowadays, perhaps a hundred of the thousand or so known varieties of oranges are eaten, and for simplification they are grouped into three major families. Navel oranges, with a small outgrowth, ripen early and have no seeds; sweet oranges have a firmer peel and light flesh; and blood oranges have a strong red flesh. A good orange should have an even color and be firm and shiny.

When preparing the ice cream, one must be vigilant, especially while reducing the milk to a third of its original quantity. This dessert must be started well ahead of time so the puff pastry can be given sufficient time to rest. If creating puff pastry from scratch seems too daunting, the frozen pastry available nowadays is of very good quality and is an acceptable substitute.

1. Peel some of the oranges and divide them into segments, retaining the juice. Set aside, and make the ice cream. Start by reducing the milk, then add the sugar and powdered milk. Bring to a boil and allow to cool. Stir and pour into an ice cream maker. Stir until it reaches a good consistency, then place in the freezer.

2. Soak the gelatin in cold water. Squeeze the remaining oranges, and add the juice to that retained in step one. Heat the orange juice with the sugar and Grand Marnier, then add the gelatin to this mixture and stir until it has dissolved. Remove from the heat, allow to cool, and then refrigerate.

Pastry and Milk Ice Cream

3. Finally, roll out the puff pastry on a flat surface sprinkled with confectioners' sugar and place on a baking tray. Place another tray on top of the pastry and bake at 375 °F / 190 °C. Cut the baked pastry into triangles.

4. On each plate, arrange a rosette of orange segments. Briefly whip the jelly with a spoon and then pour it over the orange pieces. Place a scoop of milk ice cream in the center of each plate. Arrange three triangles of pastry around it to form a pyramid and garnish with mint leaves.

Savarin with Strawberry

Preparation time: 3 hours
Cooking time: 20 minutes
Difficulty: ★★

Serves 8

For the savarin dough:
(see basic recipes)

For the syrup to soak the savarin:
³/₄ cup / 200 ml sugar syrup at
   30 °Beaumé
2¹/₂ tbsp / 40 ml lemon juice
2¹/₄ tbsp / 35 ml coconut liqueur (Malibu)
¹/₃ cup / 80 ml water and rum

For the cigarette pastry:
(see basic recipes)

For the sauce:
1¹/₄ cups / 250 g pineapple
¹/₂ cup plus 2 tsp / 135 g sugar
¹/₃ vanilla bean
1¹/₄ cups / 330 ml Malibu
1¹/₄ cups / 330 ml brown rum

For the coconut cream:
¹/₂ cup / 120 ml cream
2 tsp / 7 g confectioners' sugar
1 pinch gelatin powder
1¹/₄ oz / 35 g coconut meat
¹/₂ tsp / 3 ml Malibu

To garnish:
7 oz / 200 g strawberries
lemon juice
4 tsp / 20 g sugar

In this exotic dessert brimming with tropical smells and flavors, the pineapple and coconut conjure up images of far-away coasts and sunny lands.

Thanks to enormous advances in transport, fresh pineapples are imported by air freight from the Ivory Coast or Martinique and quickly reach grocery stores, still near their peak of flavor. Their high vitamin content and fat-absorbing properties make this a truly classic fruit. Shining red, ripe strawberries, ideally of the tasty and fleshy Pajaro variety, are excellent in combination with pineapple. When washing the berries, the stems should be left on, as they otherwise fill with water and lose much of their flavor.

If fresh coconuts are available and you are adventurous enough to try opening the hard, fibrous shells, you can retain the coco-

nut water and scoop out the meat. The ready-packed products that are available in any store are an acceptable alternative.

Malibu is another well-known import of quality. Rum, on the other hand, is available in myriad varieties and brands, and one should pay attention to quality when selecting one. Stéphane Raimbault recommends brown rum, which develops a fuller aroma, with greater nuances of flavor, than white rum.

The savarins' compact size and shape lend themselves to particularly stylish arrangements. The consistency of this simple but classic cake creates a delightful contrast with the crunchy cookies made using the cigarette pastry.

1. Prepare the savarin cake dough according to the basic recipe. Fill individual cake pans three-quarters full and allow the dough to rise to the top. Bake for 20 minutes at 390 °F / 200 °C.

2. Boil the ingredients for the syrup and allow to cool to 140°F / 60 °C. Dip the savarins into the syrup, let them drain, then sprinkle them with rum. Make the cigarette pastry as directed in the basic recipe. Cut out round cookies and place on a baking tray. Sprinkle them with the nuts and fruits. Bake for a few minutes at 355 °F / 180 °C.

and Pineapple Flower

3. For the sauce, dice the pineapple, retaining the resulting juice. To make the sauce, heat the sugar (without liquid) together with the melted vanilla pulp until it forms a pale caramel. Carefully and gradually add the rum and Malibu, together with the pineapple pieces and retained pineapple juice, stirring constantly. Allow to cool.

4. For the coconut cream, whip the cream and sugar until stiff and add the dissolved gelatin, coconut meat, and Malibu. Combine everything thoroughly. Cut the strawberries into fine sticks, sprinkle them with lemon juice and coat in sugar. Cover each plate with sauce and strawberries and place a savarin on each. Decorate with coconut cream, arrange the cookies on top and garnish with a strawberry.

Nougat Parfait à

Preparation time: 2 hours
Cooking time: 6 minutes
Cooling time: 5 hours
Difficulty: ★★★

Serves 8

For the brittle:
3¹/₂ tbsp / 50 g sugar
2 tsp / 10 ml water
²/₃ cup / 100 g almonds
²/₃ cup / 100 g hazelnuts

For the nougat:
meringue (see basic recipes)
2 cups / 500 ml cream, whipped
6 tbsp / 75 g each raisins, dried apricots
2 tbsp / 25 g maraschino cherries

2 tbsp / 25 g candied orange peel
¹/₄ cup / 40 g pistachios

For the cigarette batter: (see basic recipes)
sesame, saffron

For the spice mixture:
1 tsp / 2 g ground licorice
1 tsp / 2 g ground vanilla
1 tsp / 2 g ground pepper
2 tsp / 4 g ground cinnamon
1 whole clove
2¹/₂ tbsp / 10 g instant coffee

For the sauce:
4¹/₂ tbsp / 100 g honey
1 vanilla bean
6¹/₂ tbsp / 100 ml lemon juice
3 tbsp / 30 g peel of untreated oranges
pistachios

Our chef, born in the Vendée region of France, was inspired in his creation of this recipe by his travels to Asia. During his time there, in addition to living for a while in Japan, he retraced Marco Polo's journey along the dangerous "spice route." It was here that he gathered aromas and adapted the various flavors that give his nougat its special quality, so suited to the European palate. The spices should be selected with great care; their scent is less important than their actual taste.

The mixture of spices must be balanced, for the entire dessert can be ruined by imprecise measuring or poor ingredients. It has been said before but bears repeating: excessive use of spices is the enemy of all good cooking.

Two points are very important when preparing this complex recipe:

– All the basic components, such as the brittle and the fruit and spice mixtures should be prepared in advance.
– The light, sensitive ingredients – the meringue and the whipped cream – should be folded in very carefully so that they do not collapse.

In honor of his present home, Stéphane Raimbault uses this opportunity to incorporate the Midi region's sweet almonds, rich in calcium and magnesium, into his dessert. Along with other various delicacies and dried fruits, nougat is one of the famous "thirteen desserts" served on Christmas Eve in Provence.

1. To make the brittle, boil the sugar and water at 230 °F / 116 °C to produce a syrup. Add the blanched almonds and hazelnuts and caramelize them. Allow to cool, then crush. Make the meringue according to the basic recipe. Combine the fruits, then add the fruit mixture to the whipped cream.

2. Fold the meringue into the whipped cream, then add the crushed brittle as well. Turn the nougat into a bowl and freeze for 5 hours. Prepare the cigarette batter according to the basic recipe, incorporating the spice mixture listed above.

la "Spice Route"

3. Using a triangular stencil, spread the batter onto a non-stick greased baking tray. Sprinkle lavishly with sesame and saffron. Bake for a few minutes at 355 °F / 180 °C.

4. To make the sauce, bring the honey to a boil with the opened and scraped out vanilla bean. Remove from the heat and add the lemon juice and other ingredients. Allow to cool. Place a thick slice of nougat on each plate. Lean three spiced triangles against it and pour some of the sauce around the base. Garnish with mint.

Warm Charlotte

Preparation time: 40 minutes
Cooking time: 40 minutes
Difficulty: ★

Serves 4

1 lb / 500 g cooking apples
6–8 tbsp sugar
13 tbsp / 200 g soft butter

grated peel and juice of
¹/₂ untreated lemon
¹/₂ loaf white loaf bread

For the molds:
butter
3 tbsp sugar

The archetypal British apple, the Bramley, could be a cross between the Rennet and the Golden Delicious apple. Because of its acidic taste, it is better for cooking than for eating raw. When cooked, it does not fall apart and develops an extremely fine flavor. In our recipe, it forms the basis for a traditional, economical, and easily prepared dessert. If you are not able to find Bramley apples, substitute other cooking apples. Whichever variety you choose, the apples must be cooked in an uncovered pan so that the liquid can steam off, resulting in a smooth, thick compote that still contains a few firm pieces of fruit.

The firmness of the charlotte is produced by the slices of white bread with which the molds, preferably metal ones, are lined.

The molds have to be thoroughly sugared on the inside, so that a crisp brown crust can form. The most suitable bread is a firm white sandwich loaf, or a yeast bread made with egg and milk. It is vital that the slices of bread overlap along the edges so that the fruit filling does not leak out. After baking, this bread casing produces a firm, golden brown crust, so that the charlottes do not collapse when turned out of the molds.

Serve the dessert warm rather than hot, with custard, a caramel sauce or simple whipped cream. Your guests will love this warm sweet. And, to be completely British, indulge yourself and your guests with a cup of first-class tea!

1. Peel the apples and core them. Cut the flesh into coarse cubes and cook with the sugar, butter, lemon juice, and peel over a moderate heat to produce a thick compote. If necessary, add a little more sugar. Preheat the oven to 390 °F / 200 °C.

2. Cut the crusts off the white bread. Cut the bread into slices ¹/₄ in / 0.5 cm thick and use a pastry brush to spread butter on them. Cut out round slices of bread with the same diameter as the molds for the lids, and several strips about 1³/₄ in / 3.5 cm wide for the edges.

with Bramley Apples

3. Brush the molds with butter, sugar them and line them with the strips of bread: the strips should overlap, so that the compote cannot seep out during baking. The bread should stand about $^1/_4$ in/0.5 cm over the top edge of the molds.

4. Fill each mold seven-eighths-full with warm apple compote and firmly close with a bread lid. Bake the charlottes for 10 minutes at 390 °F / 200 °C, then reduce the oven temperature to 320 °F / 160 °C and bake for another 20 to 30 minutes. As soon as the bread is firm and golden brown, take out and serve warm.

Spiced Cake with Ginger

Preparation time: 30 minutes
Cooking time: 30 minutes
Difficulty: ★

Serves 8–10

³/₄ cup / 175 g butter
6¹/₂ tbsp / 100 g cane sugar
2 tbsp grated fresh ginger root
4 egg yolks
1 tbsp ground ginger
3 tbsp / 40 g superfine sugar
2 cups / 250 g flour
1¹/₂ tsp baking soda
¹/₂ tsp ground nutmeg

¹/₂ tsp ground cloves
³/₄ cup / 200 ml molasses
6¹/₂ tbsp / 100 ml heavy cream
8 egg whites

For the compote:
2 lb 3 oz / 1 kg rhubarb
³/₄ cup / 200 g superfine sugar
juice of 1 lemon
2 tsp Grenadine

To garnish:
whipped cream

One noble witness to Britain's colonial past is ginger, a pale brown, firm root with a strong flavor, usually cut into thin slices and given a protective coating to protect it from drying out. According to Chinese tradition, ginger is an excellent aid to digestion, whether fresh or cooked with sugar and eaten at the end of a meal.

This appetizing, moist cake contains ground ginger – a fresh, aromatic, amber-colored powder. The mix of flavors can also be broadened by adding cinnamon, coriander or curry. There should be no particular difficulty in preparing the cake batter. The cake is baked once the edges come loose from the pan and a fork inserted into its center comes out cleanly. Once cool, it can easily be kept fresh for several days by wrapping it in clear plastic wrap.

Rhubarb, long used for medicinal purposes, cannot be eaten raw because of its stringiness and acidity. For that reason it is cooked and used in cakes, sorbets, and compotes.

When buying the rhubarb, make sure that its stems are firm, smooth, and crisp. If overcooked, they will become too soft and brownish. Rhubarb usually produces a lot of juice, which should be drained off before serving. The compote will also keep for a few days in the refrigerator, if stored in an airtight container.

1. Preheat the oven to 355 °F / 180 °C. Grease a springform pan with a diameter of 10–11 in / 23–25 cm with butter. Using a mixer, beat the butter, cane sugar, and fresh ginger until creamy. Add the egg yolks gradually, while stirring continuously, until they have completely combined with the other ingredients.

2. Sift all the dry ingredients except the superfine sugar together. Add to the butter and egg yolk mixture.

and Rhubarb Compote

3. Combine the molasses and heavy cream, then add to the mixture in the mixer. Beat the egg whites and sugar until stiff. Fold them in carefully in order to produce a smooth dough. Pour into the cake pan and bake for 30 minutes at 355 °F / 180 °C.

4. Peel and chop the rhubarb. Cook with the sugar and lemon juice at a low temperature, stirring occasionally. As soon as it is tender, remove from the heat. Pour into a bowl and add the Grenadine. Arrange a piece of cake on each plate and serve with the rhubarb compote and whipped cream.

Crêpe Pouches with

Preparation time: *1 hour*
Cooking time: *15 minutes*
Difficulty: ✷

Serves 4

4 Williams pears
a little lemon juice
1 tbsp flower honey
1 vanilla bean
7 oz / 200 g raspberries
mint leaves

For the crêpe mixture:
1 cup / 125 g flour
3 eggs
1 cup / 250 ml milk
3¹/₂ tbsp / 50 g butter

The pear has been known since classical times, and countless varieties have been bred through the centuries. Ever since it was first bred 180 years ago by an Englishman of the same name, the Williams pear has experienced ongoing popularity. Due to its fine flavor and melting consistency, it is the summer pear *par excellence*, frequently preferred over other equally good pears like the Louis Bonne and Bosc varieties. It is probably only surpassed by the Vereins-Dechants, the "queen of pears," which has a harmonious, voluptuous form raved about by gourmets.

Carmelizing the pears presents no problem at all; simply warm the pears in honey, the "sweet dew" whose flavor sent the

Hebrews into raptures. Jean-Claude Rigollet recommends using a honey made with flowers, or perhaps an acacia honey whose fine flavor goes equally well with the pears.

The crêpe mixture has to be carefully stirred by hand so that no lumps form. If necessary, one could always pour the mixture through a fine sieve. Either way, it should be completely smooth and homogeneous. If the milk is poured into the flour and egg mixture gradually and mixed in immediately, the batter should be successful. The mixture is then normally set aside for a few hours before being used to make the crêpes, which improves its consistency due to the gluten in the flour.

1. Prepare the crêpe mixture. Mix the flour and eggs. Gradually add the milk as well as the melted and lightly browned butter and stir in. Allow the mixture to rest.

2. Meanwhile, peel the pears and drizzle lemon juice onto them. Quarter and core them and cut into small pieces. Make the crêpes, one for each serving.

Caramelized Pears

3. Heat the pear pieces with the honey in a pan. Arrange some of the pears in the center of each of the four thin crêpes.

4. Gather the sides of the crêpes to form little pouches and tie with a vanilla bean that has been cut lengthways into four strips. Retain several choice raspberries for garnishing, and prepare a sauce with the rest. Cover the plates with raspberry sauce, place the crêpe pouches on top and garnish with whole raspberries and mint leaves.

Prunes in Pastry

Preparation time: 30 minutes
Cooking time: 15 minutes
Difficulty: ✻✻

Serves 4

20 prunes
1¼ cups / 300 ml red wine
½ untreated orange
½ untreated lemon
1 cinnamon stick
3½ tbsp / 50 g sugar
confectioners' sugar

For the almond cream:
3½ tbsp / 50 g sugar
7 tbsp / 50 g finely ground almonds

3½ tbsp / 50 g butter
1 egg

For the custard: (see basic recipes)
2 cups / 500 ml milk
6 eggs
6½ tbsp / 100 g sugar
1 vanilla bean

For the beer pastry:
2 eggs
¾ cup / 100 g flour
4 tsp / 20 g sugar
3½ tbsp / 50 ml beer
1 pinch of salt
oil for deep-fat frying

Prunes have been used with great success in a wide variety of dishes for centuries, and in many parts of France, this long tradition continues. In the Touraine region, gourmets are familiar with the classic dish of liver medallions served with prunes. But, however well the prune goes with savory dishes, one ought not to forget that it is a fruit, even more suited as an ingredient in a dessert.

For this unusual recipe, one needs nicely shaped, extra-large prunes so that they are easy to fill with the almond cream. In order to increase their size somewhat, they are marinated in wine, which causes them to swell, and then cooked in it briefly to take on even more of its flavor. For the wine marinade, our chef recommends a sweet wine with a strawberry and raspberry bouquet that will not evaporate when heated: a French Chinon, for example, or a Pinot Noir. Or you could try a Trollinger from Baden-Württemberg in Germany.

The batter must be completely smooth, without lumps. Adding a pinch of salt and a little light beer at the last minute gives it a bitter taste. Dip the prunes in the batter and then cook them in oil, which should be hot but not steaming.

1. Marinate the prunes for 2 hours in the red wine with the citrus fruits, cinnamon stick, and sugar. Stone the prunes.

2. Cook the prunes in the wine for 10 minutes over a low heat and allow to cool in the liquid. To make the almond cream, mix the sugar and ground almonds. Then work in the soft butter and egg. Put the almond cream into a pastry bag and fill the prunes with it.

with Almond Cream

3. Prepare the custard according to the basic recipe. Now make the beer batter and dip the prunes in it to coat fully.

4. Deep-fry the prunes for about 15 seconds. Carefully drain them and sprinkle them with confectioners' sugar. Arrange the prunes on a plate with the custard.

Apple Tart "Nonette"

Preparation time: 30 minutes
Cooking time: 25 minutes
Difficulty: ★★

Serves 4

For the cakes:
5¹/₂ oz / 160 g puff pastry (see basic recipes)
4 apples (Granny Smiths)
8 tsp / 40 g butter, melted
3 tbsp / 40 g sugar

For the vanilla ice cream:
²/₃ cup / 150 ml milk
²/₃ cup / 150 ml cream
2 vanilla beans
4 egg yolks
¹/₄ cup / 60 g sugar

For the caramel sauce:
6¹/₂ tbsp / 100 g sugar
6¹/₂ tbsp / 100 ml cream

This recipe is not for the typical nonette made in Auxerre – a type of spiced cake known as *pavé* in Chartres and *chanoinesse* in Remiremont. Rather, the fine p...f pastry cakes that Michel Rochedy makes for us here are an homage to his aunt, the Mother Superior of the monastery of Saint-Sacrement, whose culinary abilities made a deep impression on him as a child. Using a cake mixture, she made three cakes covered with caramelized apples, producing a dessert that was both light, crispy and so tasty that one scarcely notices the dough. Perhaps this was the very dessert that led our chef to his vocation!

The first prerequisite of this cake is a light dough, and the second is finely sliced apples. The cakes can, by the way, be prepared in advance and baked shortly before serving. Do not bake them at too high a temperature, or the apples may become too hard. After five minutes, the temperature can be raised somewhat.

For this recipe, use apples suitable for cooking in order to avoid any unpleasant surprises. The acidic flavor of Granny Smiths forms an interesting contrast with the caramel sauce, especially when the sauce has been enriched with cream. This recipe can, however, be prepared using other apples, such as the Golden Delicious – or even with other fruit, such as oranges or grapefruit. In that case, though, it should be served with orange sorbet or rum raisin ice cream.

1. Roll out the puff pastry and cut out four circles measuring 7 in / 16 cm in diameter. For the vanilla ice cream, bring the milk to a boil with the cream and the halved vanilla beans. Beat the egg yolks and the sugar until foamy. Pour the milk and cream onto the egg yolks and cook at 185 °F / 85 °C. Beat thoroughly. Pour into an ice cream maker and let harden.

2. Peel the apples and hollow out the centers with a corer. Cut the flesh into paper-thin slices about 1 mm thick.

with Caramel Sauce

3. Place a rosette of apple slices on the puff pastry. Pour melted butter over them and sprinkle sugar on top. Bake them on a non-stick tray for 20 minutes at 355 °F / 180 °C.

4. For the caramel sauce, heat the sugar with a little water to 320 °F / 160 °C. Add the hot, liquid cream. Place a cake in the middle of each plate with a scoop of vanilla ice cream on top. Pour the caramel sauce around it.

Crème Brûlée à la Bergamotte

Preparation time: 10 minutes
Cooking time: 1 hour 30 minutes
Difficulty: ★

Serves 4

For the crème brûlée:
²/₃ cup / 150 ml cream
6¹/₂ tbsp / 100 ml milk
5 egg yolks
3¹/₂ tbsp / 50 g sugar
a little essence of bergamot

For the pineapple accompaniment:
1 fresh pineapple
4 cups / 1 l sugar syrup (2 cups / 500 g sugar,
   2 cups / 500 ml water)
butter
1 tsp pastis (aniseed schnapps)

There is probably no other dessert as simple and yet so continually popular as the crème brûlée. Despite the countless variations of this sweet made with cream, eggs, and milk over the years, it still has the power to convince and, thanks to its delicious, light flavor, deserves a place of honor among the great desserts. The bergamot flavoring recommended by our chef gives it a subtle, pleasant aftertaste.

Little is known about the origins of the little bergamot fruit, which was evidently originally imported from Turkey. Nowadays, the round, pale fruit with acidic flesh is mainly cultivated in Calabria. Despite its apparent kinship with the orange and mandarin, botanists are reluctant to classify this mysterious fruit. The bergamot is the source of the aroma used for classic Earl Grey tea, but the main use for the essence of this citrus fruit is in the manufacture of perfume and – due to its benefi-

cial effects on the digestive system – in the pharmaceutical industry.

At first glance, the combination of bergamot and pineapple appears rather daring, but this has turned out to be a real success on the part of Joël Roy: he adds a finishing touch in the form of a dash of pastis, making the dessert even more unconventional. The pastis should be added with care, as its aniseed flavor may overpower the bergamot.

When preparing the crème, it is important to stick precisely to the given quantities and cooking times. The creamy mixture should be stirred as little as possible and allowed to rest a while before baking, so that there are no air bubbles in it. The prepared crème can infuse for a few hours in the refrigerator.

1. Bring the cream and milk to a boil. Beat the egg yolks with the sugar until they become a little lighter. Add the hot milk to the egg yolk mixture. Stir in the essence of bergamot and allow everything to rest for a few minutes. Pour the mixture into ovenproof molds.

2. Bake in a water bath in the oven for 1¹/₂ hours at 210 °F / 100 °C; cover the dishes with baking paper or aluminum foil after half of the time has passed. Allow to cool in the molds. Peel the pineapple; cut off four thin, complete slices, and cut the rest into half slices. Set aside.

with Pineapple in Pastis

3. Using the water and sugar, make a syrup. Fry the half slices of pineapple in a pan with a little butter. Pour on a little glass of syrup. Reduce, then deglaze with pastis.

4. Arrange a whole fresh slice of pineapple on each of the dessert plates. Invert a crème brûlée onto each, sprinkle sugar onto the crème, and melt the sugar with a white hot salamander. The dessert can also be placed under a hot grill briefly. Garnish with the half slices of pineapple.

Hot Pineapple on

Preparation time: 15 minutes
Cooking time: 5 minutes
Difficulty: ✶✶

Serves 4

1 pineapple
3¹⁄₂ tbsp / 50 g butter
4 cups / 1 kg sugar
2 cups / 500 ml water
3¹⁄₂ tbsp / 50 ml brown rum

For the pineapple sauce:
1 medium-sized pineapple
1 tbsp sugar
1 cup / 250 m white rum
ice cubes

For the sorbet:
2 cups / 500 ml pineapple juice
6¹⁄₂ tbsp / 100 ml white rum
2¹⁄₄ oz / 70 g ice cubes

To garnish:
3 tbsp / 20 g blanched almonds

The idea for making this "hot and cold" pineapple dessert, an homage to the juicy fruit found almost everywhere in the Antilles, came to our chef during a family holiday on Puerto Rico. Though he admits that preparing savory dishes is his main preference, he worked almost unceasingly at this recipe once he returned to Spain. After a few trials, a result emerged that was completely satisfactory to him. Very likely, you will be as excited as our chef.

Pineapple originally grew in Central and South America, where Europeans discovered it in the 16th century in Brazil. It was first cultivated in France during the reign of Louis XV, but the European climate is not entirely suitable for this bromeliad, which grows so luxuriantly in the tropics; Hawaii is the leading producer of pineapple today.

Before harvesting, pineapples should be grown to a decent size and ripened in their country of origin. Santi Santamaria considers the small pineapples from the island of Réunion to be less suitable: while they have a more intense flavor, they are difficult to work with. It should be easy to remove the individual leaves of the rosette, a sign that the fruit is ripe.

If you carefully follow the instructions in the recipe, you will create a dense composition of flavors that may awaken a forgotten memory, especially if you sniff your fingertips, which will smell of the fruit. The most important ingredient in this delightfully light dessert is its scent (as suggested by the fruit's name in German, *Ananas*, which derives from the Guaraní word for "scent," *ana*). It provides a virtuoso conclusion to a meal with friends or family.

1. Peel a pineapple and quarter it. Cut the flesh from one quarter pineapple into small cubes. Slice the remaining pineapple lengthwise. Discard the peels.

2. To make the pineapple sauce, chop the flesh of the medium-sized pineapple in a blender. Pass through a fine sieve and add the sugar together with the white rum and ice cubes. Mix everything thoroughly and stir in the small pineapple cubes. Refrigerate. For the sorbet, mix all the ingredients in a blender and prepare in an ice cream maker.

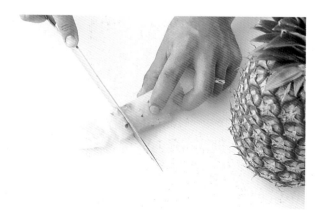

a Piña Colada Sorbet

3. In a pan, heat the butter and slightly brown the pineapple slices in it.

4. Add the sugar, water, and brown rum and reduce the syrup until it starts to caramelize. Arrange a pineapple slice in each bowl on a pool of pineapple sauce, garnish with the almonds, pour syrup over it and serve with a ball of sorbet.

Pastry Wafers with Verbena

Preparation time: 15 minutes
Cooking time: 15 minutes
Difficulty: ★★

Serves 4

For the verbena cream:
2 bunches of verbena
4 cups / 1 l milk
3/4 cup / 100 g cornstarch
1/2 cup plus 2 tbsp / 150 g sugar
8 egg yolks
1 cup / 250 ml heavy cream, whipped

For the puff pastry wafers:
3 tbsp confectioners' sugar
3 1/2 tbsp / 50 ml heavy cream
2 egg whites
3 tbsp flour

For the custard:
4 cups / 1 l milk
1 vanilla bean
1/2 cup plus 2 tbsp / 150 g sugar
8 egg yolks

To garnish:
confectioners' sugar

Santi Santamaria was so impressed with the ice cream his colleague Michaugral prepares with verbena, he is now doing his utmost to restore this fragrant herb to its former glory. Also known as lemon verbena, its Spanish name, *Maria-Louisa*, is reminiscent of one of the ships sailed by Christopher Columbus. It is evidently native to Chile, and was brought to Europe after the first voyages of discovery, as were so many spices now in everyday use. Available more frequently in dried form (but sometimes fresh, in specialized produce stores) in the United States, verbena has a potent lemon-like flavor. Our chef is firmly convinced that verbena is just as suitable as vanilla or cinnamon for making pastries.

First, a light filling is prepared using heavy cream and other ingredients. It is then spread between the pastry wafers. The name heavy cream, or double cream, does not mean twice the fat, but refers to the cream's thicker consistency as compared to light or single cream. Because these wafers are so sensitive, they should not be prepared until immediately before serving to make sure that they stay nice and crisp.

There is nothing to say about custard – it is a classic. If you want something more unusual to go with this dessert, substitute a raspberry sauce to give the pastry more of a tart taste, or other red fruits, which will enhance the refined flavor of the verbena without distorting it.

1. To make the verbena cream, first place a bunch of verbena into the milk. Proceed as for a pastry cream (see basic recipes), by mixing the starch, sugar, and egg yolks without heat. Gradually add the milk. Slowly heat, while stirring constantly. Bring to a boil, then remove from the heat immediately.

2. To make the wafers, heat the sugar to about 250 °F / 120 °C and mix in all the ingredients with a tablespoon. Spread circles about 4 1/2 in / 10 cm in diameter onto a non-stick baking tray and bake for 15 minutes.

Cream and Ice Cream

3. For the custard, bring the milk to a boil with the vanilla bean. Stir the sugar and egg yolks together until creamy. Pour the hot milk onto the egg yolks, then return to the heat at a low temperature, stirring continuously, until the custard sticks to the spoon.

4. Fold the stiffly whipped cream into the verbena cream. To make the ice cream, marinate the second bunch of verbena in half of the custard for 15 minutes, then stir thoroughly and allow to set in an ice cream maker. Place a wafer on a plate, and top with a spoonful of the verbena cream. Repeat, making three layers. Dust with confectioners' sugar and serve with the ice cream.

Hot Chocolate Pudding

Preparation time: 30 minutes
Cooking time: 15 minutes
Difficulty: ★★

Serves 6

3¹/₂ tbsp / 50 g butter
1¹/₂ oz / 45 g bittersweet chocolate
1 egg
2 egg yolks
3 tbsp / 25 g flour

¹/₂ cup / 75 g confectioners' sugar
1 cup / 250 ml milk
1 cup / 250 ml crème fraîche
12 oz / 350 g white chocolate, coarsely
   chopped

The whole Santin family helped to perfect this delightful dessert, an example of the superlative confection-making skills of the Italians. Note that the choice of ingredients produces a marvelous harmony of black and white, a classic color combination, pleasing to the eye.

If you prefer the pudding to have a somewhat more bitter flavor, use chocolate with a higher cocoa content. Experts consider the criollo beans from Venezuela to have the best flavor, but they are rare. However, excellent varieties of chocolate with a high cocoa content (70 % or higher) are available in stores, and these guarantee quite a fine flavor. Bringing all the ingredients to room temperature before preparing this dessert will help ensure its success.

Great care must be taken in choosing the white chocolate for the sauce. This ingredient is very sensitive, and unfortunately there are a few varieties of poor quality. It is best to store it in a cool, dry place. Chocolate can sometimes seem to "sweat," when the cocoa butter forms little pearls and crystallizes on the surface. This is a sign that it has been stored in an unsuitable place and should be kept in a cooler one.

This chocolate duet not only contains many nutrients, it also offers a balance between the delicate aromas. It provides the perfect excuse to quote Chateaubriand, who felt that "taste is the common sense of genius."

1. In the top half of a double boiler (85 °F / 30 °C), melt the butter and bittersweet chocolate. Beat the eggs until they are an even pale yellow. Add the flour and sugar and mix well until the dough has a thicker consistency.

2. Carefully pour in the melted chocolate and butter, stirring constantly.

with White Chocolate Sauce

3. Bring the milk and creme fraîche to a boil and pour over the coarsely chopped white chocolate. Cover and allow the chocolate to melt for a few minutes.

4. Grease four molds (3 in / 7 cm diameter, 2³/₄ in / 6 cm height) with butter and dust with confectioners' sugar. Fill them with the bittersweet chocolate mixture and bake for 10 minutes at 355 °F / 180 °C. After taking them out of the oven, slide the puddings out onto plates and pour the white chocolate sauce around them.

Creole Mousse with

Preparation time: 2 hours 30 minutes
Cooking time: 1 hour
Cooling time: 4 hours
Difficulty: ★★

Serves 4

For the cocoa meringue:
1 egg white (40 g)
3 tbsp / 40 g sugar
1 tbsp / 10 g cocoa powder
2¹/₂ tbsp / 25 g confectioners' sugar

For the chocolate mousse:
5¹/₄ oz / 150 g bittersweet chocolate
²/₃ cup / 150 ml crème fraîche

For the banana mousse:
3¹/₂ oz / 100 g banana
1 tbsp / 15 g sugar
1 tsp lemon juice
1 tsp / 3 g ground gelatin
6¹/₂ tbsp / 100 ml crème fraîche

During his honeymoon in the Antilles, Maurizio Santin, our chef's son, became enchanted with a combination of rum, chocolate mousse, and banana sorbet. He returned determined to combine these three elements, producing a special harmony, a taste rich in exotic aromas.

Bananas are native to the Antilles, and bittersweet chocolate is its ideal companion here, especially chocolate with a high cocoa content (about 70 %). However, it must be treated with care: the melted chocolate should be lukewarm when mixed with the crème fraîche. The mousse should be prepared without interruption and filled into the molds immediately.

The meringue should be made light; it is better to apply it in a thin layer so that the baking time remains short. After half the baking time has elapsed, opening the oven door a bit to let air in will make the meringue a little more crisp.

One tip (according to our chef, the key to success): Start by preparing the meringue, then make the chocolate mousse followed by the banana mousse, and finish with a chocolate sauce or custard with vanilla and rum flavoring.

1. Prepare the cocoa meringue by beating the egg white and then carefully folding in the sugar and cocoa. Spread the mixture onto a baking tray to a height of 1 in / 2 cm and bake at 210 °F / 100 °C for 45 minutes.

2. For the chocolate mousse, melt the chocolate in a double boiler, allow to cool and carefully fold in the crème fraîche, which has been stirred until creamy. Cut the baked meringue into circles with a diameter a little smaller than the cutters used in step 4.

Bananas and Chocolate

3. To make the banana mousse, mash up the bananas and mix with the sugar and lemon juice. Add the gelatin, which has been dissolved in a teaspoon of water. Stir the crème fraîche until creamy and mix into the banana mixture.

4. Cover a baking tray with plastic wrap and place on it four round cookie cutters with a diameter of 3¹/₂ in / 8 cm and height of 2 in / 4.5 cm. Place a slice of meringue in each cutter. Spread some chocolate mousse on it, then top with another slice of meringue. Finish with a layer of banana mousse. Refrigerate for about 4 hours. Place on dessert plates and decorate with a border of chocolate sauce.

Chocolate Drops

Preparation time: *20 minutes*
Cooking time: *15 minutes*
Cooling time: *1 hour*
Difficulty: *★★*

Serves 4

6¹/₂ tbsp / 100 ml cream
4 tsp / 20 g sugar
2 tbsp / 20 g cocoa powder
3¹/₂ oz / 100 g chocolate coating

For the caramel:
6¹/₂ tbsp / 100 g sugar

For the orange sauce:
The juice of 2 oranges
2 tbsp / 30 g sugar

To garnish:
caramelized orange peel

Like all Mediterranean countries, Italy grows a large variety of oranges that are used for a number of different purposes. Italy, by the way, is the first place in Europe where this member of the citrus family was cultivated.

It is best to use juicy oranges such as Tarocco or Moro oranges, but not blood oranges such as the Sanguinella. Whichever you choose, select firm oranges that are heavy in the hand and have a smooth, furrowed peel.

In this recipe, the whole fruit is used: the peel for the decoration after it has been blanched three times in boiling water, and the juice for the sauce, though you should pay particular attention to its consistency.

Our chef advises against substituting a ready-made syrup, which often contains many preservatives and other additives. Using one could impair the quality of this dessert.

Chocolate, frequently used in desserts in which it is combined with oranges, contains bitter cocoa, which further emphasizes the contrast between the flavors of the two main ingredients.

As soon as the chocolate is completely melted, use small spoons to pour it in irregular drops. This irregularity gives the dessert a very special charm.

1. Pour the cream into a bowl. Add the sugar and stir in for a minute. Add the cocoa and beat rapidly until the mixture becomes thick and stiff.

2. Using spoons, shape small drops out of the cocoa and cream mixture, place them on waxed paper and refrigerate for an hour. Melt the chocolate coating in a double boiler (120 °F / 48 °C). Take the cocoa cream drops out of the refrigerator, dip in the chocolate coating, and refrigerate again.

with Orange Sauce

3. Heat the sugar without adding water to make a caramel, then caramelize the drops. Place on a buttered serving dish or plate. Also caramelize the orange peel, which has been blanched three times in boiling water.

4. For the orange sauce, squeeze 2 oranges and reduce the juice with the sugar. Add the caramelized peel and reduce to the consistency of a syrup. Arrange the drops in a star shape and serve covered with the orange sauce and garnished with the peel.

Brittle Cake

Preparation time: 20 minutes
Cooking time: 10 minutes
Cooling time: 6 hours
Difficulty: ★

Serves 4

1 cup of coffee
6½ tbsp / 100 ml milk
10 ladyfingers
1¼ cups / 300 ml cream
3½ tbsp / 50 g sugar
1¾ oz / 50 g macaroons, crushed
3½ oz / 100 g shortbread, crumbled

For the almond brittle:
3½ tbsp / 50 g sugar
⅔ cup / 100 g almonds

For the zabaglione:
2 egg yolks
2 tsp sugar
2 tsp white dessert wine

The name of this dessert in Italian is *torta di cantucci*, which translates as "almond brittle torte." But words and names cannot do justice to this delicacy; one should instead concentrate fully on its preparation.

Very fresh almonds with a pronounced flavor are needed for the brittle. For the greatest possible freshness, look for nuts still in the shell. Almonds are grown in warm climates throughout the world, including South Africa, Australia, Asia, the Mediterranean region, and, of course, California. They are chockfull of nutrients, including protein, calcium, magnesium, and potassium.

The consistency of the almond brittle, which is rich in fat, provides a delightful contrast with the soft ladyfingers. In order for it to be firm enough, the cake must be refrigerated for at least 6 hours.

A second contrast is not evident until the very last minute, when the cold cake is served with the warm zabaglione. To give it the perfect finishing touch, it is important to serve this dessert with a truly first-class, dessert wine. Likewise, the coffee used to soak the ladyfingers must be of a high quality – if possible, a very good arabica. All these pieces of advice may seem superfluous, but once you have experienced this extraordinary cake, it becomes clear that it is worth every bit of extra effort.

1. To make the brittle, heat the sugar in a small pan without adding water. Add the almonds and stir until they are thoroughly coated. Turn the brittle onto an oiled tray. Allow to cool, then crush.

2. Combine the coffee and milk. Place the ladyfingers on a tray so that they form a square. Spoon the milk and coffee mixture over the ladyfingers to soak them. Press firmly with your fingers so that the liquid is better absorbed. Beat the cream and sugar until stiff.

with Coffee

3. Spread the whipped cream over the ladyfingers . Make the zabaglione in a double boiler using the ingredients listed above.

4. Spread half of the zabaglione over the cake. Cover it with alternating layers of macaroons, shortbread, and crushed brittle; repeat all three layers. Refrigerate for 6 hours. After taking out of the refrigerator, cut into four pieces and serve with the remaining warmed zabaglione.

Crème Brûlée

Preparation time: 20 minutes
Cooking time: 10 minutes
Difficulty: ✶

Serves 4

3 cups / 750 ml milk
¹/₂ cup plus 2 tsp / 135 g sugar
1 cinnamon stick
grated peel of 1 untreated lemon
13 egg yolks
sugar for glazing

In Portugal, there is still a certain splendor associated with religious festivities: they provide frequent occasions for social gatherings and merry goings-on, are an expression of regional customs, and provide continuity and points of contact between the different generations. Rivalries arise in only one area: when it comes to desserts and other sweet treats, Portuguese monasteries and cloisters are beehives of activity, and the results are compared mercilessly.

If legend is to be believed, this crème brûlée, along with a series of other desserts, was created by the nuns of the monastery of Alenquer, to be served at the table of King Diniz of Portugal (1279–1325), who established the University of Coimbra and was the monastery's patron. In Portugal, where a cactus is often used in place of the classic Christmas tree, this crème is a popular family Christmas dessert.

There is no particular skill involved in making the crème brûlée, but do be sure to take the crème out of the double boiler as soon as it starts to thicken and pass it through a pointed sieve so that any lumps are removed. This will also improve the fine consistency of the crème, showing off the delicate cinnamon flavor of this delicious pudding to best advantage.

By the way, we owe the introduction of cinnamon to Portuguese seafarers, who opened up the famous spice route. In Portuguese gastronomy, cinnamon is used in many ways, both as a powder and as whole sticks; it is found in meat and game dishes as well as in cakes and pastries. It is even used to give various drinks, such as wine, cocoa, and coffee, a pleasant aroma.

1. Place the milk, sugar, cinnamon stick, and grated lemon peel in a pan. Bring to a boil and then remove from the heat.

2. Beat the egg yolks vigorously with a little cold milk. Stir into the hot milk mixture.

Monastery Style

3. Allow the crème mixture to thicken in a double boiler: it must not be allowed to simmer! When it has reached the desired consistency, pour the crème through a pointed sieve into flat bowls and refrigerate.

4. Sprinkle a little sugar on top and glaze the surface with a salamander or under a hot grill. Serve warm.

Encharcada

Preparation time: 20 minutes
Cooking time: 3 minutes
Difficulty: ✶

Serves 4

15 egg yolks
1 small cinnamon stick
2 cups / 500 g sugar
2 cups / 500 ml water

For seasoning:
ground cinnamon

The Convent, or rather the *Conventual*, is a restaurant set up in a former monastery by Maria Santos Gomes, who seeks to transform the necessary act of eating into an exquisite pleasure for her guests. The nuns who lived in these places are worthy predecessors for Maria Santos Gomes, because the majority of the desserts now traditional in Portugal were invented by their religious orders in the 17th and 18th centuries.

The Portuguese specialty introduced here, *encharcada*, is a dessert in which eggs play the central role. It is vital that they be completely fresh, so be sure to check the laying and use-by dates before you purchase them. Only the egg yolk is used in this dish. Though egg yolk has been much maligned because of its relatively high concentration of cholesterol and calories (75 of the 90 calories in a 2 oz / 60 g egg), it is still an excellent source of protein, iron, and vitamins A and D. A fresh yolk retains its shape when separated: if it splits, has dark spots or flattens out, it is probably not completely fresh.

We can thank the Portuguese *conquistadors* for cinnamon. They brought the spice, actually the peeled bark of the cinnamon tree, from India. It is difficult to imagine Portuguese cooking without it. So if you finish the dessert off by seasoning it – in moderation, of course – with cinnamon, this will be a well-deserved homage to the bold discoverers of foreign territories.

1. Mix the sugar, water and cinnamon stick in a pot on the stove and simmer until small bubbles start to appear. Beat the egg yolks. As soon as the syrup is ready, remove the cinnamon stick and pass the egg yolks through a sieve into the hot syrup.

2. Over a constant low heat, allow to simmer and as it does so carefully stir with a wooden spatula or spoon from time to time.

3. Allow the encharcada to continue simmering, and use a wooden spatula or spoon to scrape the outer edge of the mass toward the middle of the pan, so that no crust forms. Remove the mixture from the heat as soon as the eggs are cooked, but a little syrup still remains.

4. Pour the encharcada onto plates, season with cinnamon and briefly grill in a hot oven until golden yellow.

Chocolate Cream

Preparation time: 45 minutes
Cooking time: 5 minutes
Difficulty: ✶✶

Serves 4

1 cup / 250 ml cream
9 oz / 250 g bittersweet chocolate
4 egg yolks
1/3 oz / 10 g mint leaves
1 1/3 cup / 40 g fresh coriander, chopped
2/3 cup / 100 g confectioners' sugar
2 tbsp / 20 g cocoa powder, if desired
4 slices of phyllo pastry

For the cherry sauce:
7 oz / 200 g cherries
3 1/2 tbsp / 50 g sugar
6 1/2 tbsp / 100 ml water

To garnish:
fresh fruit, cut into small pieces
mint leaves

Athena, goddess of wisdom and daughter of Zeus, has been the source of inspiration for countless artists. Over the years, a distinct cult developed around her. Painters, sculptors, poets, philosophers, and even politicians have appealed to her throughout the centuries. Even the capital of modern Greece bears her name, as does the Athenaeum Intercontinental Hotel, where our chef Nikolaos Sarantos has run the kitchen since 1988.

Unique in this recipe is the stunning combination of fresh coriander with high-quality chocolate. So that the flavor is not too bitter, the chocolate should not contain more than 50% cocoa and should be of the best quality. A higher cocoa content does not seem to blend well with the coriander. You can, however,

add some cocoa powder to deepen the color of the mousse and prevent the cream from making it too light.

Coriander is extremely popular in Greek cooking and is therefore found almost everywhere – in salads as an *hors d'œuvre*, as a seasoning in meat dishes (usually lamb) and sometimes simply as a decoration. Do not be afraid to use it copiously; its flavor has long been a staple of Greek cuisine.

Make sure the cherry sauce is not too sour, because this could destroy the effect of the coriander and chocolate. If you are unable to find nice, fresh cherries, make a custard instead (see basic recipes) with a discreet amount of vanilla.

1. Whip the cream until stiff. Melt the chocolate in a double boiler and carefully stir in the egg yolks, mint leaves, chopped coriander, and confectioners' sugar. Fold in the whipped cream and refrigerate the finished mousse.

2. Lay the sheets of phyllo dough over a round, ovenproof bowl so that they are given its shape, and bake in the oven until light brown. Make one pastry dome per serving,

"Athenaeum" with Coriander

3. Arrange the sheets of pastry like a dome with two balls of chocolate mousse nestled inside it. Garnish with the small pieces of fruit and mint leaves.

4. To make the cherry sauce, bring the stoned cherries to a boil with the sugar and water. Puree in a blender and pass through a pointed sieve. Pour on to the plates with the fruit.

Mastic

Preparation time: 30 minutes
Cooking time: 10 minutes
Difficulty: ★

Serves 4

3 cups / 750 ml cream
6 eggs, separated
1 cup / 250 g sugar
6$\frac{1}{2}$ tbsp / 100 ml mastic liqueur
3 tbsp / 20 g mastic powder

1 lb / 500 g kataifi dough (available in Greek and Turkish stores)

For the sauce:
$\frac{3}{4}$ cup / 200 ml milk
3$\frac{1}{2}$ tbsp / 50 g sugar
4 egg yolks
1 cinnamon stick
$\frac{1}{2}$ cup / 80 g light and dark raisins

Even Victor Hugo found worthy of a vivid poem the destruction wrought on the Aegean island of Chios in the 19th century during the battle for Greek independence. Afterward, Chios became famous for its mastic, a resin obtained from the gum mastic tree. The trees are grown on plantations on the island, and are tapped once a year in August and September. The resin itself is a clear yellow glass-like substance, which is washed and sold in crystalline form.

Mastic finds the most varied uses, from industrial adhesives to varnishes to medicines. Small packages of the crystals are sold as chewing gum in Greece. Pounded into a powder, it is a uniquely Greek flavoring commonly used in baking, as well as other sweets including puddings and ice creams. Naturally,

there is also a liqueur made from the mastic tree, called *Mastiha* or *Mastika*. Although the taste is delicate, use it carefully, as too much of it can ruin any dessert.

Another Greek specialty – sheets of kataifi dough – is used mainly for preparing small tarts filled with dried fruit. The combination of ingredients for these tarts differs according to the region and its indigenous products.

Make sure that the kataifi dough is not allowed to soak up any moisture – this will make it soft, and it will taste doughy and be unpalatably sticky. Pay particular attention to this tip if you intend to store the sheets for a few days. It is best to serve the dessert fresh.

1. Whip the cream. Beat the egg yolks with 6$\frac{1}{2}$ tbsp / 100 g of the sugar until foamy. Using the egg whites and remaining sugar prepare a meringue (see basic recipes). Gently combine the whipped cream, egg yolks, and meringue, then blend in the mastic liqueur and powder. Refrigerate for a few hours.

2. Plait braids out of the kataifi dough. Place the braids on a greased baking tray and bake them until golden yellow.

Mousse

3. For the sauce, heat the milk with half of the sugar. Mix the egg yolks with the remaining sugar, stir in the hot milk, then return to the stovetop and heat to about 175 °F / 80 °C. Add the cinnamon.

4. Form "nests" out of the braided dough and fill the center with some raisins. Place a scoop of the mastic mousse in each nest and pour some sauce around the dessert. Garnish with the remaining raisins.

Chocolate and

Preparation time: 2 hours
Cooking time: 30 minutes
Difficulty: ★★★

Serves 4

For the strips of brittle:
3¹/₂ tbsp / 50 g butter
6¹/₂ tbsp / 100 g sugar
3¹/₂ tbsp / 50 ml orange juice
¹/₄ cup / 30 g flour

For the coconut milk parfait:
1 cup / 250 ml coconut milk
1 oz / 25 g white chocolate
4 egg yolks
3¹/₂ tbsp / 50 g superfine sugar

Batida de Coco (optional)
1 cup / 250 ml cream

For the chocolate mixture:
3¹/₂ tbsp / 50 g butter
2 eggs, separated
¹/₃ cup / 75 g sugar
¹/₄ cup / 30 g flour
3¹/₂ oz / 100 g chocolate coating, melted
2¹/₂ tbsp / 25 g confectioners' sugar

For the coffee sauce:
6¹/₂ tbsp / 100 ml heavy cream
2 cups espresso coffee
1 egg yolks
4 tsp / 20 g sugar

To garnish:
sugar for glazing
bittersweet chocolate sticks (optional)

In this dessert, in which contrasting flavors are perfectly balanced, Fritz Schilling's main purpose is to introduce you to coconut milk – not to be confused with coconut water, the liquid that pours out when one opens a coconut. Coconut milk is produced from fresh coconut meat, which is mixed with water or warm milk, liquidized in a blender, and finally poured through a pointed sieve so that a homogenous, creamy liquid results. It is used in many ways in cooking, including desserts, of course, but also to season rice or subtly flavor curries for savory dishes. Coconut milk can also be bought in cans.

When preparing the parfait, it is important to make sure that the ingredients do not go through any sudden changes of temperature when mixed; for example, the coconut and chocolate mixture must be cooled off quickly by being set into ice water

after reaching the desired consistency in the double boiler so that the whipped cream does not melt when folded in.

Production of the brittle strips is a bit tricky, but there is a way around difficulty here as well. If the brittle seems too stiff after baking, simply put it back into the warm oven until it is soft enough to be rolled around a glass or similar object. If necessary, repeat this until you have enough curved brittle strips.

The chocolate tart, for which the chocolate coating can simply be melted in the oven, also requires a little skill, particularly the fine-tuning of the relevant temperatures. One ingredient is missing from our list, though in principle it is obvious and should be used liberally – patience!

1. For the brittle strips, mix all the ingredients thoroughly and allow to rest for about 2 hours. Spread thinly onto baking paper and bake at 355 °F / 180 °C. Cut the brittle into strips 1 in / 2 cm wide and wrap them around a circular object or form. To make the parfait, heat the coconut milk and white chocolate and reduce by a third.

2. Beat the egg yolks and sugar until they are light, add the warm coconut milk, and stir until cooled. Add Batida de Coco to taste. Fold in the stiffly whipped cream. Pour into a pan lined with plastic wrap to a depth of ³/₄ in / 1.5 cm. Freeze. For the chocolate mixture, stir the soft butter with the egg yolks and sugar until creamy, then add the flour and finally the melted chocolate coating.

Coconut Brittle Tarts

3. Beat the egg whites and confectioners' sugar until stiff, then carefully fold them into the chocolate mixture. Bake in a springform pan for 20 minutes at 300 °F / 150 °C. When cool, cut out circles with a cookie cutter. For the coffee sauce, bring the heavy cream and espresso to a boil. Beat the egg yolk and sugar until foamy, then add the hot cream and reduce to a thick sauce.

4. Lay a brittle ring in the center of each plate and place a chocolate round inside it, then top with a circle of parfait of exactly the same size. Sprinkle with sugar and briefly caramelize the parfaits under a grill. Garnish with coffee sauce and whipped cream, and serve with chocolate sticks if desired.

Preparation time: 3 hours
Cooking time: 40 minutes
Difficulty: ★★★

Serves 4

For the short pastry: (see basic recipes)
6¹/₂ tbsp / 100 g sugar
13 tbsp / 200 g butter
2¹/₂ cups / 300 g flour
apricot jam

For the wine cream:
3 eggs
1 egg yolk
¹/₃ cup / 75 g sugar
¹/₂ cup / 125 ml Riesling wine
¹/₂ cup / 125 ml Sauternes

For the caramel sauce:
¹/₃ cup / 75 g sugar
3 egg yolks
1 cup / 250 ml cream

For the topping:
1 lb / 500 g grapes

For the glaze:
³/₄ cup / 200 ml Sauternes
3 tbsp / 40 g sugar
2 tsp / 5 g cake glaze powder (see glossary)

For the ice cream:
1¹/₄ cups / 300 ml Sauternes
¹/₃ cup / 75 g sugar
3 egg yolks
6¹/₂ tbsp / 100 g butter

People normally leave a little room for a dessert after a fine meal. This means that after they have appropriately admired the atmosphere in the restaurant, the expertise of the chef, and the courtesy of the service, they are able to devote their full attention to the sweet temptations available. This is the motto of our chef, who firmly rejects pastries made solely with whipped cream and other ingredients rich in fat. Instead, he recommends this cake made with sweet wine, which has a delicacy to outstrip any traditional dessert.

The principle behind this recipe is a perfect balance of the flavors of grapes and sweet wine. The latter is available in

Germany in the form of a Trockenbeerenauslese, or in France as a Sauternes or muscatel. Only grapes of first quality should be used. Skinning and deseeding them is a tiresome business, but the end result more than justifies this inconvenience.

Some care is required in making the glaze. Fritz Schilling warns against exceeding the given temperature, even by only a few degrees, because it would cause the cream to lose its smooth consistency and form lumps, greatly detracting from its perfection. If it does not reach the right consistency within the given time, it is better to bake it a little longer rather than raise the temperature.

1. Prepare a short pastry using the sugar, butter, and flour and use it to line one large pie pan, or one could also use several smaller tart forms. Bake at 300 °F / 150 °C. After removing from the oven, allow to cool and brush with egg yolks or apricot jam to make the base impermeable.

2. To make the cream, beat the eggs and egg yolk with the sugar. Combine the wines and add to the eggs. Stir everything thoroughly, heat to 100 °F / 50 °C and pour the wine cream onto the tart shell. Bake at 300 °F/150 °C until the cream has thickened. Prepare the caramel sauce using the given ingredients; set aside.

Wine Tart

3. Remove the skin and seeds from the grapes. Place them on the thickened cream on the tart shell. To prepare the glaze, mix the Sauternes, sugar, and cake glaze powder and bring to a boil. Pour the glaze over the tart and allow to set.

4. To make the ice cream, cook the wine with the sugar. While stirring, pour over the whisked egg yolks, mix in the cold butter and briefly bring to a boil. After cooling, pour into an ice cream maker. Arrange a piece of tart and a scoop of ice cream on each plate and pour caramel sauce around them.

Preparation time: 1 hour
Cooling time: 4 hours
Difficulty: ✳✳✳

Serves 4

For the passion fruit mixture:
5¼ oz / 150 g passion fruit flesh
1 sheet of gelatin
2 tbsp / 35 g dextrose
⅔ cup / 150 ml cream, whipped

For the raspberry sauce:
7 oz / 200 g raspberries
⅔ cup / 100 g confectioners' sugar

For the coconut ice cream:
2¾ cups / 250 g shredded coconut
2 cups / 500 ml milk
2 cups / 500 ml cream
½ cup plus 2 tbsp / 150 g sugar
4 tbsp / 75 g dextrose

For Pierrot's chocolate ruff:
9 oz / 250 g bittersweet chocolate

This dessert is a culinary illustration of the familiar French children's song, "*Au clair de la lune*". The first step is to find a suitable mold for Pierrot's head, in which all the details of the face and the little hat are visible. Preparing the head using a coconut ice cream and chocolate decorations requires a little finesse: handle the ice cream very carefully, wipe off any excess ice cream when filling the mold and only then place the filled mold into the freezer. Before you begin, taste the shredded coconut to make sure it is fresh and has a good flavor.

Peaches can be substituted for the passion fruit, though the slightly tangy flavor of passion fruit is preferable; it provides a more intense experience for the taste buds and gives the dessert an exotic touch. Do not whip the cream for too long or it may curdle. The dextrose and gelatin are absolutely essential for the correct consistency. If you have a crescent mold, you could let the passion fruit mixture set in it rather than cutting it out.

Raspberries are not the only fruit suitable for the fruit sauce – any red fruits will do as long as they are completely fresh. The sauce turns out best if the fruits are pureed with confectioners' sugar and then passed through a pointed sieve, making the sauce fine and smooth.

1. Heat 3½ oz / 100 g of the passion fruit flesh and stir in the soaked gelatin and dextrose. Allow to cool, then carefully fold in the whipped cream. Let the cream set in the freezer for 1 hour.

2. Once the mixture has set, remove it from the freezer and cut out crescent shapes. For the raspberry sauce, puree the raspberries with confectioners' sugar and pass through a sieve. Make a sauce with the remaining passion fruit, adding sugar to taste, then brush it onto the crescents.

a Crescent

3. For the ice cream, heat the shredded coconut with the milk and cream and allow to infuse. Add the sugar and dextrose and pour everything into an ice cream maker. After it has set, press the ice cream firmly into the Pierrot molds so that there are no air bubbles. Freeze for 2 hours.

4. Take the Pierrots out of the molds. Melt the bittersweet chocolate and draw the face using a roll of paper as a tiny pastry bag. Pour the remaining chocolate out thinly onto a smooth work surface. As soon as it is firm, use a broad metal spatula or knife to carefully scrape it up to form the ruffs. Cover the bottom of the dessert plates with raspberry sauce, then place a Pierrot and crescent in the center.

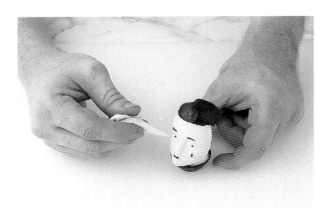

English Dessert

Preparation time: 15 minutes
Cooking time: 6 minutes
Cooling time 24 hours
Difficulty: ★

Serves 4

¹/₃ cup / 80 g butter
2 oz / 60 g sweet apples, chopped
3¹/₂ oz / 100 g each strawberries, raspberries,
  blackberries, and blueberries
sugar
6 sheets gelatin
12 slices of white loaf bread or yeast bread

To garnish:
red berries
4 sprigs of mint
4 tbsp cream, whipped
confectioners' sugar
red fruit sauce

The way our chefs prepare summer berries here is similar to a charlotte (named after the wife of the British King George III) or even the typical British pudding, a method of preparation particularly suited to fruits too ripe to be used in a fruit salad. Here they are wrapped in a coating of sliced white bread that, as long as you use firm bread cut into thin slices, forms a tasty "container" for the fruit. Sliced white bread is a traditional, extremely common food in Great Britain; it is eaten at every meal from breakfast to dinner, including the inevitable after-noon tea, which is served with a variety of sandwiches.

Take care in selecting the fruits; they should be very ripe but not too badly bruised and certainly not spoiled. It is also important that the bread casing is pressed firmly into the molds

so that none of the fruit compote can escape, or the bread casing will not be firm enough. The choice of molds is also important – if they are too high, too much compote will fit inside and the dessert will fall apart when turned onto serving plates. If the molds are too small, though, there will be too much bread in proportion to fruit. In order to make it easier to turn the dessert out of the molds, you can put a layer of plastic wrap between the bread and the sides of the molds.

It is recommended that an apple be added to the berry com-pote, because its sweetness counterbalances the slight acidity of the berries. Its consistency also makes the compote a little firmer. Bramley, Cox's Orange Pippin or Golden Delicious would all work well.

1. Melt the butter in a saucepan over low heat. Add the chopped apple and stew for 1 minute. Add the berries, sugar to taste, and a half glass of water. Bring everything to a boil, then remove from the heat and add the sheets of gelatin.

2. Brush oil into four molds with a height and diameter of 2³/₄ in / 6 cm, or line them with plastic wrap. Cut the crusts off the sliced bread and cut the bread into strips. Use it to line the forms.

with Summer Fruits

3. Carefully close any gaps between the bread strips. Pour the fruit compote into the bread-lined molds, soaking the bread thoroughly.

4. Finish the compote off with a round slice of bread on top. Allow to infuse in the refrigerator for 24 hours. Invert onto plates and pour a red fruit sauce over the dessert. Garnish with fresh berries, whipped cream, and sprigs of mint.

Fritters with

Preparation time: 45 minutes
Cooking time: 5 minutes
Cooling time: 30 minutes
Difficulty: ★★

Serves 4

For the chocolate truffles:
³/₄ cup / 200 ml crème fraîche
5 cups / 500 g grated chocolate
6¹/₂ tbsp / 100 g butter, very soft

For the fritter mixture:
2 cups / 250 g flour
7 tbsp / 50 g cocoa powder
a pinch of salt
3¹/₂ tbsp / 50 g sugar
1 cup / 250 ml champagne
3¹/₂ tbsp / 50 g butter, melted
2 eggs
oil for deep frying

Both chocolate, a noble concoction, and its fans are worthy of closer examination. Lovers of chocolate meet all over the world to taste it. And it is not simply a craving for sugar that is behind the need to taste and compare the sublime fruit of the cocoa tree – even medical books attribute a considerable therapeutic effect to chocolate!

Roger Souvereyns is himself a lover of chocolate. His recipe, taste-tested by chocolate experts, was inspired by a fritter filled with pig's liver once served to him by his colleague Marc Meneau in Burgundy.

Cocoa, available in several quality grades, varies depending on its origins. The one our chef recommends is the rarest and most refined, though at the same time the most sensitive: criollo. It comes from Indonesia and Latin America and has a distinct aroma. Another fine quality cocoa you might use instead is a mixture called trinitario, a combination of two cocoa beans from the Caribbean and Brazil. The cocoa content of the chocolate should not be less than 60 to 70%. The chocolate and cream mixture for the truffles must be prepared a day in advance and refrigerated overnight.

In a departure from Belgian tradition, the fritter mixture in our recipe is prepared with champagne instead of beer. Make sure that there is enough oil in the deep-fryer, and fry the fritters about an hour before serving so that the chocolate filling, which melts during the frying process, has a chance to set again. Immediately before serving, you can briefly re-warm the fritters in the oven.

1. Heat the crème fraîche and pour onto the grated chocolate. Stir, allow to cool and then add the butter. Refrigerate.

2. Using a pastry bag, pipe truffle sized pralines onto a tray lined with baking or waxed paper. Refrigerate.

Chocolate Truffles

3. For the fritter dough, combine the flour, cocoa, salt, sugar, eggs, and champagne in a mixing bowl to produce a smooth batter, then add the melted butter.

4. Dip each of the truffles in turn into the fritter mixture and fry in a deep-fryer for about 3 minutes at 355 °F / 180 °C. Arrange the finished fritters on a plate and garnish with an apricot sauce.

Preparation time: 45 minutes
Cooking time: 25 minutes
Difficulty: ☆

Serves 4

1 cup / 125 g wheat flour
1 egg
1 egg yolk
3¹/₂ tbsp / 50 g butter, melted
1 cup / 250 ml fresh whole milk
butter for frying

For the sauce:
³/₄ cup / 200 ml cream
2¹/₂ tbsp / 40 ml juniper schnapps
2 egg yolks
3 tbsp / 30 g confectioners' sugar
2¹/₂ tbsp / 40 ml Heidebitt (liqueur made out of heather, a speciality of Hasselt)

For the filling:
acacia honey
4 tsp sugar

Though it is not yet widely known in gastronomic circles, the processing of heather is a particular specialty of the city of Hasselt, the administrative center of the Flemish province of Limburg. Traditionally, the plants are harvested by school children from Limburg, giving them hands-on experience of nature.

Crêpes Hasselt Style is Roger Souvereyns's contribution to the efforts of a friend of his who brews beer, to create a menu with which one can drink beer from start to finish, all the way through dessert. Juniper schnapps was used in the very first version of this dessert; the dry alcohol reduces the sweetness of the crêpes so that they go better with the taste of beer. This effect is heightened by the acacia honey, a natural and aromatic sweetener. The recipe was further modified a few years ago,

when the distillation of heather led to the invention of Heidebitt liqueur. This is now used in place of the original Cointreau, intensifying the regional character of this delicious recipe.

The ingredients and preparation of the crêpe mixture are entirely in keeping with the classic recipe. Make sure that the crêpes are hot when served, so that they do not soak up the sauce. They also taste much better hot. The sauce itself contains whipped cream and must be stirred with some care.

We were very impressed by the generosity that is characteristic of both this recipe and the chef, who says, "I put my heart and soul into everything that I do. I am by nature very creative and do not hide my talents. I always give my all."

1. To make the sauce, whip the cream until stiff. Mix the juniper schnapps, egg yolks, confectioners' sugar, and Heidebitt together. Add to the whipped cream and carefully combine.

2. Stir the ingredients for the crêpes together to form a creamy, liquid batter. Preheat the oven to 390 °F / 200 °C. Heat a little butter in a small cast iron pan (5¹/₂–6³/₄ in / 12–15 cm in diameter) and make the crêpes using a good tablespoon of the batter for each. Keep warm.

Hasselt Style

3. Spread acacia honey onto the crêpes, fold in half and sprinkle with half a teaspoon of sugar. Place the serving dishes with the crêpes into the warm oven.

4. Place two crêpes on each plate and pour sauce over them. Brown them briefly under a hot grill.

Puff Pastry Pouches with

Preparation time: 30 minutes
Cooking time: 15 minutes
Difficulty: ★★

Serves 4

puff pastry (see basic recipes)
confectioners' sugar
2 cups / 500 ml sour sheep's milk
5 tsp / 25 g sugar
1 sheet of gelatin

For the caramelized apples:
4 small apples (e.g. Rennets), peeled and
    quartered
butter

$3^1/_2$ tbsp / 50 g sugar
$3^1/_2$ tbsp / 50 ml water
2 tbsp / 30 ml Sagardoz (apple schnapps)

For the apple sauce:
7 oz / 200 g apple flesh, chopped
$^1/_2$ cup / 125 ml water
3 tbsp / 40 g sugar
juice of 1 lemon
1 cinnamon stick
2 tbsp / 30 ml Sagardoz

To garnish:
red berries

Soured sheep's milk (*mamía* in Spanish) is a traditional Spanish dessert prepared with Sagardoz, a spirit made with apples.

It is not particularly complicated to use soured sheep's milk as long as you make sure to remove the whey produced by the process. You should beat it with sugar, add a sheet of gelatin, and allow it to curdle again. Too much gelatin, however, will give the soured sheep's milk a too-firm, tough consistency. If the necessary utensils are available, you can follow the traditional method of burning off the top layer of the soured sheep's milk with a hot piece of iron.

The only addition to this main ingredient are apples of the *Errecilla* variety, which used to be plentiful in the countryside of Spain. Farmers stored them bedded in sand and straw so that

a supply was available year round. *Errecilla* apples have been almost totally forgotten today, though Pedro Subijana still has a few of these special apple trees in his orchard and is making every effort to restore them to their former glory. But you can quite happily use different kinds of apples, such as Rennets.

Sagardoz, an apple schnapps produced during the distillation of cider, is an extremely tasty spirit. It flows like water, and not just during the Txox competitions between cider makers. During the entire competition, the most exciting dishes are available for sampling: beef ribs, cod omelette and, of course, soured sheep's milk with nuts. The Sagardoz adds a very special delicacy to this dessert. Our chef even had the honor of serving King Juan Carlos and his wife, Queen Sophie, in person.

1. Roll out the puff pastry to a thickness of $^1/_4$ in / 0.5 cm. Cut eight triangles measuring $6\,^3/_4$ in / 15 cm × $6\,^3/_4$ in / 15 cm × $2\,^1/_2$ in / 6 cm out of the puff pastry and bake. Remove the pastry from the oven, dust the triangles with confectioners' sugar and put them back in the oven to caramelize. Allow to cool.

2. Beat the sour sheep's milk and mix in the sugar and gelatin, which has been soaked in water. Do not stir again. Place a layer of the sour sheep's milk mixture between two puff pastry triangles.

Mamía and Sagardoz

3. Peel, quarter, and core 4 apples. Brown them until golden brown in a saucepan with melted butter. Caramelize the apples in the sugar, then carefully and gradually add the water and boil until the caramel dissolves. Stir in the apple schnapps and allow to cool in the pan.

4. For the sauce, bring the chopped apple to a boil in the water with the sugar, lemon juice, and cinnamon. Mash and pass through a pointed sieve. Stir in the apple schnapps. Pour a ladle of apple sauce in the center of each plate, place a puff pastry pouch on top, and arrange the apple pieces with the caramel sauce around the edge.

Pineapple with Saffron

Preparation time: 35 minutes
Cooking time: 25 minutes
Difficulty: ★★

Serves 4

1 large pineapple
light sugar syrup
saffron butter

For the coconut cookies:
1/3 cup / 80 g sugar
3/4 cup / 70 g shredded coconut
3 tbsp / 20 g flour
2 large egg whites
4 tsp / 20 g butter, melted

For the coconut cream:
1/2 cup / 125 ml milk
1/2 cup / 125 ml coconut milk
1 vanilla bean; 3 eggs
3 1/2 tbsp / 50 g sugar

4 tsp / 20 ml Grand Marnier
3 tbsp / 25 g flour
3 1/2 tbsp / 50 ml cream

For the sauce:
1 3/4 oz / 50 g fresh root ginger
3 1/2 tbsp / 50 ml fresh pineapple juice
Grand Marnier

For the syrup:
1/2 cup plus 3 tbsp / 150 g dextrose
5 1/4 oz / 150 g fondant
6 1/2 tbsp / 100 g butter
a pinch of ground saffron
1/3 cup / 50 g almonds, colored pink and
   roasted

The visible refinement and variety of exotic flavors in this recipe will transform the end of your meal into a culinary journey through sunny realms.

As in most European languages, the German word for pineapple, *Ananas*, is derived from the Guaraní word, *ana-ana*, which means "scent of scents." The English name refers to its resemblance to a pine cone. Pineapples have long been a symbol of hospitality. Native to South and Central America, pineapples are now grown in Hawaii and Florida as well, though our chef prefers fruits from Martinique or the Ivory Coast, and are available year-round. They should be quite heavy and have a good amber color, a firm peel with flat "eyes" and leaves that can be detached readily.

The greatest difficulty in this dessert is preparing the syrup. The dextrose and fondant must, with a little skill, be reduced

until they have formed a dense mixture that must nonetheless remain smooth and fluid enough not to form lumps. The ideal temperature for the syrup from which the spun sugar is made is 320–340 °F / 160–170 °C.

The combination of steamed pineapple and saffron, which produces decorative red spots of color on the flesh even when used very moderately, creates a dish that is a true delight for the eyes and the taste buds.

The coconut cookies are a traditional accompaniment. As soon as they take on their characteristic curved shape, they should be stored in a cool, dry place so that they do not flatten out again.

1. Peel the pineapple, leaving it whole. Cut horizontally into 12 even pieces of approximately the same thickness and cut out the woody section in the middle of each slice. To make the coconut cookies, combine the ingredients listed above, drop small amounts of the mixture onto a baking tray lined with baking paper and bake at 465 °F / 240 °C.

2. Steam the pineapple slices for about 5 minutes in a light sugar syrup, then cool and drain. Retain the syrup. Steam the pineapple slices again, this time in a pan with saffron butter.

and Grand Marnier

3. For the coconut cream, bring the milk and coconut milk to a boil with the vanilla bean, then set aside and allow to infuse. Beat the eggs and sugar slightly, then add the Grand Marnier and flour. Combine with the milk mixture and bring everything to a boil. Allow to cool and finally stir in the cream carefully with a whisk. Spread the coconut cream onto the pineapple slices and layer on top of each other.

4. To make the sauce, simmer the chopped ginger in the pineapple syrup retained in step 2. As soon as a caramel has been formed, remove from the heat and deglaze with the pineapple juice. Flavor the sauce with a little Grand Marnier. Combine the ingredients for the syrup and use it to "spin" fine threads of sugar. Garnish the dessert with the spun sugar and scatter pieces of almond on top.

Parfait with Aniseed

Preparation time: 30 minutes
Cooking time: 12 minutes
Cooling time: 4 hours
Difficulty: ★★

Serves 4

3 egg yolks
$^1/_4$ cup / 60 g superfine sugar
$^1/_4$ oz / 8 g aniseed
$^1/_3$ cup / 17 g ground coffee
$^3/_4$ cup / 180 ml cream, stiffly whipped
$2^1/_2$ tbsp / 50 g fruit jelly
$^1/_2$ cup / 130 ml sugar syrup

For the custard: (see basic recipes)
$6^1/_2$ tbsp/100 ml milk
1 tsp cream

2 egg yolks
2 tbsp / 30 g sugar
1 pinch of instant coffee
2 tsp / 10 ml half-and-half

For the almond cookies:
$1^1/_4$ cups / 135 g finely ground almonds
$^1/_2$ tsp / 5 g confectioners' sugar
1 cup plus 1 tbsp / 135 g flour
10 egg whites
2 tbsp / 30 g butter, melted
2 oz / 60 g light nut icing
shelled walnuts

To garnish:
$1^3/_4$ oz / 50 g bittersweet chocolate coating
$3^1/_2$ tbsp / 50 ml sauce made with red fruits, to taste

This astonishing dessert tastes of licorice – but there is none in it. The licorice flavor is produced by the combination of aniseed and coffee. Such discoveries have led to the creation of exceptional, brilliant recipes.

There are a few products made with aniseed, such as anisette or pastis, which are reminiscent of the sunshine of Provence. But aniseed is also found in different variations in Burgundy and Alsace, as well as many other regions of France.

The myriad varieties of coffee available – there are close to 200 – means that the coffee must be selected with care; not every type is suitable. Our chef recommends pure *arabica* of good quality from Central or South America (Costa Rica, Guatemala). In El Salvador, there are a few milder varieties. The custard flavored with coffee complements the taste of the aniseed perfectly.

The almond cookies served with the dessert should be lukewarm, crunchy on the outside, soft on the inside, and browned enough to be pleasant to the eye. If they are decorated with walnuts, make sure that the walnuts are fresh, so that there is nothing to impair the taste of this magnificent treat.

1. Using a mixer, beat the egg yolks with the sugar. Add the aniseed and coffee, then fold in the stiffly whipped cream. Pour into round molds and freeze for about 4 hours.

2. Combine the fruit jelly and syrup; coat the parfaits with this mixture. Prepare a custard according to the basic recipe from the ingredients listed above, using 1 tbsp of the sugar and adding the instant coffee. Pass through a sieve and cool rapidly. Stir in the half-and-half.

and Coffee Sauce

3. For the cookies, mix the ground almonds, confectioners' sugar and flour. Add the egg whites and stir with a spatula. Stir in the melted butter and frosting. Fill small greased forms and place half a shelled walnut on each. Bake the almond cookies at about 410 °F / 210 °C, then turn out of the forms immediately.

4. Place the parfaits, decorated with chocolate coating, onto chilled plates and pour the coffee custard around them. Decorate the plates with the red berry sauce and arrange the almond cookies on them.

Tortelloni with Cream

Preparation time: 1 hour
Cooking time: 25 minutes
Difficulty: ★★

Serves 4
2 lb 3 oz / 1 kg lard (for deep-fat frying)
confectioners' sugar

For the dough:
4 cups / 500 g flour
3 eggs
3 tsp light oil
3 tsp grappa
3 tsp sugar

For the cream:
2 cups / 500 ml milk
4 vanilla beans
6 egg yolks
1 cup / 250 g sugar
$^1/_2$ cup plus 2 tbsp / 80 g flour

For the coffee sauce:
$^3/_4$ cup / 200 g sugar
$6^1/_2$ tbsp / 100 ml water
6 cups espresso coffee

Not everyone knows that the fresh pasta frequently served as an appetizer in Italian restaurants can also be served as a dessert. This recipe is certain to astonish those not in on the secret. The preparation of the dough pouches (tortellos) differs in no way from the preparation of the usual Italian noodles. Like many pasta dishes, this dessert also combines economy and tradition.

Three elements typical of Italian cuisine are noticeable in this delicacy. Lard, which is frequently used for sponge cakes and pastries, produces an even dough. Grappa, a marc originally produced using the Nebbiolo grape from the Barolo (Piedmont) region, gives the dough its malleability and minimizes the taste of the fat used for frying. It is frequently used to make

pastries but can also be drunk as a *digestif* with friends. And finally coffee, to which Italians have become addicted, even though the Finns and other northern peoples consume the largest quantities. The quality of the Italian roasting houses should not be underrated, however, and neither should the coffee specialties, such as espresso and cappuccino, prepared throughout the peninsula.

Romano Tamani is willing at least to tolerate the thought that one might wish to serve this dessert with a bittersweet chocolate sauce made from a caramel base. For the coffee sauce, an *arabica* mixture from a good source should be chosen, from Ethiopia or Kenya for instance. Its fine flavor will emphasize the charm of this dessert all the more.

1. Mound the flour on a flat work surface and place the other ingredients for the dough in a well in the center. Mix by hand until the dough is even. Roll it out and cut out squares with sides 2$^1/_2$ in / 5 cm long.

2. For the cream, bring the milk to a boil with the vanilla beans. Beat the egg yolks and sugar for 10 minutes in another pan. Carefully add the flour to the egg yolks, stir into the milk, bring to a boil and simmer gently for another 3 minutes. Allow to cool on the stove. Fill the squares with the cream, and fold the edges over and press the unfilled ends together to form a circle.

and Coffee Sauce

3. Heat the lard in a large, tall pot. Once the fat is hot enough, deep-fry the tortelloni until golden brown. Drain and dust with the confectioners' sugar.

4. To make the sauce, dissolve the sugar in the water in a saucepan. Add the coffee and caramelize the mixture. Refrigerate for a few minutes. Cover a deep plate with the coffee sauce and arrange the tortelloni on top.

Tagliarini Cake with

Preparation time: 40 minutes
Cooking time: 50 minutes
Difficulty: ★★

Serves 4

1¹/₃ cups / 200 g almonds
³/₄ cup / 200 g sugar
1 glass sassolino (Italian liqueur)
butter

For the tagliatelle dough:
2¹/₂ cups / 300 g flour
1 egg
2 egg yolks

For the zabaglione:
4 egg yolks
4 tsp sugar
4 tsp / 20 ml Marsala (De Bartoli)
4 tsp / 20 ml muscatel (Moscato d'Asti)
1 pinch of cornstarch

This cake, typical of the region around Mantua, is even better if prepared an evening in advance. It is especially good if the tagliarini is very fine (a task left to the nimble fingers of young girls in Italy). The cake originated in a small town on Sicily, but the Venetians have made it known worldwide.

The zabaglione (a wine cream) should not be prepared until shortly before serving, and the eggs should be beaten in a copper bowl to give them more body. They are easier to beat if Marsala and bubbly muscatel are added in equal parts. If you are afraid that this will not work, add half a teaspoon of corn-

starch when nobody is looking. This tip, also very useful when preparing custard, will help less experienced cooks avoid unpleasant disappointments. If you are still hesitant to make a zabaglione, you can serve the cake with a rich chocolate sauce instead.

Another Italian liqueur used in this cake is sassolino, whose peach and prune flavor sparks childhood memories of autumn days in the country for Italians. If you cannot find it, you can substitute another liqueur, such as a walnut liqueur.

1. For the tagliarini, combine the flour, egg, and egg yolks. Roll out small portions of the dough into long oblong shapes and allow it to dry for several minutes. Roll each oblong starting with a short end and cut into thin tagliarini. Chop the almonds finely and roast them.

2. Grease a baking dish and place a layer of tagliarini in it, followed by sugar and then almonds, and continue until all the ingredients have been used.

Marsala Zabaglione

3. Bake the cake for 40 minutes at 320 °F / 160 °C. After half an hour, pour the sassolino over the cake and dot the surface with a few pieces of butter.

4. To make the zabaglione, whisk all the ingredients in a heat-resistant mixing bowl for 8 to 10 minutes over low heat. After taking the cake out of the oven, break it into pieces by hand, place some of it on each plate and serve with the zabaglione.

Crispy Wafers

Preparation time: 1 hour
Cooking time: 10 minutes
Cooling time: 10 minutes
Difficulty: ★★

Serves 4

For the wafers:
$^3/_4$ cup / 100 g chopped almonds
$^2/_3$ cup / 100 g confectioners' sugar
7 tbsp / 50 g flour
grated peel of 1 untreated orange
$3^1/_2$ tbsp / 50 g butter
$^3/_4$ cup / 200 ml Grand Marnier
$2^1/_2$ tbsp / 40 ml orange juice

For the quark sorbet:
12 oz / 350 g quark
$6^1/_2$ tbsp / 100 g sugar
$6^1/_2$ tbsp / 100 ml water
juice of $^1/_2$ lemon

For the prunes:
$6^1/_2$ tbsp / 150 g plum jam
$5^1/_4$ oz / 150 g quark
$3^1/_2$ tbsp / 50 ml cream, whipped
1 cup / 250 ml water
$^1/_3$ cup / 80 g sugar
1 vanilla bean
8 prunes

The view that any variety of plum is suitable for making into prunes is an unfortunate mistake. All the experts in the French department of Lot-et-Garonne will tell you the same thing: only the variety of plum brought by the Knights Templar from Palestine can be turned into prunes with a perfect flavor. Few fruits are so perfectly suited to being baked in the oven, without burning or bursting under the pressure of the juice.

There are, of course, other varieties of plums that have an entirely honorable history. Cultivated by the Romans, they were extremely popular during the Renaissance, and in the 17th century caused a sensation due to the interest of Gaston, Duc d'Orléans, the brother of Louis XIII. In 18th-century France, they were known as "sergeants' jackets," a way of making fun of the uniforms worn by the police at the time.

It is easy to produce wafers that are simultaneously crunchy and soft. They turn out particularly well if the dough is allowed to rest for a good half hour. The wafers are baked in a pre-heated 320 °F / 160 °C oven until golden brown. Afterward, allow them to cool off completely before filling them evenly with the refreshing quark and plum jam mixture.

People who are trying to keep their sweet tooth in check a little will be relieved to hear that the quark sorbet does not contain any cream at all. The dessert as a whole can be served with custard, or even with a mint sauce.

1. For the wafers, place the chopped almonds in a mixing bowl. One after the other stir in the confectioners' sugar, flour, and grated orange peel. Make a hollow in the center and place the butter, Grand Marnier and orange juice in it. Mix the ingredients and allow to rest for 30 minutes.

2. On a baking tray, fill round cookie cutters with a diameter of $4^1/_2$ in / 10 cm with the mixture, making three per serving. Bake in the oven at 320 °F / 160 °C until the wafers are golden brown. Allow to cool.

with Prunes

3. Prepare the quark sorbet using the ingredients listed above and freeze. Using a whisk, combine the plum jam and quark. Fold in the whipped cream. Using the water, sugar, and vanilla bean, make a syrup and marinate the prunes in it.

4. Spread a small amount of the prune cream onto a wafer and cover with another wafer; repeat. Arrange on a plate with two of the marinated prunes and a spoonful of quark sorbet.

Creamy Rice with

Preparation time: *1 hour*
Cooking time: *1 hour*
Difficulty: ★★

Serves 4

1 pineapple
8 dates
butter

For the creamy rice pudding:
6 tbsp / 80 g rice
1²/₃ cups / 400 ml milk
1 vanilla bean
3¹/₂ tbsp / 50 g superfine sugar
2 egg yolks
6¹/₂ tbsp / 100 ml heavy cream

For the syrup:
1 cup / 250 g sugar
1 cup / 250 ml water
1 vanilla bean
a little brown rum

For generations, medicinal and purifying properties have been attributed to rice. There are thousands of varieties of rice, but it is enough to name the three main types: short grain, medium grain and long grain rice. It is also fascinating to realise just how extremely widespread rice is, in all countries worldwide, and that it connects gourmets everywhere.

Our chef, who has settled in St. Tropez, considers long grain rice most suitable for this dessert, and he draws his inspiration from the creamy rice pudding traditional in many European countries for generations. To start with, the rice has boiled in water, which softens the surface of the grains somewhat. After draining it, cook the rice in the vanilla milk in the usual way

until it is ready. The most difficult aspect is probably to achieve a creamy consistency while definitely retaining the distinct flavor of rice.

Our chef has an interesting method of cooking the rice pudding: the mixture is placed in a casserole dish and the lid is sealed to the pan with a dough made of water and flour. This ensures that the cooking process is hermetic, so that all the flavor and various aromas of the rice are retained.

The consistency and delicacy of this unusual dessert will delight anyone who tries it; on top of everything else, it is also very healthy.

1. Wash the rice in water; drain. Cover it with water in a pot and bring to a rolling boil. Drain again. Bring the milk to a boil. Add the rice and the slit vanilla bean. Simmer over a low heat for 25 minutes without stirring.

2. Peel the fresh pineapple and cut into eight slices. Using a corer, remove the hard flesh in the center. Retain the peel. Using the sugar, water, and vanilla bean, prepare a syrup. Poach the pineapple and dates in the syrup; drain.

Pineapple and Dates

3. Poach the pineapple peels in the same syrup. Add the rum. Blend and pass through a pointed sieve. Once the rice has finished cooking, add the sugar, the egg yolks, and the heavy cream.

4. Place the rice into a casserole dish. Seal the lid as described above and cook at 275 °F / 140 °C for 15 minutes. Slightly brown the pineapple and dates in butter. Arrange both on a plate and cover with the rum mixture. Serve the rice separately.

Roasted Figs with Banyuls

Preparation time: 30 minutes
Cooking time: 15 minutes
Difficulty: ★★

Serves 4

1¼ cups / 300 ml Banyuls (or another dessert wine)
1 orange
1 lemon
2 tbsp / 30 g sugar
¼ oz / 5 g peppercorns
¼ oz / 5 g cardamom
12 figs
1 cup / 250 ml vanilla ice cream (see basic recipes)

Until about the 17th century, glazed sweets were reserved for the ruling classes. Today they remain an inexhaustible base for the most delicious desserts. Imagination has led to many variations being served, including filled and warmed fruits. The fig has long been associated with a good and trouble-free life, and the Romans considered it a sign of luxury. Romulus and Remus were suckled directly beneath a fig tree by the famous she-wolf. According to biblical tradition, this tree, grown throughout the Mediterranean region, is a symbol of fertility.

In this recipe, it is best to use violet figs, which are less juicy than green ones and as a result less sensitive to heat. They grow in France, Italy, Spain, and Turkey and are normally eaten complete with the peel.

It is not easy to fill the fruits with the vanilla ice cream without tearing them. To start with, the figs have to be poached, but not boiled. They are then carefully hollowed out and put into the freezer; once they have started to freeze, they are more firm and easier to fill. Finally, the fruits are filled with the vanilla ice cream by means of a pastry bag.

The various accompanying flavors are worthy of mention: Banyuls is a highly prized dessert wine produced in the area around Perpignan, traditionally produced since the 18th century using the grapes from a particular location, and cardamom is a sweet spice from India whose peppery flavor highlights the elegance of this hot and cold dessert, which can be enjoyed any time during the fig season.

1. In a saucepan, combine the dessert wine and thin slices of orange and lemon. Stir in the sugar, then the peppercorns and cardamom. Bring everything to a boil and simmer for 5 minutes.

2. Add the figs. Poach them with the other ingredients for 3 minutes. Remove the saucepan from the heat and allow the figs to cool in the liquid. Drain the fruits and freeze briefly.

and Vanilla Ice Cream

3. Continue to reduce the cooking liquid until it takes on a syrupy consistency. Keep warm. Carefully hollow out the figs.

4. Use a pastry bag to fill the inside of the hollowed-out figs with vanilla ice cream. Bake briefly in order to slightly warm the outside. Pour the warm syrup over the figs and serve.

Apple Lattice with

Preparation time: 45 minutes
Cooking time: 25 minutes
Difficulty: ★

Serves 4

3 lb 4 oz / 1¹/₂ kg apples (e.g. Granny Smith)
6¹/₂ tbsp / 100 g sugar
the juice and grated peel of 1 untreated lemon
3¹/₂ tbsp / 50 g butter
9 oz / 250 g puff pastry
1 egg, slightly beaten

For the marinade:
¹/₃ cup / 50 g prunes
¹/₄ cup / 50 g dried apricots
¹/₄ cup / 50 g candied orange peel

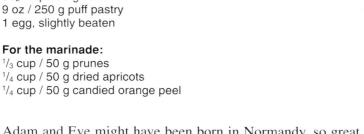

3¹/₂ tbsp / 50 ml Bénédictine
2 whole cloves
1 pinch of cinnamon

For the apricot sauce:
1 lb / 500 g apricots
1²/₃ cups / 400 g sugar

For the spiced ice cream:
2 cups / 500 ml milk
2 cups / 500 ml cream
12 egg yolks
¹/₂ cup plus 2 tbsp / 150 g sugar
2¹/₂ tbsp / 50 g honey
1 pinch of cinnamon

Adam and Eve might have been born in Normandy, so great is the passion that people have developed for apples in this French region filled with orchards. Like our Biblical ancestors, they would gladly brave disaster in order to taste of their fruit. We have them to thank for this quintessential fruit, with its crunchy flesh and fine, sweetish taste. Who could possibly care that it all started with a sin?

The possibilities for using the apple for desserts are seemingly endless. They can also, of course, be eaten raw just as they are or used to flavor cider, Calvados, and apple schnapps. In this dessert, our chef from Rouen uses cinnamon, a spice frequently used with apples and an important ingredient of the spiced ice cream. Choose a variety of apple suitable for cook-

ing, such as the Rome Beauty, Cortland or the Granny Smith particularly favored by Gilles Tournadre. The most important thing is that the jam be reduced slowly and stirred with a wooden spoon, rather than a metal or plastic one.

One consideration of the different seasons is that apricots and apples do not ripen at the same time. This should not cause too many headaches, however, because the flavor of dried apricots would also complement the apples very well.

The lattice is made out of puff pastry that is refrigerated and then cut into thin strips. The pastry base can be a little larger than the form, because it will shrink a little during baking.

1. To make the marinade, cut all the dried fruits into small cubes and marinate for 24 hours in the Bénédictine with the spices. Prepare an apricot sauce. To do this, wash and stone the apricots, then chop them. Mix the fruit with the sugar, add a little water and simmer gently until the fruit is soft. Cool and pass through a pointed sieve.

2. Peel and chop the apples into relatively large pieces. Cook with the sugar, lemon juice, and a piece of lemon peel; add the butter. After the jam has cooled, stir in a little grated lemon peel.

Spiced Ice Cream

3. Roll out the puff pastry. Use half of it to form four circles with a diameter of at least 4½ in / 10 cm. Make the lattice out of the other half. Prepare the spiced ice cream using the ingredients listed, pour into an ice cream maker and allow to set. Add the fruits that have been marinating in the Bénédictine.

4. Set round cookie cutters with a diameter of 4½ in / 10 cm and height of 1½ in / 3 cm on the pastry circles. Fill the forms with the jam and cover with the lattice. Use a pastry brush to glaze the pastry with the beaten egg and bake for 25 minutes at 355 °F / 180 °C. Serve with the apricot sauce and a spoonful of ice cream.

Preparation time: 30 minutes
Cooking time: 40 minutes
Difficulty: ✫

Serves 4

For the apricot compote:
7 oz / 200 g apricots
3¹/₂ tbsp / 50 g sugar
water

For the vanilla ice cream (see basic recipes):
2 cups / 500 ml

For the puff pastry (see basic recipes)

For the filling:
2 eggs
3¹/₂ tbsp / 50 g sugar
6 tbsp / 40 g ground almonds
¹/₃ cup / 80 ml crème fraîche
2 tbsp / 20 g confectioners' sugar

The well-traveled writer Flaubert had a weakness for beautiful women and fine pastries, especially those produced in his native city of Rouen. He derived great pleasure from watching his beloved women savoring *mirlitons à la Rouen* (tartlets dusted with confectioners' sugar) and how the sugar gave "their sweet mouths a white moustache." There is no clear explanation of how these tartlets came by their unusual name (*mirliton* means "reed pipe"), given that they neither have the shape of a flute, nor is there another sense of the word that could explain the name.

Gilles Tournadre attributes the invention of the *mirlitons* to his own grandfather, a pastry cook whom Flaubert most likely did not even know. Usually, such traditions change over the years, and their very charm lies in the fact that they contradict each other. Now, as then, the most important thing is that the tartlets are made using a first-class puff pastry, and ground almonds

and fully ripe apricots of the very best quality. Dried sweet almonds are a popular ingredient for fine pastries, and with their high content of oil, protein, and nutrients, they are very nourishing.

Two elements of the preparation are vital: the pastry base should be pierced several times with a fork to prevent rising during baking, and the confectioners' sugar should be dried briefly before the tartlets are put in the oven. When apricots are out of season, our chef recommends substituting another fruit, like a fig compote or other stewed autumn fruits.

One final note: *mirlitons* are a specialty of Rouen, *not* of Normandy. In the shadow of the Gros-Horloge clock tower and the Cathedral of Notre-Dame, such subtle distinctions are no laughing matter.

1. Halve the apricots and, with the sugar and a little water, reduce them over a low heat for 15 minutes to make a compote. Make the vanilla ice cream according to the basic recipe.

2. For the filling, combine the eggs, sugar, ground almonds, and crème fraîche in a mixing bowl and set aside.

Rouen with Apricots

3. Prepare the puff pastry (see basic recipes). Line four molds with a diameter of 4 ½ in / 10 cm with the puff pastry. Prick the base with a fork. Fill the tartlet with some apricot compote and then a layer of filling.

4. Close the tart with a layer of puff pastry, dust with confectioners' sugar and allow to infuse in the refrigerator for 5 minutes so that the sugar starts to dry. Bake for 40 minutes at 355 °F / 180 °C. Serve the warm tart with a scoop of vanilla ice cream and a spoonful of apricot jam.

Almond Crêpes with

Preparation time: 30 minutes
Cooking time: 10 minutes
Difficulty: ✶✶✶

Serves 4

2 tsp / 10 g butter

For the crêpe mixture:
¹/₃ cup / 45 g flour
4 tsp / 20 g sugar
5 egg yolks
a pinch of salt

³/₄ cup / 200 ml milk
3 tbsp / 50 g almond paste (or crushed almonds)

For the zabaglione:
6 egg yolks
3 tbsp sugar
³/₄ cup / 200 ml champagne

To garnish:
10¹/₂ oz / 300 g raspberries
3 tbsp / 30 g confectioners' sugar

In this zabaglione, the qualities of the egg are exploited to their fullest. The egg contains important nutrients – protein, fat, and vitamins – and, thanks to its consistency, is able to unite ingredients as apparently incompatible as butter and water. Yolks are also brushed on cakes and cookies to give them a pleasing golden-brown glaze; they are also responsible for the thick, creamy consistency of custard.

The eggs are beaten with a whisk in this zabaglione and warmed slightly to give them volume. Add the egg yolks one at a time and whisk until foamy. To do this, stir the whisk in a figure of eight, using an absolutely regular stroke.

But other techniques can be used as well. For example, the cream can be whisked at room temperature to begin with and then stirred over a low heat, with white wine or Marsala, until finished. In this recipe, José Tourneur uses champagne, but this is only a suggestion.

Whatever utensils you use to prepare the zabaglione, make sure that they are absolutely free of dirt or grease; the mixing bowl, for example, should be thoroughly rinsed beforehand, ideally with a mix of water and vinegar, and dried with a clean towel.

All precautions aside, luck does play a part in making this sensitive cream. Do not despair if you do not succeed at first! Even the best chefs have experienced such disappointments.

1. To make the crêpe batter, beat the flour, sugar, and egg yolks with a whisk until they form a shiny, foamy mixture; add a pinch of salt. Stir the milk in gradually so that the batter remains smooth. Stir in the almond paste and allow to rest for 30 minutes.

2. Make golden-brown crêpes and keep them warm. Set aside several choice raspberries for garnishing and make a raspberry sauce with the rest. To do so, puree the raspberries with the confectioners' sugar and pass through a sieve.

Zabaglione and Raspberries

3. Begin the zabaglione by beating the egg yolks in a pan at room temperature. Gently heat the foamy eggs over a low heat, then beat in the sugar. Finally, add the champagne and whisk continuously to produce a thick, foamy cream.

4. Place the crêpes on the plates, pour a portion of zabaglione in the center and fold each crêpe once so that the zabaglione runs out a little at the sides. Arrange the raspberries around the edge of the plates and dust the crêpes with confectioners' sugar.

Preparation time: *4 hours*
Cooking time: *15 minutes*
Difficulty: ★★★

Serves 6

For the almond ice cream:
8 1/2 cups / 2 l milk
2 cups / 500 ml cream
1/2 cup plus 2 tbsp / 150 g sugar
20 egg yolks, beaten
bitter almond extract
1/2 cup / 75 g dextrose

For the ice soufflé:
14 oz / 400 g wild strawberries
1 2/3 cups / 400 g superfine sugar
2 cups / 500 ml cream

For the tulips (see basic recipes)

For the almond cookies (see basic recipes)

To garnish:
6 almond cookies
6 mint leaves
1 cup / 250 ml cream, whipped
wild strawberries

In the Bible we are told the story of Joseph, who was sold into slavery by his brothers. Later, when he became the Pharaoh's Grand Vizier, they crawled back to him with arms full of almonds (Genesis 43:11). This biblical scene turns the almond into a symbol of reconciliation and reveals that it was already highly valued in ancient times.

In the pâtisserie, almonds are used in many ways, whether whole, ground or as a paste: white nougat, marzipan, and roasted almonds are just a few examples. Almond oils are also widely used in the cosmetics industry.

The preparation of the ice soufflé, which should be made only with completely fresh fruits in season, requires a little patience.

Wild strawberries are very sensitive and must be used soon after purchase. The success of the soufflé depends mainly on the firmness of the whipped cream, which also gives it its creamy consistency. The whipped mixtures have to be combined with the greatest care – thoroughly and evenly.

The "three colors" of the title are the black, red, and yellow of the Belgian national flag. They are also an allusion to José Tourneur's restaurant *Des Trois Couleurs*, which is in a house of the same name. Les Trois Couleurs is located in the capital city, Brussels, where the birth of Belgian independence was celebrated in 1831.

1. Make the almond ice cream using the ingredients listed above, using the basic recipe as a guide. Allow it to set in an ice cream maker. For the soufflé, wash the wild strawberries, mash them and pass them through a sieve. Mix the strawberry puree with an equal quantity of sugar. Whip the cream with a little sugar until very stiff and fold into the strawberry puree.

2. Grease parchment paper and use it to line individual soufflé dishes or little beakers. The top edge of the paper should stand higher than the forms; press the paper firmly against the sides. Fill the forms with the strawberry mixture and place in a container filled with ice cubes. Once the soufflés have set, turn them out and remove the paper.

Three Colors

3. Follow the basic recipe to make the dough for the "tulips." Bake and form them as described. Prepare the dough for the almond cookies, again according to the basic recipe.

4. Spoon small amounts of the almond cookie dough onto a greased, floured baking tray. Bake until they begin to turn brown. Arrange a soufflé on each plate with some almond ice cream in a tulip, garnished with almond cookies and wild strawberries. Decorate with whipped cream and mint leaves, if desired.

Tiramisù

Preparation time: 30 minutes
Cooling time: 4 hours
Difficulty: ★

Serves 4

5 egg yolks
$^1/_3$ cup / 50 g confectioners' sugar
1 lb / 500 g mascarpone cheese
5 tsp Cognac
24 firm ladyfingers
4 cups very strong coffee
3 tsp cocoa powder

You would think that tiramisù is so well known outside Italy these days that there is no need to publish the recipe. You might also believe, like Luisa Valazza, that it is important for exactly that reason to look toward tradition and do away with the recipes that call just about any dessert a tiramisù.

Ideally, one should use savory Italian ingredients such as ladyfingers from Savoy (which has been part of France only since 1860), mascarpone, and certain varieties of coffee. Tiramisù was originally prepared using leftovers, which explains the use of coffee for soaking what was probably stale sponge cake. It

appears to have originated in Lombardy, and can now be found on the menus of the most exclusive restaurants. The special feature of this dessert is the sweet/bitter contrasts among the sponge cake, cocoa, and coffee. Between the layers is mascarpone, a creamy, soft cheese with a high fat content and a mild, cream-like flavor.

The ladyfingers should have a texture that enables them to soak up the liquid well without completely disintegrating. Our chef recommends serving the dessert with maraschino, a liqueur made from wild cherries grown near Trieste.

1. To make the mascarpone cream, beat the egg yolks and confectioners' sugar in a bowl until creamy. Add the mascarpone and Cognac and beat for a few minutes.

2. Soak the ladyfingers in the coffee and set aside until needed.

3. In an attractive dish or individual forms, alternate layers of mascarpone cream, the coffee-soaked ladyfingers, and cocoa powder.

4. Finish with a layer of mascarpone. Refrigerate for 4 hours. Before serving sprinkle confectioners' sugar and sifted cocoa on top.

Preparation time: 20 minutes
Cooking time: 10 minutes
Difficulty: ★★

Serves 4

20 prunes
7 oz / 200 g marzipan
2 cups / 500 ml whole milk
8 egg yolks
1$\frac{1}{2}$ cups / 225 g confectioners' sugar

3$\frac{1}{2}$ oz / 100 g lebkuchen
3$\frac{1}{2}$ oz / 100 g spekulatius (spiced cookies)
6$\frac{1}{2}$ tbsp / 100 ml cream
6$\frac{1}{2}$ tbsp / 100 ml dark beer (preferably Belgian
    beer from Leffe)
6$\frac{1}{2}$ tbsp / 100 ml cream, whipped

Marzipan, traditional in certain regions of France, Italy, and central Europe, is made of crushed almonds, sugar, and egg whites. It is used to make small cakes and pastries that are sometimes glazed or made into pralines like those available in Belgium over the New Year. In Austria, marzipan is used at Easter to make eleven balls that decorate a cake made with dried fruits, representing the eleven apostles left after Judas betrayed Christ. In southern Italy, among other places, marzipan is used to make small figures that look like fruits, vegetables, even animals and people.

Prunes are dried plums that have retained their consistency, juice, and softness. They are best kept in an airtight container in a cool place, as they quickly dry out and become tough.

Belgians are particularly fond of spekulatius, a dry cookie flavored with cinnamon and cloves, but it is also very popular in other countries.

Despite the decline of so many Belgian breweries – of the 3,200 in existence at the beginning of the century, only about a hundred still survive – the incomparable Leffe Abbey still continues the centuries-old tradition of monks brewing beer. Particularly popular is the fine, delicious Radieuse, and their dark beer has a somewhat more bitter flavor that is valued highly by experts. Try to resist the temptation to add more beer than is called for, because it easily overpowers the flavor of the dessert.

1. Stone the prunes. Roll out the marzipan and cut pieces 1$\frac{1}{2}$ in / 3 cm long. Place the marzipan pieces inside the prunes.

2. Heat the milk. Whisk 6 egg yolks with $\frac{3}{4}$ cup plus 1 tbsp / 125 g confectioners' sugar. Pour the hot milk onto the egg yolks and continue stirring at 175 °F / 80 °C until the mixture has a creamy consistency. Pass the custard through a pointed sieve.

Marzipan and Beer

3. Add the crumbled lebkuchen and crushed spekulatius cookies to the custard. Add the cream and stir thoroughly in an ice cream maker.

4. Combine the two remaining egg yolks and $2/3$ cup / 100 g confectioners' sugar. Add the beer and whisk until foamy. Blend in the whipped cream. Arrange the prunes on deep plates. Pour the beer mixture over them and glaze under a hot grill. Serve with the ice cream and, optionally, petits fours.

Chocolate Pastry

Preparation time: 1 hour
Cooking time: 30 minutes
Difficulty: ★★

Serves 4

For the chocolate sand cake:
(see basic recipes)
6¹/₂ tbsp / 100 g butter
³/₄ cup / 120 g confectioners' sugar
2 egg yolks
1 pinch of vanilla powder
1 pinch of salt
1¹/₂ cups / 180 g flour
3 tbsp / 20 g cocoa powder
¹/₃ cup / 40 g dry cake or cookie crumbs

For the orange cream and garnish:
6 egg yolks
6¹/₂ tbsp / 100 g sugar

peel and juice of 2 untreated blood oranges
6¹/₂ tbsp / 100 g butter
3¹/₂ tbsp / 50 ml Grenadine

For the ganache:
1 vanilla bean
³/₄ cup / 200 ml cream
14 oz / 400 g bittersweet chocolate
6¹/₂ tbsp / 100 g butter

For the tea ice cream:
¹/₂ oz / 15 g Earl Grey tea leaves
2 cups / 500 ml whole milk
6 egg yolks
¹/₂ cup / 125 g sugar
6¹/₂ tbsp / 100 ml cream

Although the inhabitants of Sablé-sur-Sarthe have recently started making it their specialty, "sand cake" (*sablé* in French, actually pound cake in English) does not derive its name from this town, but from its consistency – the cake crumbles between one's fingers after baking and feels "sandy."

For our chef, preparation of the dough starts with a very even mixture of butter, confectioners' sugar, and eggs. Once this is complete, the vanilla, salt, and dry ingredients are added. Make sure that the dough is not worked too vigorously, as that would make it rubbery and impair the flavor. After preparing the mixture, it is very important to let the dough rest so that it loses its stickiness. The same care should be taken with the ganache:

the mixture of cream and chocolate (as always, of the best quality) will quickly reach its boiling point and should not be allowed to exceed it. Use it quickly, because it does not keep well.

The tea ice cream may seem unusual, but one taste will convince you how perfectly fitting it is. In this case, Earl Grey is used, a very popular tea mixture flavored with bergamot.

Assemble the dessert by alternating layers of sand cookies, ganache, and orange cream. Finally, dust with some confectioners' sugar, decorate with the glazed orange peel, and serve with the ice cream.

1. Mix the ingredients for the sand cake, stirring as little as possible, cover with a towel and allow to rest for 1 hour. Roll the dough out to a thickness of ¹/₄ in / 4 mm and cut out circles measuring 3¹/₂ in / 8 cm. Place these on a greased baking tray and bake for 15 minutes at 355 °F / 180 °C. Allow to cool on a rack.

2. To make the orange cream, beat the egg yolks with the sugar in a pan. Add the juice of the blood oranges. Stirring constantly, whisk until foamy over a low heat. Remove from the heat and stir in the butter. Refrigerate.

with Tea Ice Cream

3. For the ganache, infuse the vanilla bean in the cream. Add the chopped bittersweet chocolate and slowly melt in the top of a double boiler, then allow to cool slightly. Beat the butter until creamy. Fold in the chocolate mixture; allow to cool completely. Blanche the orange peel and cut into thin strips. Cook with the grenadine. Drain on paper towels.

4. For the ice cream, steep the tea in the milk over a medium heat for 5 minutes, then strain. Meanwhile, beat the egg yolks and sugar until they are thick. Pour the hot milk onto the eggs, combine, and return to the pan. Simmer over moderate heat and stir. Pass through a pointed sieve. Add the cream and mix for 15 minutes in an ice cream maker. Assemble the dessert as described above and garnish.

Apple Jelly

Preparation time: 30 minutes
Cooking time: 15 minutes
Cooling time: 2 hours
Difficulty: ★ ★

Serves 4

4 apples (Granny Smiths)
3 sheets of gelatin
1²/₃ cups / 400 ml juice from green apples
1 pinch of cinnamon

For the sorbet:
4 cups / 1 l apple juice
6¹/₂ tbsp / 100 g sugar
5 tbsp / 50 g dextrose

For the zabaglione:
3 egg yolks
6¹/₂ tbsp / 100 g sugar
6¹/₂ tbsp / 100 ml juice from green apples
²/₃ cup / 150 ml hard cider (slight alcohol
    content)
²/₃ cup / 150 ml Calvados
4 tsp / 20 ml cream, whipped

For as long as humanity has known the meaning of despair – surely since the beginning of time – we have also known sugar's capacities to restore morale and vitality. But it was not until the 18th century that dessert became a fixed part of a meal. Nowadays, a wide range of sweets tempts us.

The apple is the quintessential fruit and, in this recipe, appears in three different forms: as a jelly, a sorbet, and as Calvados in the zabaglione. The zabaglione will certainly be the most difficult part of the recipe, as some skill is required to prepare it. The challenge is to prevent the eggs from becoming too firm and impairing the smooth texture, while still cooking them so that the cream as a whole does not collapse. The degree to which you achieve this balance will determine the success of the entire recipe. The typical Normandy combination of cider and Calvados gives the zabaglione a distinct apple flavor.

Green Granny Smith apples are used for the zabaglione and jelly because they are one of the varieties of apples best able to withstand cooking without becoming mushy or flavorless.

Our chef, eager to simplify the preparation of his recipe, suggests preparing the jelly and sorbet a day in advance. Aside from the fact that this allows you to devote your entire attention to the zabaglione, the consistency of the jelly and sorbet actually benefit from the extra resting time. Be careful with the amount of cinnamon – too much could ruin the flavor of the dessert.

1. Mix the ingredients for the sorbet and place in the freezer. Peel the apples and dice them. Soak the gelatin in cold water for 5 minutes. Bring the apple juice to a boil with the cinnamon.

2. Add the diced apples to the hot apple juice, then add the gelatin. Stir carefully, remove from the heat and allow to cool until the mixture is lukewarm.

with Calvados

3. Spoon equal amounts of the apple jelly into four deep dishes. Allow to set in the refrigerator for about 2 hours.

4. For the zabaglione, whisk the egg yolks and sugar and gently heat them. Add the apple juice, then the cider. Remove from the heat and continue to beat the cream with a whisk as it cools. Stir in the Calvados and whipped cream. Cover the apple jelly with some zabaglione. Sprinkle with superfine sugar and brown briefly. Serve with the sorbet.

Chocolate Soufflé

Preparation time: 20 minutes
Cooking time: 15 minutes
Difficulty: ★★

Serves 4

4³/₄ oz / 130 g bittersweet chocolate
4 tsp / 10 g cocoa powder
¹/₄ cup / 60 ml green walnut liqueur
2 eggs, separated
¹/₃ cup / 50 g confectioners' sugar
4 tsp / 20 g superfine sugar

For the pastry cream:
1 cup / 250 ml milk
¹/₂ vanilla bean
2 egg yolks
3 tbsp / 40 g sugar
3 tbsp / 20 g flour
2 tbsp / 15 g cornstarch

Christopher Columbus brought chocolate to Europe from a place he mistakenly believed to be India, where the cocoa bean was apparently used as a unit of currency by the natives. Chocolate has been popular ever since it was first introduced to the French court by Queen Anne, the wife of Louis XIII, and countless recipes have been developed using pure, bitter, hard chocolate that melts in the mouth. This is the very chocolate that our chef has selected for his soufflé, prepared with all the expertise customary in Belgium. The exceptional quality of Belgian chocolate has made it one of the country's most widely exported products.

Apart from the beaten egg whites, which should be folded in at the last minute, all the ingredients for the soufflé can be pre-pared in advance. Carefully watch the baking time and serve the soufflé as soon it is ready, to avoid any danger of collapse. For the same reason, this dessert cannot be kept or reheated.

The green walnut is a liqueur with a flavor sure to surprise those who have not experienced it. If necessary, it can be replaced by Banyuls, a Catalan dessert wine that has been pro-duced since the 13th century using black Grenache grapes, which are exposed to 325 days of sun every year.

Even though the preparation is a little risky, the triumphant moment when this soufflé is served makes it all worthwhile.

1. To make the pastry cream, bring the milk to a boil with the halved vanilla bean. In another bowl, beat the egg yolks with the sugar, then add the flour, cornstarch, and hot milk. Return everything to the pan and stir constantly until the cream briefly boils. Remove from the heat. In a double boiler, melt the chocolate, then stir in the lukewarm pastry cream, cocoa powder, and one-third of the walnut liqueur.

2. Remove from the heat and stir in the egg yolks. Whisk the egg whites until very stiff; add the confectioners' sugar while continuing to beat.

with Walnut Liqueur

3. Fold the beaten egg whites into the chocolate mixture and carefully blend with a wooden spatula or spoon. Grease four ovenproof soufflé dishes and sprinkle them with superfine sugar.

4. Pour the chocolate mixture into the dishes and sprinkle some sugar on top. Place halved walnut or egg shells with the open sides facing upward in the center, and bake for 12 minutes at 430 °F / 220 °C. Remove from the oven, pour the remaining liqueur into the shells, flambé, and serve immediately.

Baked Pears with

Preparation time: *1 hour 15 minutes*
Cooking time: *1 hour*
Difficulty: ✳

Serves 4

5 pears
lemon juice
4 cups / 1 l red wine
7 oz / 200 g black currants
2 cups / 500 ml crème de cassis (black currant liqueur)
1 cup / 250 g butter

For the pepper ice cream:
2 cups / 500 ml water
1¼ cup / 300 g sugar
1¾ oz / 50 g Szechuan pepper
9 oz / 250 g mango flesh
1 cup / 250 ml passion fruit juice
juice of 1 lime
½ cup / 50 g grated chocolate

Serving a dessert flavored with pepper may seem incongruous, all the more so when the dish actually tastes sweet, but Gérard Vié takes care to respect and retain the original flavors of the ingredients he uses. This recipe is no joke on the part of our chef – it was created in honor of Giscard d'Estaing's visit to the Trianon Palace.

Since the pears will be baked, choose a variety that will hold up well in the heat. This dessert could also be prepared using peaches.

Many an enthusiastic cook considers the preparation of black currant liqueur to be a worthy challenge. But it is a tremendous effort; and the resulting liqueur will not keep for very long. It is much simpler and perfectly acceptable to buy a bottle of ready-made crème de cassis.

Szechuan pepper, also spelled Sichuan, is actually the berry of the prickly ash tree native to the Chinese province of the same name. Its strong and distinctive flavor contributes to a perfect balance between the mango and passion fruit juice. The Chinese consider it to be rich in healing properties.

1. Peel the pears without removing their stems and place them in a bowl of water with the lemon juice to prevent them from turning brown too quickly. Bring the red wine and the stemless black currants to a boil in a pan.

2. Poach the pears in the red wine. Add the cassis and simmer for 30 minutes at a low temperature. Allow to cool and marinate in the liquid for 24 hours.

Peppered Cassis Liqueur

3. Drain the pears and place them in an ovenproof dish with the butter and a little of the cooking liquid. Bake for 30 minutes at 355 °F / 180 °C, regularly spooning the liquid over the pears.

4. For the ice cream, bring the water, sugar, and pepper to a boil, then remove from the heat. Let steep until cooled, then pass through a pointed sieve. Add the mango flesh, passion fruit juice, and lime juice. Stir thoroughly. Finally add the grated chocolate and allow to set in an ice cream maker. Arrange the pears on plates with the black currants and a little of the cooking liquid. Serve with the pepper ice cream.

Preparation time: 3 hours
Cooking time: 1 hour
Cooling time: 12 hours
Difficulty: ★★★

Serves 8–10

For the caramel cream:
6¹/₂ tbsp / 100 g (ml) each sugar and cream

For the caramel sauce:
6¹/₂ tbsp / 100 g sugar; 2 tbsp / 30 ml water

For the custard:
6¹/₂ tbsp / 100 ml milk; 4 tsp / 20 g sugar
2 egg yolks; ¹/₂ vanilla bean

For the nougat parfait:
2 egg whites, 6 tbsp / 90 g sugar
³/₄ cup / 170 ml cream, whipped
1¹/₄ cups / 150 g caramelized nuts

For the apple cake:
³/₄ cup / 300 g apple sauce
¹/₃ cup / 80 g butter; 1 egg

For the baked caramel custard:
1 cup / 250 ml milk; 1 egg plus 1 egg yolk
3¹/₂ tbsp each: cream and sugar
1 vanilla bean

For the caramel flan:
sponge cake (see basic recipes)
1 egg yolk; ¹/₄ cup / 60 ml cream
1 sheet of gelatin
¹/₃ cup / 80 ml caramel cream
2 egg whites; 2 tbsp / 30 g sugar
¹/₄ cup / 60 ml cream, whipped

There is surely something for everyone in this stunning array of sweets: cake, nougat parfait, caramel flan, and ice cream. A selection like this requires high-quality ingredients, and that is just what Jean-Pierre Vigato makes sure he has on hand when he begins.

Nuts with intense flavor for the nougat, apples for the apple sauce – all must withstand Vigato's scrutiny. Choose good cooking apples, the Golden Delicious for example, or another to your own taste. The vanilla beans used to refine the flavor of both the custard and the caramel custard should be tender and fleshy.

Though caramel is prepared in myriad ways all over the world, little is known about the origins of the name itself. It first appeared in Spain in the 16th century, a term derived from the Latin word for cane sugar, *cannamella*. The word "caramel-ized" means that something has the color or flavor of caramel.

But how to celebrate this balance of flavors and consistencies – melting and crunchy, lukewarm and cold, sweet and bitter? Such contrasts, perfectly managed by an experienced and talented chef, lead to a dessert that will surely leave a lasting impression on everyone fortunate enough to partake of it.

1. Prepare the caramel cream by caramelizing the sugar in a pan without water, then carefully and gradually adding the cream to it. Make the caramel sauce in the same way adding the water in place of cream. Prepare a custard (see basic recipes) with the above ingredients. To make the caramel ice cream, combine the custard and caramel cream. Allow to set in an ice cream maker.

2. Make the nougat parfait a day in advance: begin with a meringue made from the egg whites and sugar (see basic recipes). Allow to cool, then fold in the whipped cream. Blend in a mixture of chopped and caramelized nuts. Freeze.

Feast

3. For the apple cake, start by making a greatly reduced apple sauce. Beat in the egg and butter. Spoon the mixture into a greased and sugared cake pan and bake for 1 hour at 340 °F / 170 °C in a water bath. Prepare the baked caramel custard using the ingredients given and bake in a water bath for 30 minutes. Allow the cake and baked custard to cool. Pour the caramel sauce onto the baked custard.

4. To make the caramel flan, whisk the egg yolk with the cream. Pass through a pointed sieve. Stir in the dissolved gelatin, 1/3 cup / 80 ml caramel cream and a meringue (see basic recipes) made with the egg whites, sugar, and whipped cream. Pour into a pan that has been thinly lined with sponge cake and allow to set. Arrange everything on plates with caramel cages, if desired.

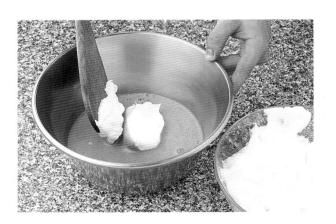

Coffee Leaves with

Preparation time: 25 minutes
Cooking time: 15 minutes
Difficulty: ★★

Serves 4

6 large sheets of phyllo dough

For the milk ice cream:
3¼ cups / 800 ml milk
¾ cup / 80 g powdered milk

For the coffee cream:
3 egg yolks
1¼ cups / 300 ml milk

3½ tbsp / 50 g sugar
3 tbsp / 20 g pudding powder
4½ tbsp / 65 ml cream, whipped

For the mocha sugar:
confectioners' sugar
instant coffee

For the mocha sauce:
1¼ cups / 300 ml water
4 tsp / 12 g cornstarch
¼ cup / 65 g sugar
2 tbsp / 8 g instant coffee

When looking at this dessert many of us will note the fine layer of confectioners' sugar covering this pastry, so light it could be blown away by the slightest breath of air. For Jean-Pierre Vigato, this recipe calls to mind memories of grandmothers who generously distributed cookies and candy, maybe even jelly doughnuts covered with confectioners' sugar . . .

For the end product to live up to these memories, it is important to start by choosing milk of acceptable quality. Milk is among the oldest foods in the world, rich in carbohydrates, protein, fat, and several other nutrients, and has been used in a variety of different ways since ancient times.

According to expert opinion, milk is stimulating and nutritious, and the best basis for ice cream. Our chef recommends adding a small amount of commercially prepared pudding mix to give the coffee cream body. He also adds a finishing touch to the flavor of this elegant dessert by adding powdered milk, produced according to the formula that made the Swiss chemist Henri Nestlé (1814–1890) famous. Also take care when measuring the instant coffee, for too much coffee flavor would overpower everything else.

1. To make the milk ice cream, mix the milk and powdered milk. Stir vigorously, then pour into an ice cream maker and let harden. Prepare the coffee cream using the egg yolks, milk, sugar, and pudding powder, using the basic recipe for custard as a guide. Allow to cool, then blend in the stiffly whipped cream.

2. From the sheets of phyllo dough, cut out rectangles 4½ in / 10 cm long and 2½ in / 5 cm wide. Dust with a mixture of nine parts confectioners' sugar and one part instant coffee. Bake and caramelize the pastry under a hot grill.

Milk Ice Cream

3. To make the mocha sauce, bring the water, cornstarch, and sugar to a boil, then add the instant coffee. Pass the sauce through a pointed sieve.

4. Divide the pastry rectangles into four equal portions. For each serving, place a rectangle of pastry in the center of a plate and top it with a spoonful of coffee cream. Continue alternating layers of pastry and cream, finishing with a sheet of pastry. Dust the top piece of pastry with confectioners' sugar. Pour some of the mocha sauce around it, and serve with the ice cream.

Neapolitan

Preparation time: 30 minutes
Cooking time: 1 hour
Difficulty: ★★

Serves 4

For the short pastry: (see basic recipes)

For the filling:
9 oz / 250 g ricotta cheese
1²/₃ cups / 250 g confectioners' sugar
1²/₃ cups / 400 ml cream
9 oz / 250 g cooked corn

2 egg yolks
2 eggs
³/₄ cup / 75 g candied fruits
rose or orange blossom extract
sour cherries

For the sauce:
1¹/₄ cups / 300 ml cream
2 eggs
6¹/₂ tbsp / 100 g sugar
6¹/₂ tbsp / 100 ml Grand Marnier

The excellent Neapolitan and Sicilian desserts are famous well beyond the borders of Italy, and this recipe offers further proof of the skill of Italian pastry chefs. The unusual combination of ricotta and cooked corn in this dessert would pique anyone's interest.

Ricotta, a fresh cheese made using sheep's milk in Italy, has a surprisingly light consistency. A few drops of rose or orange blossom extract go well with its fresh taste. So that it retains its creamy consistency, the ricotta must be passed through a sieve. If stirred with a mixer, for example, it easily forms lumps that greatly detract from the ideal of a perfectly smooth filling.

The sauce with Grand Marnier is made the same way as a custard. You can substitute a different flavoring, if you wish; depending on your taste, you might add an Italian herbal liqueur or French Armagnac. One important tip: after baking, the tartlets must cool off at room temperature for a short time before being served.

The taste of this dessert transports us to Naples, directly beneath the Mediterranean sun. The local cuisine there is a remarkable one based on traditions that are still very much alive; they remain open to new trends and are enriched, rather than altered or diminished by them.

1. Make the short pastry and refrigerate. Pass the ricotta through a sieve. In a bowl, use a whisk to combine thoroughly the ricotta, confectioners' sugar, cream, cooked corn, eggs, candied fruits, and rose or orange blossom extract.

2. Roll out the short pastry thinly. Line the greased tart forms with the pastry and prick the bottoms with a fork.

Cake

3. Fill the tart shells with the ricotta mixture. For the sauce, beat the sugar and eggs until light. In a pan, bring the cream to a boil. Pour the hot cream onto the eggs, add the Grand Marnier and return to the heat. Continue as for a custard and pass through a sieve.

4. Cover the tarts with a lattice of interlaced strips of short pastry. Bake for about 1 hour at 340 °F / 170 °C. Pour a small ladle of sauce on the center of each plate and place the cake on top. Decorate with a few cherries.

Parfait with Madeira

Preparation time: 20 minutes
Cooking time: 10 minutes
Cooling time: 3 hours
Difficulty: ✷✷

Serves 4

For the parfait:
³/₄ cup / 200 g sugar
6 egg yolks
6¹/₂ tbsp / 100 ml Madeira
2 cups / 500 ml cream

For the blueberry sauce:
6¹/₂ tbsp / 100 g sugar
6¹/₂ tbsp / 100 ml water
Peels of an untreated lemon and orange
3¹/₂ oz / 100 g blueberries
juice of 1 lemon

Whether served as the centerpiece of a family celebration, to mark the close of a contract or to reflect the sweetness of a tryst, this dessert is always an uplifting moment and needs to be treated accordingly.

Keep precisely to the recommended ingredients of the parfait and their quantities, and allow it to freeze for at least 3 hours. This is the only way to insure the dessert has a light consistency and can be turned out of the mold later without falling apart. This dangerous enterprise can be simplified somewhat by dipping the base of the molds in hot water first, but do not do this until the very last minute.

The sauce can be made using other fruits, or even a mixture of them if you would like to add a personal touch by varying the colors and flavors of the dessert. For example, the blueberry sauce could be accompanied by a sour cherry sauce or a sauce from any other berries (strawberries, raspberries, red currants or black currants). Before serving, it is important to pass every fruit sauce through a fine pointed sieve to remove the berries' small seeds and other bits. You could even use a chocolate sauce, whose dark color would produce the same visual contrast with the light color of the parfait.

Depending on your taste, the parfait itself can be flavored using spirits other than the Madeira – a clear fruit schnapps, for instance, which will give it more bite and firmness, or perhaps a fine Cognac or old Armagnac.

1. To make the parfait, place the sugar and egg yolks in the top of a double boiler and beat until the mixture is even and foamy.

2. Over moderate heat, add the Madeira and continue to beat until a creamy mixture has been produced. Remove from the heat and allow to cool while continuing to beat with a whisk.

and Blueberry Sauce

3. Whip the cream until stiff. Carefully fold in the completely cooled Madeira mixture. Fill individual molds with the parfait mixture and freeze for at least 3 hours.

4. Prepare a syrup using the sugar, water, and orange and lemon peel. Bring to a boil, then remove from the heat and let steep until completely cooled. Pass through a pointed sieve. Add the blueberries to the syrup and cook for 4 to 5 minutes. Allow to cool completely, then add the lemon juice, mix the sauce in a blender and again pass it through a pointed sieve. Serve the parfaits on a bed of sauce, garnished with whole blueberries.

Prickly Pears with Raspberries

Preparation time: 25 minutes
Difficulty: ★

Serves 4

4 ripe prickly pears

For the almond cream:
6$^1/_2$ tbsp / 100 ml almond milk
6$^1/_2$ tbsp / 100 ml heavy cream
3$^1/_2$ tbsp / 50 g sugar syrup
$^3/_4$ cup / 200 ml cream, whipped

To garnish:
raspberries

The world is changing faster and faster, and every day there are more opportunities to enjoy fruits from other countries around the globe. One example is the oval, interestingly colored prickly pear, which is widely popular in Mexico, Central and South America and increasingly available in the United States.

This fruit has many delightful qualities, though they are hidden beneath its most uninviting skin; the aptly named prickly pear is covered with stiff hairs and spines that are very painful to touch. Also known as the cactus pear, it is the fruit of several varieties of cactus plants. Once they have ripened and developed their full flavor, the fruits have a nice red or reddish-orange color and give slightly when pressed (obviously, wear a glove when doing this). Cutting open the prickly pear reveals a yellowish orange flesh that is very acidic and contains small dark, firm seeds.

This invigorating, refreshing fruit is even used for medical purposes in some countries. It can be used to prepare a tasty sorbet, and lends a unique touch to a fruit salad.

The almond cream, based on whipped cream, provides a pleasant sweetness in contrast with the acidity of the prickly pears and raspberries crowning this dessert. This recipe is a combination of finesse and adventurousness, and it should only be served to unprejudiced gourmets who are open to its slightly exotic qualities.

1. In a mixing bowl, combine the almond milk, heavy cream and sugar syrup thoroughly. (To make your own almond milk, grind $^1/_3$ cup / 65 g almonds and three bitter almonds finely and infuse in 2 cups / 500 ml hot milk; press through a cloth before using.) Carefully fold in the stiffly whipped cream.

2. Before using the prickly pears, put on a glove and remove the spines. Halve the prickly pears, scoop out the flesh and retain the skins. Select the raspberries for the decoration.

and Almond Cream

3. Generously fill the prickly pear skins with the almond cream and place a few raspberries on each filled half.

4. Divide the remaining almond cream between the dessert plates. Place the filled prickly pear skins next to the cream and garnish with the remaining raspberries. Decorate with a sprig of mint.

Quark Omelette with Pears

Preparation time: 1 hour
Cooking time: 30 minutes
Difficulty: ★★

Serves 4

2 large pears

For the marinade:
2 tbsp / 30 g sugar
1 cup / 250 ml red wine
$^1/_2$ cup / 125 ml port
1 whole clove
1 small cinnamon stick
1 piece of ginger

For the ice cream:
1 cup / 250 ml each milk, cream

6 egg yolks, $^1/_3$ cup / 75 g sugar
$4^1/_2$ oz / 125 g white chocolate coating, melted

For the quark omelette:
$5^1/_4$ oz / 150 g quark

3 eggs, separated
3 tbsp flour
1 pinch of salt
1 vanilla bean
grated peel of 1 untreated lemon

For the sauce:
4 egg yolks
$3^1/_2$ tbsp / 50 g sugar
$^1/_2$ cup / 125 ml milk
$^1/_2$ cup / 125 ml cream
1 vanilla bean

To garnish:
1 tbsp raspberry sauce
1 tbsp mango sauce
4 sprigs of mint

The expertise of the chef at the Schwarzwaldstube ranges from exquisite appetizers to delicious desserts. This small restaurant, opened in 1984, has earned a good reputation through the excellent recipes and its welcoming atmosphere, and this quark omelette certainly does nothing to dispel that. It is also a worthy tribute to Germany's superb and manifold dairy products.

Harald Wohlfahrt suggests using Williams pears, but other varieties are also delicious. For the accompaniment, our chef sticks to old traditions: the quark, ice cream, sauce, and carefully selected spices (increasingly popular since the Middle Ages) combine to provide wonderful taste and texture experiences.

Cinnamon, which comes from Sri Lanka, gives the liquid in which the pears are prepared a touch of bittersweetness. Use cinnamon sticks to achieve a more intense flavor than ground cinnamon. Cinnamon is used in many meat dishes in northern Africa and the Middle East, though in the west it is found primarily in desserts. Cloves can also be used, though without onions as is so often the case in European broths; for example, they are used by the Japanese to flavor their famous sushi.

1. For the marinade, caramelize the sugar in a pan, then carefully and gradually add the red wine and port. Add the whole clove, cinnamon stick, and ginger and cook over a low heat until reduced by half. Peel the pears and add them to the pan. Bring the marinade briefly to a boil, then remove from the heat and let stand for 4 to 5 hours.

2. To make the ice cream, boil the milk and cream. Beat the egg yolks and sugar, then add the hot milk and beat with a whisk in a double boiler until creamy. Pass through a pointed sieve. Add the chocolate coating and whisk thoroughly. Allow to set in an ice cream maker. For the omelette, combine the quark, egg yolks, flour, salt, vanilla bean and grated lemon peel in a mixing bowl.

and Chocolate Ice Cream

3. Beat the egg whites until stiff and gradually add to the quark mixture. Prepare the vanilla sauce by beating the egg yolks with the sugar, adding the boiling milk and cream mixture and the vanilla bean and stirring in a double boiler until the sauce thickens. Allow to cool.

4. Fill the quark mixture into four greased and floured forms. Cut the pears into thin slices and arrange on top of the quark mixture in the shape of a rosette. Bake for 15 to 20 minutes at 355 °F / 180 °C. After baking, sprinkle sugar over the pears and caramelized under a grill. Pour some sauce onto the serving plates, turn the omelettes out of the forms onto it, garnish with the remaining pears and the mango and raspberry sauces and add a spoonful of ice cream.

Chestnut Soufflé with

Preparation time: 1 hour
Cooking time: 50 minutes
Difficulty: ✶✶

Serves 4

For the marinated oranges:
6 untreated oranges
3¹/₂ tbsp / 50 ml grenadine
6 cups / 1¹/₂ l sugar syrup at 28 °Beaumé
1 cinnamon stick
4 star anise
1 vanilla bean

For the soufflé:
²/₃ cup / 100 g shelled chestnuts
2 cups / 500 ml milk
2 tbsp / 30 g butter
confectioners' sugar
1 vanilla bean
2 eggs, separated
¹/₂ egg white
6¹/₂ tbsp / 100 ml kirsch
3¹/₂ tbsp / 50 g sugar

Our chef, a great lover of old traditions, reminds us of Christmas with this dessert. The best sweet chestnuts are to be found at that time of year, and their firm, shining shells and dense nutmeat tempt gourmets of any age. Harald Wohlfahrt is particularly fond of sweet chestnuts, and although he occasionally burns his fingers when shelling them, the result is worth every effort.

Turning them into a soufflé makes chestnuts more digestible; tempered a little, their flavor works better with others. The kirsch gives the soufflé an aroma reminiscent of the Black Forest, famous throughout the world for its fruit schnapps and huge orchards.

It is important to concentrate when preparing the soufflé, which needs to be served at just the right moment. Baking it in a water bath provides the even temperature essential for the egg whites to rise properly. For this reason, never open the oven door while a soufflé is baking.

The unique combination of oranges with sweet chestnuts is enticing, thanks to the balance and originality of these two beloved fruits. Use only very fresh fruits in season, and allow them to marinate in the liquid long enough to absorb the various flavors of the star anise, cinnamon, and grenadine.

Arranging the orange segments on the plates in the shape of a star is another way of echoing Christmas tradition.

1. Cut the peel of all the oranges into thin strips. Blanch the peel and rinse in cold water. Pour the grenadine over the peel and marinate for 24 hours.

2. Remove the pith from the oranges and divide them into segments. Cook the sugar syrup with the cinnamon stick, star anise, and the scraped out vanilla bean. Pour the boiling liquid onto the orange segments and allow them to marinate in it for 24 hours. Then remove the orange segments and set aside in a bowl.

Marinated Oranges

3. To make the soufflé, simmer the sweet chestnuts, milk, butter, and half of the vanilla bean over a low heat in a double boiler until the chestnuts are soft. Take out the vanilla bean and pass the mixture through a pointed sieve. Combine the half egg white, the egg yolks, and the kirsch, then add to the chestnut mixture. Allow to cool.

4. Grease four ovenproof soufflé dishes, sprinkle sugar in them and refrigerate. Whisk the remaining egg whites with a little sugar until stiff and fold into the cooled chestnut mixture. Fill the dishes and bake for 30 minutes in a water bath at 390 °F / 200 °C. Sprinkle confectioners' sugar on top shortly before serving. Arrange the orange segments on a plate in the form of a star and decorate with the orange peel.

Panna Cotta with

Preparation time: 20 minutes
Cooling time: 12 hours
Difficulty: ★

Serves 4

¹/₂ oz / 12 g ground gelatin
1¹/₄ cups / 300 ml milk
1 tbsp almond milk
¹/₂ cup / 125 g sugar
1¹/₄ cups / 300 ml cream

1 lb / 500 g raspberries, blueberries, wild strawberries or red currants

A traditional dish from the Piedmont region, *panna cotta* (Italian for "cooked cream") may have originated during the reign of Charles Albert, King of Sardinia and Piedmont (1798–1849), who was forced to abdicate after being defeated by Austria. The dessert is prepared using milk, almond milk, and gelatin. In order to assure the success of the dessert, either use cream with a fat content between 30% and 35%; or add more gelatin. The cream must then be slowly warmed over a moderate heat, so that it does not turn yellow.

Armando Zanetti has no interest in forcing the use of almond milk on anyone, especially since it puts some people off with its distinctive, unusual aroma. Since it is not a decisive ingredient in this dessert, it can simply be omitted. Other flavors, such as melted chocolate or vanilla, will also produce a delicious result. The preparation of this *panna cotta* is quite straightforward, requiring no further elaboration.

The subtle grace of this dessert supports northern Italy's generations-old claim of being able to compete with the south when it comes to pastry and ice cream-making. While it cannot be compared with a Sicilian cassata or other familiar southern Italian desserts, the eye-catching forest berries add their own acidic flavor to this presentation, and its simple elegance is an irresistible temptation.

1. Soak the gelatin in cold water. Bring the milk and almond milk to a boil with the sugar, and then stir in the soaked gelatin. Add the cream and slowly whip with a whisk.

2. Pour the panna cotta mixture into ovenproof dishes with a height of 2³/₄ in/6 cm to 3¹/₂ in / 8 cm. Refrigerate for at least 12 hours.

Forest Berries

3. Carefully turn the chilled panna cotta out of the dishes. Wash the berries briefly (do not soak them). Do not remove the stems from the strawberries.

4. Place a panna cotta on the center of each dessert plate, and arrange the various colored berries in circles around it. Serve with a red berry sauce and garnish with mint leaves.

Filled Pastry Rolls

Preparation time: 30 minutes
Cooking time: 45 minutes
Difficulty: ✳✳

Serves 4

For the short pastry:
6 cups / 750 g flour
3 eggs
3¹/₂ tbsp / 50 g sugar
3¹/₂ tbsp / 50 ml Cognac
2 cups / 500 g butter
grated peel of 1 untreated lemon

For the walnut cream:
8 cups / 2 l milk
1 cinnamon stick
2¹/₂ cups / 250 g shelled walnuts
1 cup / 250 g sugar
4 tsp / 10 g flour

confectioners' sugar for dusting

The unusual word in our recipe title is the Basque term for the walnut cream described below, an expression of our chef's attachment to his native region. The walnut, a classic autumn nut, is held in particularly high regard in southwestern and northern Spain. The best nuts are those harvested in November or December, the small ones in particular, with their more concentrated flavor. Fresh walnuts keep for about two weeks after ripening but then quickly turn rancid. If dried nuts are used, remove the bitter skin around the kernels by soaking the nuts in salt water for three days.

Do not chop the nuts in an electric blender, because this tends to pulverize them and give them an oily consistency. Instead, use a chopping knife, or better still, crush the nuts with a pestle and mortar. That way, the consistency of the nuts will remain intact. Set aside some nuts for garnishing and caramelize them; this allows the nuts to form a crunchy contrast with the delicate cream.

As odd as this may sound, a small quantity of water in which a cod has been soaked is traditionally added to the nut cream. In that way, the bounties of land and ocean unite to form a stunning combination of flavors. Unfortunately, this ancient tradition has been all but forgotten because most people today have difficulty imagining that the intensive flavor of cod could go with the sweetness of such a dessert.

If the walnut cream does not appeal to you, the rolls could also be filled with a pastry cream flavored to your own taste, or with a creamy rice pudding.

1. To make the short pastry, mound the flour on a work surface, make a hollow in the middle and put the eggs, sugar, Cognac, grated lemon peel, and softened butter into it. Knead by hand to form a dough. Shape the pastry into a ball and refrigerate.

2. Roll out the pastry and, using a pastry wheel, cut out strips of pastry 3 in / 7 cm wide and 9 in / 20 cm long. Roll these onto metal tubes with a diameter of 1¹/₂ in / 3 cm and bake at 375 °F / 190 °C. Alternatively, the rolls can also be deep-fried.

"Intxaursaltza"

3. Prepare the cream: bring half of the milk to a boil with the cinnamon stick; stir in the crushed or chopped nuts (see text above) and the sugar and simmer. Add the second liter of milk to the simmering mixture in two or three portions. Continue cooking until the liquid has reduced to the consistency of a caramel. Refrigerate. Fill the baked rolls with the cream using a pastry bag.

4. Before serving, dust the pastry rolls with confectioners' sugar and briefly glaze with a salamander or under a hot grill. Arrange on a plate, decorate with caramelized nuts, and serve cold or warm.

Apple Ring with

Preparation time: 20 minutes
Cooking time: 20 minutes
Difficulty: ★★

Serves 4

4 apples (Golden Delicious)
1/2 cup / 120 g butter, softened
3 cups / 750 ml sugar syrup
1/2 cup / 100 g dried figs

4 apples (Rennets or other cooking apples)
6 1/2 tbsp / 100 g sugar
1 cup plus 2 tbsp / 200 g raisins
1/3 cup / 50 g prunes
2 cups / 500 ml red wine

For the custard:
(see basic recipes)

In this case, our chef has created no mere variation of the traditional upside-down apple cake: Alberto Zuluaga has invented an apple ring that – apart from the compote filling – consists entirely of fruit.

Two different varieties of apples are used, Golden Delicious and Rennets. The former, as its name suggests, has a golden color and delicate, sweet flesh that nonetheless holds up well when cooked and is perfectly suited for baked desserts. Be sure to add enough sugar when cooking Golden Delicious apples so that they remain tender. Rennets are a type of cooking apple popular in Europe. They are frequently used to make compote, and their characteristically acidic taste provides an interesting contrast to the dried fruits. They are not generally available in the United States, but many excellent varieties would be acceptable substitutes, such as Baldwin, Cortland, Rome Beauty, or Winesap.

The dried fruit mixture conjures up the Middle Ages, when Muslims and Crusaders fought one another: raisins from Damascus, eaten since ancient times, first appeared in southern Spain at this time, or the equally exquisite raisins from Málaga. Figs have also been popular since ancient times – in the Bible, the fig tree symbolizes fertility.

The apple ring is produced using a ring-shaped mold. A sorbet could be substituted for the fig cream in the center (which can, of course, be placed next to the ring instead). The sorbet can be flavored to taste with an alcohol like Calvados, Cognac or Armagnac. Or, depending on the season, try a tasty mixture of fresh red berries.

1. Peel and slice the Golden Delicious apples approximately 1/4 in / 0.5 cm thick. Add half of the butter to 2 cups / 500 ml of the sugar syrup and poach the apple slices in it. Once they are soft, drain and allow to cool.

2. Line a ring-shaped form with the cooled apple slices. To make the fig cream, prepare a custard according to the basic recipe. Chop the dried figs and simmer them in 1 cup / 250 ml sugar syrup for 20 minutes or until they resemble a thick puree. Fold the figs into the custard.

Compote Filling

3. Prepare a compote using the diced cooking apples, sugar and remaining half of the butter. Add the raisins, which have been soaked in water. For the fruit syrup, carefully reduce the prunes, some raisins and diced apple with the red wine to form a thick syrup; pass through a pointed sieve.

4. Fill the apple-lined tins with the apple and raisin compote. Firmly press the remaining apple slices on top. Turn out of the tins, sprinkle sugar on top and glaze under a hot grill. Pour fig cream in the center of each ring and pour the fruit syrup around the base.

Basic Recipes

Apple Sorbet

Recipe: Normandy Delight by Michel Bruneau

Ingredients:
2 apples (Granny Smith) – juice of 1 lemon – freshly ground pepper – 6¹/₂ tbsp/100 ml sugar syrup at 30 °Beaumé (3¹/₂ tbsp/50 g sugar – 3¹/₂ tbsp/50 ml water)

Cooking steps:
Cut the apples into small pieces and place them in the freezer to freeze the skin. Mix with the lemon and pepper in a blender, stir into the syrup and place in an ice cream maker.

Meringue

Recipe: Nougat Parfait by Stéphane Raimbault

Recipes: Sloe Gin Soufflé and Puff Pastry with Creamy Rice Pudding by Hilario Arbelaitz

Ingredients:
4¹/₂ tbsp/100 g pine honey – 1 tbsp/25 g glucose – ¹/₂ cup/120 ml water – 3¹/₂ tbsp/50 g sugar – 4 egg whites – a pinch/2 g gelatin

Cooking steps:
Place the honey, glucose, water and sugar in a small pan. Reduce at 250 °F/121 °C. Beat the egg whites until stiff, then pour the hot syrup onto them. Beat with an electric mixer at high speed for 4 minutes, then at medium speed until the mixture has completely cooled. Stir in the dissolved gelatin.

Sponge Cake Dough

Recipe: Cassata alla Siciliana by Carlo Brovelli

Recipe: Caramel Feast by Jean-Pierre Vigato

Ingredients:
1 cup/250 g sugar – 8 eggs – 2 cups/250 g flour

Cooking steps:
Whisk the sugar and eggs until foamy over low heat in the top of a double boiler. Remove from the heat when lukewarm. Beat at high speed with an electric mixer. Reduce the speed and continue to stir the mixture as it cools and thickens. Using a skimmer, carefully fold in the sifted flour. Turn into a greased and floured cake pan and bake for about 30 minutes at 390 °F/200 °C.

Puff Paste

Recipe: Normandy Delight by Michel Bruneau

Recipe: Fried Fruit Dessert by Philippe Dorange

Recipe: Cake with Caramelized Apples by Michel Haquin

Recipe: Puff Pastry with Creamy Rice Pudding by Hilario Arbelaitz

Recipe: Orange Jelly with Puff Pastry by J. & L. Pourcel

Recipe: Cake with Fresh Figs and Cinnamon Cream by Jean-Louis Neichel

Recipe: Delicate Apple Cake by Jean Crotet

Recipe: Puff Pastries with Strawberries by Paul Pauvert

Recipe: Little Apple Cake "Nonette" by Michel Rochedy

Recipe: Puff Pastry Pouches with Mamía and Sagardoz by Pedro Subijana

Recipes: Apple Lattice and Mirliton à la Rouen by Gilles Tournadre

Ingredients:
4 cups/500 g flour – 1 tbsp/15 g salt – 1 cup/250 ml water – 2 cups/500 g butter

Cooking steps:
Mound the flour on a smooth work surface. Add the salt and water and make a ball of dough without kneading excessively. Allow to rest for 20 minutes, then roll out into a rectangle on a marble slab. Place the butter in the center and fold the dough in thirds over the butter to form a square. Immediately, and gently, roll out to form a long strip of dough, without pressing the butter out. Fold the ends of the strip into the center, then fold the dough together in the middle and refrigerate for 20 minutes.

Turning (folding and rolling out):
Turn six times (3 times 2 turns) at 20 minute intervals.

Cigarette Paste

Recipes: Savarin with Strawberry and Pineapple Flower, and Nougat Parfait by Stéphane Raimbault

Ingredients:
13 tbsp/200 g butter – 1¹/₃ cups/200 g confectioners' sugar – 7 egg whites – 1¹/₄ cups/150 g flour – 1 tsp/5 ml vanilla extract – 2 tbsp/20 g pistachios – 1 tbsp/20 g raisins – ¹/₄ cup/20 g shredded coconut – 2 tbsp/20 g almonds – 3 tbsp/20 g flaked almonds

Cooking steps:
Beat the butter until fluffy, then add the confectioners' sugar and in rapid succession the egg whites, flour, and vanilla extract. Spread the mixture evenly onto a non-stick baking tray using a round spatula. Sprinkle it with the pistachios, raisins, shredded coconut, almonds and flaked almonds. Bake for a few minutes at 355 °F/180 °C.

Custard

Recipes: Chocolate Variations and Burgundy Pear by Michel Blanchet

Recipe: Apple Ring with Compote Filling by Alberto Zuluaga

Recipe: Ice Soufflé with Figs and Armagnac by Michel Libotte

Recipe: Prunes in Pastry with Almond Cream by Jean-Claude Rigollet

Recipe: Apple Tarts with Raisin Streusel by Émile Jung

Recipe: Sweet Chestnut Dessert by Georges Paineau

Recipe: Parfait with Aniseed and Coffee Sauce by Émile Tabourdiau

Ingredients:
2 cups/500 ml milk – 1 vanilla bean – 6 egg yolks – ¹/₂ cup plus 2 tbsp/150 g sugar

Cooking steps:
Bring the milk to a boil with half of the sugar and the vanilla bean, which has been cut open lengthwise. Thoroughly whisk the egg yolks and remaining sugar until foamy. Add a little hot milk to the egg yolks, then pour everything into the pan with the milk and stir constantly with a wooden spatula or spoon until the desired consistency is reached. Do not allow to boil! Remove from the heat and continue to stir until completely cooled. Pass the custard through a pointed sieve.

Spice Cookies

Recipe: Quince Sorbet with Rhubarb Compote by Jean-Louis Neichel

Ingredients:
³/₄ cup/100 g flaked almonds – ³/₄ cup/100 g sugar – 3 tbsp/20 g flour – 2 eggs – spices to taste

Cooking steps:
Mix the almonds, sugar, flour, eggs and spices in a bowl. Allow to rest and infuse for about 2 hours. Spoon the batter onto a greased tray and bake at 465 °F/240 °C.

Pastry Cream

Recipe: Crispy Wafers with Raspberries by Patrick Jeffroy

Recipe: Sand Cake with Oranges and Bittersweet Chocolate by Jean-Pierre Bruneau

Recipe: Normandy Delight by Michel Bruneau

Recipe: Almond Crackers with Berries by Francis Chauveau

Recipe: "Chocolat-Café" with Walnuts by Louis Grondard

Recipe: Mocha Charlotte with Ice Cream and Nuts by André Jaeger

Recipe: Cake with Fresh Figs and Cinnamon Cream by Jean-Louis Neichel

Recipe: Basque Cake by Firmin Arrambide

Recipe: Fruit Gratin with Almonds by Jean Fleury

Ingredients:
4 cups/1 l milk – 1 vanilla bean (optional) – 10 egg yolks – ³/₄ cup/200 g sugar – ¹/₂ cup plus 2 tbsp/80 g cornstarch

Cooking steps:
Bring the milk to boil in a large pan with the vanilla bean, which has been slit lengthwise. In a bowl, beat the egg yolks and sugar until creamy. Add the cornstarch. While stirring, pour the boiling milk onto the egg yolks, then pour everything back into the pan and simmer for 2 minutes while stirring continuously. Make sure the cream does not burn! Pour into a bowl and top with a little butter to prevent a crust from forming.

Almond Cookies

Recipe: Delicacy in Three Colors by José Tourneur

Recipe: Ice Soufflé with Figs and Armagnac by Michel Libotte

Ingredients:
¹/₂ cup/125 g superfine sugar – 1 cup/125 g flaked almonds – 3 tbsp/20 g flour – 1 small pinch of vanilla powder – 2 egg whites – 5 tsp/25 g butter, melted

Cooking steps:
Combine the sugar, flaked almonds, flour, vanilla and finally the egg whites in a bowl, using a wooden spatula or spoon. Add the melted butter and mix thoroughly. Place small amounts of the mixture onto a tray lined with baking paper, press flat with a fork moistened in water, and bake at 465 °F/240 °C.

Mango Sorbet

Recipe: Mango and Honey Rolls by Fernando Adría

Ingredients:
2 large mangoes (c. 24–27 oz/700–800 g) – 1²/₃ cups/400 ml sugar syrup at 28 °Beaumé – juice of 1 lemon

Cooking steps:
Peel the mangoes. Carefully remove the flesh from the stones. Puree it in a blender, then add the syrup and lemon juice. Stir everything thoroughly, pass through a pointed sieve and then freeze.

Short Paste

Recipe: Neapolitan Cake by Gianfranco Vissani

Recipe: Sweet Wine Tart by Fritz Schilling

Ingredients:
4 cups/500 g flour – 4 tsp/20 g superfine sugar – 1 tbsp/15 g salt – 1¹/₂ cups/350 g butter – 2 eggs – 2–3 tbsp water

Cooking steps:
Mound the flour on a smooth work surface and make a hollow in the middle. Place the sugar, salt, softened butter, eggs and water in the hollow. Combine. Briefly knead the dough, finally only kneading with the balls of the hands. Form the dough into a ball, wrap in a clean towel, and allow to rest at least 1 hour before using. It is best to make the dough a day in advance.

Pancake Batter

Recipe: Pancake Ravioli with "Suzette" Orange Butter by Philippe Dorange

Recipe: Variations of Pineapple by Dieter Kaufmann

Ingredients:
2 cups/250 g flour – ¹/₃ cup/80 g sugar – 1 large pinch of salt – 4 eggs – 2 cups/500 ml milk – 6¹/₂ tbsp/100 g butter

Cooking steps:
Combine the sifted flour, sugar and salt in a bowl. Stir in the eggs with a whisk and gradually add the milk in order to produce a smooth mixture. Melt the butter in a pan, and once it is brown remove from the heat and add to the batter while stirring. Pass through a pointed sieve. Allow the batter to rest for half an hour before cooking the pancakes.

Pistachio Ice Cream

Recipe: Hot and Cold Cherries by Jean Bardet

Ingredients:
²/₃ cup/100 g fresh pistachios – ¹/₂ cup plus 2 tbsp/150 g sugar – 6 egg yolks – 2 cups/500 ml milk

Cooking steps:
Crush the pistachios and half of the sugar with a pestle and mortar and add to the milk. Bring it to a boil, remove from the heat, cover, and allow to infuse for 40 minutes. Beat the egg yolks and remaining sugar until creamy. Pass the milk through a pointed sieve, then bring it to a boil again. Pour a little hot milk onto the egg yolks. Return this mixture to the pan and, without stopping, thoroughly combine while stirring with a wooden spatula or spoon. Do not allow it to boil! Remove from the heat and stir until completely cooled, then pour into an ice cream machine.

Quince Sorbet

Recipe: Quince Sorbet with Rhubarb Compote by Jean-Louis Neichel

Ingredients:
1 lb/500 g fresh quinces – water – 1 tsp rosemary, freshly chopped – 2 cups/500 g sugar – 1 untreated lemon – 1 small glass of quince liqueur

Cooking steps:
Peel the quinces, cut them into pieces and place in a pan. Cover with water and cook for 15 minutes over low heat with the rosemary, sugar, quince liqueur, lemon juice and a piece of lemon peel. Allow to cool, stir again in a blender, and then freeze.

Sand Cake Dough

Recipe: Chocolate Sponge Cake with Tea Ice Cream by Guy Van Cauteren

Recipe: Sand Cake with Oranges and Bittersweet Chocolate by Jean-Pierre Bruneau

Ingredients:
6¹/₂ tbsp/100 g butter – ¹/₃ cup/80 g superfine sugar – 2 egg yolks – 1 pinch of vanilla powder – 1 pinch of salt – ³/₄ cup/100 g flour – 2¹/₂ tbsp/20 g cocoa powder, very low fat – 6 tbsp/40 g finely ground almonds – ¹/₄ cup/40 g confectioners' sugar

Cooking steps:
Cream the butter and sugar in a bowl until light, then beat in the egg yolks, vanilla and salt. Combine the remaining dry ingredients and add to the creamed mixture in 2 or 3 portions. Cover the bowl with a cloth and let the dough rest for about 1 hour before being used.

Savarin Dough

Recipe: Savarin with Strawberry and Pineapple Flower by Stéphane Raimbault

Ingredients:
2 cups/250 g flour – 1 tsp/5 g salt – 1 tbsp/15 g superfine sugar – peel of 1¹/₂ untreated lemons – ¹/₂ oz/15 g powdered milk – 1 oz/30 g baker's yeast – 7¹/₂ tbsp/110 ml water – 2 eggs – 5 tbsp/75 g butter

Cooking steps:
Combine the flour, salt, sugar and lemon peel in a mixing bowl. In another bowl, dissolve the powdered milk and yeast in lukewarm water (80 °F/28 °C). Add the eggs without stirring. Add the liquid mixture to the dry ingredients and beat with an electric mixer, at first at low speed and then for a few minutes at a higher speed. Add the softened butter and beat for another 2 minutes. Fill individual forms two thirds full, dry in the oven at 120 °F/50 °C and then bake for 20 minutes at 390 °F/200 °C.

Tulip Dough

Recipe: Delicacy in Three Colors by José Tourneur

Recipe: Banana Soufflé with Honey Ice Cream by Paul Heathcote

Ingredients:
6¹/₂ tbsp/100 g butter – ²/₃ cup/100 g confectioners' sugar – 3 egg whites – ¹/₂ cup plus 3 tbsp/85 g flour

Cooking steps:
Mix the softened butter with the confectioners' sugar, gradually adding the egg whites and finally the flour. Spread circles of dough with a diameter of 7 in/15 cm on a greased and floured baking tray. Bake and brown in the oven. Use a small bowl to shape into "tulips" while still warm.

Vanilla Ice Cream

Recipe: Roasted Figs with Banyuls and Vanilla Ice Cream by Dominique Toulousy

Recipe: Mocha Charlotte with Ice Cream and Nuts by André Jaeger

Recipe: Mirliton à la Rouen by Gilles Tournadre

Recipe: Rhubarb Soup "Bagatelle" by Eyvind Hellstrøm

Ingredients:
2 cups/500 ml milk – ¹/₂ cup plus 2 tbsp/150 g sugar – 1 vanilla bean, slit lengthwise – 6 egg yolks – 1 cup/250 ml crème fraîche

Cooking steps:
Combine the milk, half of the sugar and the vanilla bean and bring to a rolling boil. In a bowl, beat the egg yolks and the remaining sugar until creamy. Pour a little hot milk onto the eggs, then return to the pan with the hot milk and continue to cook while stirring continuously with a wooden spatula or spoon. Do not allow to boil! Remove from the heat and continue to stir until completely cooled, then pass through a pointed sieve. Stir in the crème fraîche and place in an ice cream machine to harden.

Introducing the Chefs

Fernando Adría

born May 14, 1962

Restaurant: **El Bulli**
Address: 30, Apartado de Correos Cala
Montjoi 17480 Rosas, Spain
Tel. (9)72 15 04 57; Fax (9)72 15 07 17

As a young, talented 21-year-old back in 1983, Fernando Adrìa received two Michelin stars for his culinary achievements in El Bulli, his restaurant on the Costa Brava whose kitchens had previously been run by his friend Jean-Louis Neichel. Awarded 19 points and four red chef's hats by Gault-Millau, Adrìa has also fared well with the Spanish restaurant guides: four stars in Campsa and 9.5/10 in Gourmetour. A winner of the "Spanish national gastronomy award", Fernando Adrìa also received the "European culinary grand prix" in 1994. When his work leaves him time, this chef is a great supporter of the Barcelona soccer team.

Hilario Arbelaitz

born May 27, 1951

Restaurant: **Zuberoa**
Address: Barrio Iturrioz, 8
20180 Oyarzun, Spain
Tel. (9)43 49 12 28; Fax (9)43 49 26 79

Born in the heart of the Spanish Basque Country, whose gourmet traditions form the emphasis of his cooking, Hilario Arbelaitz began his career in 1970 at Zuberoa, where he became chef in 1982. Since then, he has received numerous French and Spanish awards: two Michelin stars and three red chef's hats and 17 points in Gault-Millau, as well as four Campsa stars. In 1993 he was named "Best Chef in Euzkadi" (the Basque Country), after being named "Best Chef in Spain" in 1991. He brings equal measures of enthusiasm to the Basque game of pelota and family life, and is very interested in the history and future of his profession.

Firmin Arrambide

born September 16, 1946

Restaurant: **Les Pyrénées**
Address: 19, place du Général de Gaulle
64220 Saint-Jean-Pied-de-Port, France
Tel. (0)5 59 37 01 01; Fax (0)5 59 37 18 97

Firmin Arrambide has been at the helm of this restaurant not far from his place of birth since 1986, garnering two Michelin stars and three red chef's hats and 18 points in Gault-Millau for Les Pyrénées. His regionally inspired cuisine won him second place in the 1978 Taittinger awards and carried him to the finals of the Meilleur Ouvrier de France competition in 1982. True to his Basque origins, Arrambide hunts woodpigeon and woodsnipe in the fall, and also loves mountain climbing; occasionally, though, he enjoys simply soaking up the sun by the side of the swimming pool.

Jean Bardet

born September 27, 1941

Restaurant: **Jean Bardet**
Address: 57, rue Groison
37000 Tours, France
Tel. (0)3 47 41 41 11; Fax (0)3 47 51 68 72

Before opening a restaurant in Tours under his own name in 1987, Jean Bardet traversed the whole of Europe, working mainly as a sauce chef at the Savoy in London. A member of Relais et Châteaux, Relais Gourmands and the Auguste Escoffier Foundation, he was awarded four red chef's hats in Gault-Millau (19.5) and two Michelin stars. In 1982 he had the honor of preparing dinner for the heads of state at the Versailles Summit. Jean Bardet is an enthusiastic cigar smoker (American Express awarded him the title of "Greatest Smoker in the World" in 1984) and in the fall indulges his passion for hunting together with friends.

Giuseppina Beglia

born May 16, 1938

Restaurant: **Balzi Rossi**
Address: 2, Via Balzi Rossi
18039 Ventimiglia, Italy
Tel. (0)18 43 81 32; Fax (0)18 43 85 32

Since 1983 her restaurant has towered over this famous vantage point and the caves of the Balzi Rossi ("red cliffs"), but Giuseppina Beglia herself is just as well known in Italy for the television cookery programs broadcast under her direction between 1985–90. A member of Le Soste, the prestigious Italian restaurant chain, she holds two Michelin stars, three red chef's hats in Gault-Millau (18) and 82/100 in the Italian Gambero Rosso guide. In 1992 she won the first "Golden Key of Gastronomy" to be awarded by Gault-Millau to chefs outside of France. Giuseppina Beglia is very interested the flower arrangements in her restaurant, and loves skiing in the nearby Alps.

Michel Blanchet

June 16, 1949

Restaurant: **Le Tastevin**
Address: 9, avenue Eglé
78600 Maisons-Laffitte, France
Tel. (0)139 62 11 67; Fax (0)1 39 62 73 09

After a top-notch training from 1967–71 at Maxim's, *Lutétia* and *Ledoyen*, Michel Blanchet took over the reins at *Tastevin* in 1972; today, the restaurant boasts two Michelin stars. Blanchet's talents have more than once carried him through to the final rounds of prestigious awards: the Prosper Montagné prize (1970 and 1972); the Taittinger prize (1974); and the Meilleur Ouvrier de France competition in 1979. Michel Blanchet is a MaÓtre Cuisinier de France and a member of the "Culinary Academy of France". A great lover of nature, he enjoys rambles through the woods – during which he sometimes also collects mushrooms – as well as cycling and hiking.

Michel Bourdin

born June 6, 1942

Restaurant: **The Connaught**
Address: Carlos Place, Mayfair
London W1Y 6AL, England
Tel. (0)171 491-0668; Fax (0)171 495-3262

One of the old and distinguished line of French chefs in Great Britain, Michel Bourdin has been delighting London diners at the *Connaught* since 1975. The recipient of numberous prizes (Prosper Montagné, Taittinger) since training at *Ledoyen* and under Alex Humbert at *Maxim's*, he has been Chairman of the British branch of the "Culinary Academy of France" since 1980. In addition, he is a member of the "100 Club", and like Paul Haeberlin is also an honorary member of the Chefs des Chefs association. His pastry-chef colleagues, the twins Carolyn and Deborah Power, have made the *Connaught* famous for its desserts.

Carlo Brovelli

born May 23, 1938

Restaurant: **Il Sole di Ranco**
Address: 5, Piazza Venezia
21020 Ranco, Italy
Tel. (0)3 31 97 65 07; Fax (0)3 31 97 66 20

One "sun" – it was only fitting that the Italian restaurant guide Veronelli should pay tribute to this restaurant with the sun in its name by awarding it this distinction. Looking back on a 120-year-old family tradition, Il Sole di Ranco is run in a masterly fashion by Carlo Brovelli, who took over the reins in 1968 after training at the college of hotel management in La Stresa. A member of the Le Soste, Relais et Châteaux and Relais Gourmands chains, Brovelli has received many accolades: two Michelin stars, three chef's hats in Gault-Millau (18), 84/100 in the Italian Gambero Rosso. Carlo Brovelli loves cycling and soccer, as well as his favorite sport, hunting.

Jean-Pierre Bruneau

born September 18, 1943

Restaurant **Bruneau**
Address: 73-75, avenue Broustin
1080 Brussels, Belgium
Tel. (0)24 27 69 78; Fax (0)24 25 97 26

For a good 20 years now, Jean-Pierre Bruneau has run the restaurant bearing his name which stands in the shadow of the important Koekelberg Basilica in the center of Brussels. The sophisticated creations of this Belgian Maître Cuisinier" have won him many distinctions: three Michelin stars, four red chef's hats in Gault-Millau, three stars in Bottin Gourmand and 94/100 in the Belgian restaurant guide Henri Lemaire. He is also a member of Traditions et Qualité. Outside of the kitchen, he enjoys hunting and car racing (first hand); in addition, he collects old cars.

Michel Bruneau

born February 11, 1949

Restaurant **La Bourride**
Address: 15-17, rue du Vaugueux
14000 Caen, France
Tel. (0)2 31 93 50 76; Fax (0)2 31 93 29 63

"Normandy is proud of herself" – this is the motto of Michel Bruneau, who never tires of enumerating the sumptuous produce of the Calvados region on his exhaustive, tempting menu. Starting off his career in the midst of the plantations in Ecrécy, on the banks of the Guigne (1972–82), he then moved to *La Bourride* in Caen, where he has been since 1982. Here he continues to delight gourmets with his inventive cooking, steeped in regional traditions, which has also impressed the critics: two Michelin stars, three red chef's hats in Gault-Millau (18). In his spare time, Michel Bruneau enjoys cooking for friends. He plays soccer and sometimes accompanies his son to the skating rink.

Alain Burnel

born January 26, 1949

Restaurant **Oustau de Baumanière**
Address: Val d'Enfer
13520 Les Baux-de-Provence, France
Tel. (0)4 90 54 33 07; Fax (0)4 90 54 40 46

Alain Burnel served his apprenticeship in Beaulieu at *La réserve de Beaulieu* (1969–73), in Nantes at *Frantel* under Roger Jaloux, in Marseilles at *Sofitel* and in Saint-Romain de Lerps at the *Château du Besset*, where he served as chef from 1978-82 before taking over the reins from the famous Raymond Thuillier in Baux, whose restaurant is now owned by the Charial family. Alain Burnel has earned two Michelin stars, three white chef's hats in Gault-Millau (18) and is a member of Traditions et Qualité, Relais et Châteaux and Relais Gourmands. In his free time this chef is a keen cyclist, and was even once a participant in the Tour de France.

Jan Buytaert

born October 16, 1946

Restaurant **De Bellefleur**
Address: 253 Chaussée d'Anvers
2950 Kapellen, Belgium
Tel. (0)3 664 6719; Fax (0)3 665 0201

Despite being a dyed-in-the-wool Belgian who has spent a large part of his career in his native country (first at the *Villa Lorraine* in Brussels from 1973–4), Jan Buytaert worked for two years in the kitchens of *Prés et Sources d'Eugénie* in Eugénie-les-Bains under Michel Guérard (1974–5). In 1975, after this French interlude, he opened his current restaurant, which has earned him two Michelin stars and is one of the best in the region. This Belgian Maître Cuisinier loves gentle activities such as hiking and riding, and also enjoys working in the garden.

Jacques Cagna

born August 24, 1942

Restaurant **Jacques Cagna**
Address: 14, rue des Grands Augustins
75006 Paris, France
Tel. (0)1 43 26 49 39; Fax (0)1 43 54 54 48

This distinguished chef has worked the most famous restaurants of the French capital (1960 at *Lucas Carton*, 1961 at *Maxim's*, 1964 at *La Ficelle*), and was even Chef to the French National Assembly (1961–62) before opening his own restaurant under his own name in 1975, for which he has received high honors: two Michelin stars, two red chef's hats in Gault-Millau (18) and three stars in Bottin Gourmand. Jacques Cagna is a Knight of the Mérite nationale des Arts et des Lettres. He knows his way around Asia very well, speaks fluent Japanese and is keen on classical music, opera and jazz.

Stewart Cameron

born September 16, 1945

Restaurant Turnberry Hotel & Golf Courses
Turnberry KA26 9LT, Scotland
Tel. (0)1655 331 000; Fax (0)1655 331 706

Since 1981, the kitchens of the *Turnberry* Hotel – one of only two 5-star Scottish restaurants – have had a real Scot at the helm: Stewart Cameron, who previously worked at *Malmaison*, the restaurant of the *Central Hotel* in Glasgow. This chef is also a member of the "Taste of Scotland" and of the British Branch of the "Culinary Academy of France". In 1986 and 1994 he was privileged to play host in his restaurant to the participants of the British Golf Open. When he gets the chance, Stewart Cameron goes hunting or fishing. A rugby fan (of course!), he is one of the Scottish Fifteen's most faithful supporters.

Mario Cavallucci

born May 20, 1959

Restaurant **La Frasca**
Address: 38, Via Matteoti
47011 Castrocaro Terme, Italy
Tel. (0)543 76 74 71; Fax (0)543 76 66 25

Two Michelin stars, 4 chef's hats in Gault-Millau (19), one sun in Veronelli, 89/100 in Gambero Rosso: what more could Mario Cavallucci want? Working in perfect harmony with the restaurant's proprietor and cellarman, Gianfranco Bolognesi, this young, energetic chef has already received many accolades. A member of the Le Soste restaurant chain, he has vigorously supported Italy's great culinary tradition since 1978. This extraordinarily busy chef nevertheless manages to find a little spare time for fishing, reading, seeing the occasional movie, and playing cards, soccer and billiards.

Francis Chauveau

Born: September 15, 1947

Restaurant: **La Belle Otéro**
Address: Hôtel Carlton (7th floor)
58, La Croisette
Cannes 06400, France
Tel. (0)4 93 69 39 39; Fax (0)4 93 39 09 06

Although born in Berry in the northwest of France, Francis Chauveau's encounter with Provencal cooking has led to outstanding results, which visitors to the legendary Palace-Hotel in Cannes – holder of two Michelin stars – have been enjoying since 1989. Francis Chauveau gained his first experience as a chef in the *Hôtel d'Espagne* in Valencay, continuing his career at the *Auberge de Noves* in 1965. Later, he worked in prestigious restaurants such as the Auberge du Père Bise, the Réserve de Beaulieu, the Terrasse in the Hotel Juana in Juan-les Pins, and in the famous restaurant *L'Amandier* in Mougins from 1980–89.

Jacques Chibois

Born: July 22, 1952

Restaurant: **La Bastide St-Antoine**
Address: 45, avenue Henri Dunant
06130 Grasse, France
Tel. (0)4 92 42 04 42; Fax (0)4 92 42 03 42

During the course of a career involving many moves, Jacques Chibois has met many famous names in French gastronomy: Jean Delaveyne in Bougival, Louis Outhier in La Napoule, Roger Vergé in Mougins, and the famous pastry chef Gaston Lenôtre. Since 1980 he has repeatedly worked under Michel Guérard, and was awarded two Michelin stars during his time at *Gray d'Albion* in Cannes (1981–95). He opened La Bastide Saint-Antoine in Grasse in 1995. In his spare time, Jacques Chibois is an enthusiastic cyclist and nature-lover, as well as a keen hunter and angler.

Serge Courville

Born: December 9, 1935

Restaurant: **La Cote 108**
Address: Rue Colonel Vergezac
02190 Berry-au-Bac, France
Tel. (0)3 23 79 95 04; Fax (03) 23 79 83 50

Serge Courville names his three teachers – Roger Petit, Robert Morizot and Jean-Louis Lelaurain – with warmth. Although not much interested in accolades, he has nevertheless reached the final of numerous culinary competitions (Prosper Montagné prize, 1971; Trophée national de l'Académie Culinaire, 1972; Taitinger prize, 1973). Since 1972, he and his wife have together run *La Cote 108*, which in 1982 received one Michelin star. When not working, Serge Courville enjoys cooking for friends; he is also a passionate reader and cyclist and spends a lot of time in the wilds, fishing or hunting for mushrooms.

Bernard Coussau

Born: September 15, 1917

Restaurant: **Relais de la Poste**
Address: 40140 Magescq, France
Tel. (0)5 58 47 70 25; Fax (0)5 58 47 76 17

Bernard Coussau's name is synonymous with the culinary essence of the Landes region in the southwest of France. At the *Relais de la Poste*, opened in 1954 and the continuous holder of two Michelin stars since 1969, this Honorary Chairman of the Maîtres Cuisiniers de France offers diners fine regional cuisine in the surroundings of a superbly preserved old coaching inn. At the summit of an extraordinary career, this chef is an officer of the Mérite agricole and a knight of the Legion of Honor and of the Palmes académiques. An old rugby fan, he supports Dax, and is also a car enthusiast.

Jean Coussau

Born: May 6, 1949

Restaurant: **Relais de la Poste**
Address: 40140 Magescq, France
Tel. (0)5 58 47 70 25; Fax (0)5 58 47 76 17

A worthy heir to the mantel of his father Bernard, Jean Coussau is a Maître Cuisinier de France, and a member of the J.R.E. ("Young Restauranteurs of Europe") and of the French Haute Cuisine association. following an exemplary Franco-Spanish career at the *Café de Paris* in Biarritz, the *Plaza-Athénée* in Paris and the Ritz in Madrid, since 1970 he has worked together with his father in the kitchens of the Relais de la Poste in Magescq. In 1976 he reached the finals of the "Best Cellarman in France" competition. Jean Coussau shares his father's passion for hunting and is also an enthusiastic and frequent golfer.

Jean Crotet

Born: January 26, 1943

Restaurant: **Hostellerie de Levernois**
Address: Route de Combertault
21200 Levernois, France
Tel. (0)3 80 24 73 68; Fax (0)3 80 22 78 00

Amidst a splendid park of Louisiana cedar, willow and ash, through which a small river flows, Jean Crotet offers discerning diners a sophisticated cuisine which has been awarded two Michelin stars and three stars in Bottin Gourmand. He is a Maître Cuisinier de France, as well as a member of Relais et Châteaux and Relais Gourmands chains. In 1988, after working for 15 years at the *Côte d'Or* in Nuits-Saint Georges, he settled down in Levernois, near Beaune. In his spare time Jean Crotet enjoys fishing, flying a helicopter, playing tennis, hunting and gardening.

Michel Del Burgo

Born: June 21, 1962

Restaurant: **La Barbacane**
Address: Place de l'Église
11000 Carcassonne-La Cité, France
Tel. (0)4 68 25 03 34; Fax (0)4 68 71 50 15

This young man from the northern province of Picardy has worked in the kitchens of Alain Ducasse in Courchevel, Raymond Thuillier in Baux-de-Provence and Michel Guérard in Eugénie-les-Bains, all in the south of France. After a short stay in the Rhône valley and Avignon (1987–90), Michel Del Burgo was in 1991 appointed chef of *La Barbacane* in the center of Carcassonne by Jean-Michel Signoles. In 1995 he was awarded his second Michelin star, the "Lily of the restaurant trade" and the Gault-Millau "golden key", as well as three red chef's hats and 18 points in the latter guide. Michel Del Burgo rates the cooking of his fellow chefs in the "Land of the Cathars", but is also fond of music, motor sport and hiking.

Joseph Delphin

Born: September 4, 1932

Restaurant: **La Châtaigneraie**
Address: 156, route de Carquefou
44240 Sucé-sur-Erdre, France
Tel. (0)2 40 77 90 95; Fax (0)2 40 77 90 08

A Maître Cuisinier de France and member of the "Culinary Academy of France", Joseph Delphin delights gourmets from the Nantes area with his culinary skills. A knight of the Mérite agricole, this chef has also received the Vase de Sèvres award from the French President. His restaurant, *La Châtaigneraie* (one Michelin star), sits right on the banks of the Erdre, and can be reached by road, river or helicopter...You are sure to be won over by the warmth of the welcome from the Delphin family, as Jean-Louis, a member of the "Young Restauranteurs of Europe", works here together with his father.

Philippe Dorange

born: May 27, 1963

Restaurant: **Fouquet's**
Address: 99, avenue des Champs Élysées
75008 Paris, France
Tel (0)1 47 23 70 60; Fax (0)1 47 20 08 69

Does one actually need to to introduce the legendary *Fouquet's* in these pages? Surely not, nor the prestigious restaurants in which Philippe Dorange has worked in the past: Roger Vergé's *Le Moulin de Mougins* (1977–81), Jacques Maximin's *Negresco* in Nice (1981–88), and lastly *Ledoyen* in Paris, where he was chef from 1988–92. All in all, a fine career path for a young chef whose Mediterranean origins are reflected in his culinary preferences, a fact which is particularly esteemed by his Champs-Elysées clientele. When not in the kitchen, Philippe Dorange likes to box, drive sports cars or play soccer.

Claude Dupont

born: June 7, 1938

Restaurant: **Claude Dupont**
Address: 46, avenue Vital Riethuisen
1080 Brussels, Belgium
Tel (0)2 426 0000; Fax (0)2 426 6540

The Belgian and French gourmet restaurant guides have positively showered awards on Claude Dupont's cooking: two Michelin stars since 1976, three stars in Bottin Gourmand, three white chef's hats in Gault-Millau (17) and 92/100 points in the Belgian Henri Lemaire guide. In 1967 he was awarded the Prosper Montagné prize, and in 1973 the "Oscar of Gastronomy". In addition, this chef ran the Belgian Pavillion at the 1970 World Fair in Osaka, before opening a restaurant under his own name in Brussels. In his leisure time Claude Dupont occupies himself by making things with his hands, gardening, playing tennis and swimming.

Éric Dupont

born: April 16, 1966

Restaurant: **Claude Dupont**
Address: 46, avenue Vital Riethuisen
1080 Brussels, Belgium
Tel (0)2 426 0000; Fax (0)2 426 6540

Éric Dupont has had a truly star-studded training, serving successive apprenticeships with the Brussels Masterchef Freddy Van Decasserie (*Villa Lorraine*), Pierre Wynants (*Comme chez soi*) and Willy Vermeulen (*De Bijgaarden*). Nowadays he works with his father Claude Dupont in the family business. The apple never falls far from the tree, and it does not seem unreasonable to place high hopes on this young chef who founded the Brussels college of hotel management C.E.R.I.A. Éric Dupont is a keen traveler and loves sporting activities such as swimming, tennis and riding.

Lothar Eiermann

born: March 2, 1945

Restaurant: **Wald- & Schloßhotel Friedrichs-ruhe**
Address: 74639 Friedrichsruhe, Germany
Tel (0)7941 60870; Fax (0)7941 61468

For over 20 years now Lothar Eiermann has worked at Friedrichsruhe, the summer residence of the Prince von Hohenlohe-Öhringen which belongs to the Relais et Châteaux chain. Before this, he traveled throughout the whole of Europe, working as a chef in Switzerland between 1964-72 in the *Grappe d'Or* in Lausanne and in the Hotel *Victoria* in Glion. He then worked in the *Gleneagles* Hotel in Scotland, traveled south to England, and returned to Scotland, where he managed a hotel from 1972-3. This Bordeaux-wine enthusiast also has a degree in Economics from the University of Heidelberg, and depending on the season, enjoys skiing, cycling or playing tennis.

Jean Fleury

born: April 22, 1948

Restaurant: **Paul Bocuse**
Address: 69660 Collonges-au-Mont-d'Or, France
Tel (0)4 72 42 90 90; Fax (0)4 72 27 85 87

After a highly promising début in his home town of Bourg-en-Bresse – the chief town of Bresse, a region renowned for its outstanding produce – Jean Fleury achieved fame as a chef in the Hotel *Royal* in Évian (1968–9) and in the Brussels *Hilton* (1971–78). Winner of the Prosper Montagné prize in 1976, he was named "Best Chef in Belgium" in the same year, and won the Meilleur Ouvrier de France competition in 1979. In 1985 he left the kitchens of the *Arc-en-ciel* in Lyons, following Paul Bocuse to his famous restaurant in Collonges. Jean Fleury loves traveling and hiking and collects antique cookbooks, from which he enjoys drawing inspiration.

Constant Fonk

born: September 1, 1947

Restaurant: **De Oude Rosmolen**
Address: Duinsteeg 1
1621 Hoorn, the Netherlands
Tel (0)229 014752; Fax (0)229 014938

Thanks to Constant Fonk, the town of Hoorn in North Holland has had a two-Michelin-starred restaurant since 1990. After his first highly promising steps in the Amsterdam *Hilton* (1965–6), and the *Amstel Hotel* (1966–7), our chef returned to his home town, where in 1967 he began work in *De Oude Rosmolen*, finally taking over the reins of the kitchen in 1976. A lover of fine cuisine and good wines, he especially enjoys partaking of both with like-minded people. As far as sport is concerned, golf is his favorite form of exercise, and makes a change from the kitchen.

Louis Grondard

born: September 20, 1948

Restaurant: Drouant
Address: 16-18, rue Gaillon
75002 Paris, France
Tel (0)1 42 65 15 16; Fax (0)1 49 24 02 15

It is no easy task to have catered for the members of the jury of the prestigious Goncourt literary prize every year since 1990; rather, it requires someone with the skills of this chef, who was named Meilleur Ouvrier de France in 1979. Louis Grondard served his apprenticeship at *Taillevent* and at *Maxim's*, first in Orly, then in Roissy. He then achieved his first successes in the Eiffel Tower restaurant and in the famous *Jules Vernes*, which opened in the Tower in 1983. To quote Michel Tournier, "The stars [two in Michelin] fall as his due from heaven." Louis Grondard has also been favored with three white chef's hats and 17 points in Gault-Millau. He loves literature, Baroque music and opera, and enjoys going diving when on vacation.

Philippe Groult

born: November 17, 1953

Restaurant: **Amphyclès**
Address: 78, avenue des Ternes
75017 Paris, France
Tel (0)1 40 68 01 01; Fax (0)1 40 68 91 88

A devoted pupil and colleague of Joël Robuchon at *Jamin* from1974–85, this native Norman now runs his own restaurant, to the satisfaction of diners and critics alike. Named Meilleur Ouvrier de France in 1982, today Philippe Groult has two Michelin stars and three red chef's hats (18) in Gault-Millau. In 1988 he was a contender in the "Culinary Olympics" in Tokyo, and one year later took over the reins in the kitchen at *Amphyclès*. He has been a member of Devoirs Unis since 1978. Philippe Groult is a keen traveler, a connoisseur of the Far East and an enthusiastic martial arts practitioner.

Marc Haeberlin

born: November 28, 1954

Restaurant: Auberge de L'Ill
Address: 2, rue de Collonges-au-Mont-d'Or
68970 Illhaeusern, France
Tel. (0)3 89 71 89 00; Fax (0)3 89 71 82 83

This worthy heir to the Haeberlin dynasty will on no account disappoint the gourmets who, once lured by the success of his father Paul, return to this temple of Alsatian cuisine. Three Michelin stars, four red chef's hats (19.5!) in Gault-Millau and four stars in Bottin Gourmand are the impressive distinctions garnered by this former student at the college of hotel management in Illkirch. Completing his training with Paul Bocuse and the Troisgros brothers, he proved his skills in Paris at the *Lasserre* back in 1976. When time allows, Mark Haeberlin occupies himself with painting and cars. In winter he goes downhill-skiing on the slopes of the Vosges.

Michel Haquin

born: September 27, 1940

Restaurant: **Le Trèfle à 4**
Address: 87, avenue de Lac
1332 Genval, Belgium
Tel. (0)2 654 0798; Fax (0)2 653 3131

Not far from Brussels, on the shores of Lake Genval, Michel Haquin successfully pursues a culinary career which began in 1961 in the Belgian capital. There, from 1977–85, he ran a restaurant under his own name. As a Belgian Maître Cuisinier and member of the Culinary Academy of France, this chef was admitted to the Order of the Thirty-three Masterchefs and was awarded the "Oscar of Gastronomy". The guidebooks have showered him with honors: two Michelin stars, three red chef's hats in Bottin Gourmand and 91/100 in the Belgian guide Henri Lemaire. In his leisure time, Michel Haquin enjoys reading and traveling.

Paul Heathcote

born: October 3, 1960

Restaurant: Paul Heathcote's
Address: 104 – 106 Higher Road,
Longridge PR3 3 SY, England
Tel. (0)1772 784969; Fax (0)1772 – 785713

This young British chef is very open to culinary influences from the other side of the English Channel. After working with Michel Bourdin at the *Connaught*, he spent two years with Raymond Blanc at the *Manoir au Quatr'Saisons* in Oxfordshire, and worked at the *Broughton Park Hotel* in Preston before finally opening his own restaurant (two Michelin stars) in 1990. In 1994, the Egon Ronay guidebook awarded him the enviable title of "Best Chef of the Year". An enthusiastic sportsman, Paul Heathcote loves soccer, squash and skiing.

Eyvind Hellstrøm

born: December 2, 1948

Restaurant: **Bagatelle**
Address: Bygdøy Allé 3
0257 Oslo, Norway
Tel. 22 44 63 97; Fax 22 43 64 20

No other chef in Scandinavia has received as many accolades as Eyvind Hellstrøm. This chef is strongly influenced by French gastronomy, with which he became familiar in the course of his training under famous chefs such as Guy Savoy, Alain Senderens, Bernard Loiseau and Fredy Girardet. A member of Eurotoques and Traditions et Qualité, Eyvind Hellstrøm was awarded two Michelin stars for his restaurant in 1982. A passionate wine connoisseur and a lover of Burgundies in particular, this chef often visits the wine cellars of Beaune and the surrounding area. He enjoys traveling and skiing, and is a self-confessed fan of the Swedish skier Ingmar Stenmark.

Alfonso Iaccarino

born: January 9, 1947

Restaurant: **Don Alfonso 1890**
Address: Piazza Sant'Agata,
80064 Sant'Agata sui due Golfi, Italy
Tel. (0)81 878 0026; Fax (0)81 533 0226

In 1973, Alfonso Iaccarino named his restaurant, with its marvelous view of the Gulf of Naples and Salerno, after his grandfather. A member of the Le Soste, Relais Gourmands and Traditions et Qualité chains, this chef has garnered numerous honors: two Michelin stars, four chef's hats in Espresso/Gault-Millau, one sun in Veronelli and 92/100 in Gambero Rosso. In 1989 he was awarded the title of "Best Winecellar in Italy" for his collection of noble Italian and French wines. In his private life, Alfonso Iaccarino is a true sportsman and particularly enjoys racing and cycling. He also loves nature, painting and traveling.

André Jaeger

born: February 12, 1947

Restaurant: **Rheinhotel Fischerzunft**
Address: Rheinquai 8,
8200 Schaffhausen, Switzerland
Tel. (0)52 625 3281; Fax (0)52 624 3285

André Jaeger can proudly claim to have successfully inspired Swiss and even European gastronomy with an oriental flavor. His restaurant, which he opened in 1975, boasts two Michelin stars and four red chef's hats in Gault-Millau (19). Named 1995 "Chef of the Year" by Gault-Millau, he was awarded the "Golden Key of Gastronomy" in 1988 and appointed Chairman of the Grandes Tables in Switzerland. He is also a member of Relais et Châteaux and Relais Gourmands. A connoisseur of wines from around the world, André Jaeger is also very interested in contemporary art and collects cars.

Roger Jaloux

born: May 20, 1942

Restaurant: **Paul Bocuse**
Address: 69660 Collonges-au-Mont-d'Or,
France
Tel. (0)4 72 42 90 90; Fax (0)4 72 27 85 87

As the loyalest among the loyal pupils of Paul Bocuse, Roger Jaloux followed his mentor into the latter's own restaurant in 1965, which incidentally received its third Michelin star in the same year. Everything there is to say about this celebrated restaurant in Collonges and the accolades it has received has already been said: it was here that Roger Jaloux prepared for the competition for the prestigious title of Meilleur Ouvrier de France, which he won in 1976. In his spare time, Roger Jaloux enjoys artistic activities such as painting and singing, and numerous sports, including tennis, cycling and skiing.

Patrick Jeffroy

born: January 25, 1952

Restaurant: **Patrick Jeffroy**
Address: 11, rue du Bon Voyage
22780 Plounérin, France
Tel. (0)2 96 38 61 80; Fax (0)2 96 38 66 29

A Breton with a penchant for solitude, Patrick Jeffroy settled down in a village in the Côtes-D'Armor département, where he serves innovative, delicious food in his restaurant, established in 1988 and now boasting one Michelin star and three red chef's hats in Gault-Millau (17). The earlier part of his career was spent in Abidjan in the Ivory Coast (1972) and the *Hôtel de l'Europe* in Morlaix back in France (1977–87). Patrick Jeffroy has had his Michelin star since 1984; he is also a Maître Cuisinier de France, and a recipient of the Mandarine Impériale first prize. Outside of working hours, he enjoys going to the theatre and the movies.

Émile Jung

born: April 2, 1941

Restaurant: Le Crocodile
Address: 10, rue de l'Outre
67000 Strasbourg, France
Tel. (0)3 88 32 13 02; Fax (0)3 88 75 72 01

Behind the sign of the crocodile – an allusion to Napoleon's Egyptian campaign – can be found Émile Jung's restaurant, highly rated by food lovers and a veritable temple of Alsatian cuisine, boasting no fewer than three Michelin stars, three white chef's hats in Gault-Millau (18) and three stars in Bottin Gourmand. The awards hardly come as a surprise, when one considers that this chef's career took him from *La Mère Guy* in Lyons to *Fouquet's* (1965) and *Ledoyen* (1966) in Paris. Émile Jung is a Maître Cuisinier de France and member of Relais Gourmands and Traditions et Qualité. A passionate enologist, he is particularly well versed in Alsatian wines.

Dieter Kaufmann

born: June 28, 1937

Restaurant: **Zur Traube**
Address: Bahnstraße 47,
41515 Grevenbroich, Germany
Tel. (0)2181 68767; Fax (0)2181 61122

Dieter Kaufmann harbors a great love of France, and that country knows how to repay him in kind: with two Michelin stars and four red chef's hats in Gault-Millau (19.5) he figures among the most highly esteemed non-French chefs, and was named Gault-Millau 1994 "Chef of the Year". He is a member of the prestigious Traditions et Qualité, Relais et Châteaux and Relais Gourmands chains. With over 30 000 bottles and some remarkable vintages, his restaurant, which he has run since 1962, boasts what is without a doubt the most important wine cellar in Germany. A bibliophile and polyglot, Dieter Kaufmann is also an enthusiastic traveler.

Örjan Klein

born: May 15, 1945

Restaurant: K.B.
Address: Smalandsgatan, 7
11146 Stockholm, Sweden
Tel. 86 79 60 32; Fax 86 11 82 83

At the pinnacle of a career based largely in the Swedish capital (*Berns* from 1966–7 and *Maxim's* of Stockholm from 1971-9), Örjan Klein joined forces with Ake Hakansson in 1980 to open K.B., which boasts one Michelin star. Named "Chef of the Year" in 1993, Örjan Klein is also a Nordfishing Trondheim and Swedish Academy of Gastronomy gold-medallist (1976 and 1983, respectively). A nature lover, our chef enjoys gardening and hiking. He also writes (cook)books and keeps fit by playing tennis and skiing.

Robert Kranenborg

born: October 12, 1950

Restaurant: **La Rive/Hotel Amstel
Inter-Continental**
Address: Prof. Tulpplein, 1
1018 GX Amsterdam, the Netherlands
Tel. (0)20 622 6060; Fax (0)20 520 3277

One doesn't become chef of La Rive (one Michelin star) – the restaurant of the *Inter-Continental*, the most prestigious hotel in Amsterdam – overnight. In point of fact, Robert Kranenborg had a string of successes as glowing references when he began work there in 1987: *Oustau de Baumanière* in Baux-de-Provence (1972-4), *Le Grand Véfour* in Paris (1975-7) and *La Cravache d'Or* in Brussels (1979-86). In 1994, Robert Kranenborg was named "Chef of the Year". When he is able to escape from the kitchen, he enjoys playing the drums or sports – golf being his favorite.

Étienne Krebs

born: August 15, 1956

Restaurant: L'Ermitage
Address: 75, rue du Lac
1815 Clarens-Montreux, Switzerland
Tel (0)21 964 4411; Fax (0)21 964 7002

As chef-proprietor of a magnificent house on the shores of Lake Geneva, Étienne Krebs is a happy man: a member of the "Young Restauranteurs of Europe" and Grandes Tables Suisses, he boasts one Michelin star and three red chef's hats in Gault-Millau (18), as well as the title of "Chef of the Year" 1995 for French-speaking Switzerland. After training with the greatest Swiss chefs – Fredy Girardet in Crissier and Hans Stucki in Basel – he ran the *Auberge de la Couronne* in Cossonay from 1984–90, before finally opening L'Ermitage in Montreux. Étienne Krebs enjoys walking and cycling around the lake, as well as cooking for his family.

Jacques Lameloise

born: April 6, 1947

Restaurant: Lameloise
Address: 36, place d'Armes
71150 Chagny, France
Tel. (0)3 85 87 08 85; Fax (0)3 85 87 03 57

The third generation of his family to bear the name, Jacques Lameloise has since 1971 also carried on the tradition of running the family restaurant. Cutting his professional teeth at Ogier's in Pontchartrain, from 1965–9 he worked at the Parisian temples of gastronomy *Lucas Carton*, *Fouquet's*, *Ledoyen* and *Lasserre*, not forgetting the Savoy in London. The *Lameloise* can boast three stars in both Michelin and Bottin Gourmand, as well as three red chef's hats in Gault-Millau (18), and is a member of the Relais et Châteaux, Relais Gourmands and Traditions et Qualité chains. Our chef is especially keen on antiques and old cars, and enjoys golfing and the occasional ski.

Erwin Lauterbach

born March 21, 1949

Restaurant: Saison
Address: Strandvejen, 203
2900 Hellerup, Denmark
Tel. 39 62 48 42; Fax 39 62 56 57

From 1972–3, Erwin Lauterbach served up the cuisine of his native Denmark at the *Maison du Danemark* in Paris – a time of which he has many fond memories. From 1977–81 he cooked in Malmö, Sweden at *Primeur*, after which he returned to Denmark. Opened in 1981, Saison boasts one Michelin star. Our chef is also member of the Danish Academy of Gastronomy, and is a virtuoso proponent of Danish culinary traditions. An admirer of naive painting, he is a passionate museum-goer and visitor of exhibitions. Of all the sports, he enjoys playing soccer the most.

Michel Libotte

born May 1, 1949

Restaurant: Au Gastronome
Address: 2, rue de Bouillon
6850 Paliseul, Belgium
Tel. (0)61 53 30 64; Fax (0)61 53 38 91

Since 1978, Michel Libotte has presided over the kitchens of *Au Gastronome*, rated 94/100 in the Belgian restaurant guide Henri Lemaire. French critics have also been unstinting in their praise, awarding our chef's establishment two Michelin stars and three stars in Bottin Gourmand. Michel Libotte has won the title of "Best Cook in Belgium", and is a member of Eurotoques and the Culinary Academy of France. His restaurant, which lies close to the Franco-Belgian border, serves a highly individual, imaginative cuisine. Michel Libotte collects firearms as a hobby, and keeps fit by swimming and playing tennis regularly.

Léa Linster

born April 27, 1955

Restaurant: **Léa Linster**
Address: 17, route de Luxembourg
5752 Frisange, Luxembourg
Tel. 66 84 11; Fax 67 64 47

Léa Linster is the first, and to date the only woman to receive the highest gastronomic accolade, the Bocuse d'Or, awarded to her in Lyons in 1989 by the Master himself in well-earned recognition of her daily efforts to make the generous cuisine of Luxembourg better known to the dining public. Converting her parents' inn into an haute cuisine restaurant in 1982, this chef received her master craftsman's diploma in 1987. In addition to her obvious enthusiasm for fine cuisine, Léa Lister enjoys walks in the wild and stimulating conversations with diners in her restaurant.

Régis Marcon

born June 14, 1956

Restaurant: **Auberge et Clos des Cimes**
Address: 43290 Saint-Bonnet-le-Froid, France
Tel. (0)4 71 59 93 72; Fax (0)4 71 59 93 40

In 1995, at only 39 years of age, Régis Marcon was awarded the Bocuse d'Or, with his neighbor Michel Troisgros serving as godfather – just one more glowing distinction in a career already crowned with accolades: the Taittinger prize in 1989, the Brillat-Savarin prize in 1992 and several-time finalist in the Meilleur Ouvrier de France competition (1985, 1991, 1993). In 1979 our chef opened a restaurant in his village which has earned him three red chef's hats in Gault-Millau (17), and which was designed to resemble "a cloister bathed in light". Here one recognizes the eye of the painter, which is what Régis Marcon, a great sportsman and medal-winning skier, as well as a passionate lover of nature, at one time hoped to become.

Guy Martin

born February 3, 1957

Restaurant: Le Grand Véfour
Address: 17, rue de Beaujolais
75001 Paris, France
Tel. (0)1 42 96 56 27; Fax (0)1 42 86 80 71

It would be impossible to summarize Guy Martin's career in just a couple of sentences – two Michelin stars, three white chef's hats in Gault-Millau (18), three stars in the Bottin Gourmand and 18.5/20 in Champérard. This young prodigy of gastronomy studied first with Troisgros, then in his native region, chiefly in Divonne. In 1991 he took over the reins of Le *Grand Véfour*, that jewel among Parisian restaurants at which the litterati of the French metropolis have rubbed shoulders for over 200 years, made famous by Raymond Oliver. Guy Martin remains true to the memory of his mother and to his native region of Savoy, of whose culinary history he is a fervent devotee. He also loves music, painting and Gothic art.

Maria Ligia Medeiros

born August 9, 1946

Restaurant: **Casa de Comida**
Address: 1, Travessa das Amoreiras
1200 Lisbon, Portugal
Tel. (0)1 388 5376; Fax (0)1 387 5132

Since 1978, Maria Ligia Medeiros has run the kitchens of a cozy restaurant owned by Jorge Vales, a former stage actor of the *Casa de Comedia* theater – hence the pun of the restaurant's name (comida = "food"). There, in the heart of the historic Old Town of the capital, she dishes up traditional Portuguese dishes with skill and flair, for which she was awarded a Michelin star several years ago. In addition to haute cuisine, our chef loves classical music and spends a large part of her leisure hours reading.

Dieter Müller

born July 28, 1948

Restaurant: **Dieter Müller**
Address: Lerbacher Weg,
51469 Bergisch Gladbach, Germany
Tel. (0)2202 2040; Fax (0)2202 204940

Dieter Müller had already beaten a career path across several countries and continents by the time he settled down in his native Germany in 1992: from 1973 onward he served as head chef of various establishments in Switzerland, Australia (Sydney), Japan and Hawaii, collecting numerous awards along the way, including the title of "Chef of the Year" in the Krug guidebook in 1982 and in Gault-Millau in 1988. Today, he boasts two Michelin stars and four red chef's hats (19.5), as well as a National Gastronomy prize. A member of Relais et Châteaux and Relais Gourmands, his hobbies are photography and collecting old recipes, as well as playing ice hockey and soccer.

Jean-Louis Neichel

born February 17, 1948

Restaurant: **Neichel**
Address: Beltran i Rûzpide, 16 bis
08034 Barcelona, Spain
Tel. (9)3 203 8408; Fax (9)3 205 6369

Thanks to his training under such culinary celebrities as Gaston Lenôtre, Alain Chapel and Georges Blanc, Jean-Louis Neichel is a European chef par excellence. For 10 years he brought his invaluable experience to bear while running *El Bulli* in Rosas, where Fernando Adrìa is now head chef, before opening his own restaurant in Barcelona in 1981, esteemed in particular for its collection of old Armagnacs and Cognacs. Awarded two Michelin stars and 9/10 in Gourmetour, Jean-Louis Neichel is also a member of Relais Gourmands. His leisure hours are devoted to oil painting (landscapes), his family, and sports (tennis, cycling, skiing).

Pierre Orsi

born July 12, 1939

Restaurant: **Pierre Orsi**
Address: 3, place Kléber
69006 Lyons, France
Tel. (0)4 78 89 57 68; Fax (0)4 72 44 93 34

Pierre Orsi's career reads like a dream: named Meilleur Ouvrier de France in 1972, he has worked with the culinary greats of his generation: with Bocuse from 1955–8, then at *Lucas Carton*; with Alex Humbert at *Maxim's*, and at *Lapérouse* in Paris. There followed a stint in the USA from 1967–71, after which he returned to Lyons and put out his shingle at the edge of the Tìte d'Or quarter. His superb restaurant, which boasts one Michelin star and three stars in Bottin Gourmand, is a mecca for gourmets. A member of Relais Gourmands and Traditions et Qualité, Pierre Orsi is also interested in table decoration and collects art objects and antiques.

Georges Paineau

born April 16, 1939

Restaurant: **Le Bretagne**
Address: 13, rue Saint-Michel
56230 Questembert, France
Tel. (0)2 97 26 11 12; Fax (0)2 97 26 12 37

Georges Paineau had the unusual good forture to start off his career under Fernand Point at *La Pyramide* in 1960. Since then, he drew ever closer to Brittany, stopping off in La Baule (1962) and Nantes (1963), before settling at *Le Bretagne* in Questembert, close to the Gulf of Morbihan, where he now collects stars (two in Michelin and four in Bottin Gourmand) and Gault-Millau chef's hats (four red, 19 points). Our chef works with his son-in-law, Claude Corlouer. His restaurant, an old coaching inn, is a member of Relais Gourmands and Relais et Châteaux. A gifted painter, Georges Paineau also loves literature and rugby.

Paul Pauvert

born July 25, 1950

Restaurant: **Les Jardins de la Forge**
Address: 1, place des Piliers
49270 Champtoceaux, France
Tel. (0)2 40 83 56 23; Fax (0)2 40 83 59 80

Professionally speaking, Paul Pauvert took his first steps at the *Café de la Paix* in Paris; from 1972-4 he served a stint in the kitchens of the Transatlantic Shipping Company's famous ocean liner *Grasse*, after which he worked at the Hotel *Frantel* in Nantes at the invitation of Roger Jaloux. In 1980 he opened his own restaurant in his home town, on the same spot where his ancestors had once run a forge. The holder of one Michelin star, Paul Pauvert is also a member of the Culinary Academy of France and the "Young Restauranteurs of Europe". The border area between Anjou and Nantes where our chef lives offers ample opportunity for the hunting, fishing and riding which he enjoys.

Horst Petermann

born May 18, 1944

Restaurant: Petermann's Kunststuben
Address: Seestraße 160,
8700 K¸snacht, Switzerland
Tel. (0)1 910 0715; Fax (0)1 910 0495

After serving his apprenticeship in Hamburg, Horst Petermann continued his career in Switzerland, in Saint Moritz, Lucerne and Geneva. He cooked in the kitchens of Émile Jung at *Le Crocodile* in Strasbourg, and at the Culinary Olympics in Tokyo in 1985, where he figured among the prizewinners. Further accolades received were the "Golden Key of Gastronomy" in 1987, "Chef of the Year" in 1991, four red chef's hats in Gault-Millau (19) and two Michelin stars. The success of his restaurant is also ensured by his master pastrycook, Rico Zandonella. As well as being a keen sportsman, Horst Petermann is passionate about his work and enjoys cultivating the friendships he has made through it.

Roland Pierroz

born August 26, 1942

Restaurant: **Hôtel Rosalp-Restaurant Pierroz**
Address: Route de Médran,
1936 Verbier, Switzerland
Tel. (0)27 771 6323; Fax (0)27 771 1059

Since 1962, Roland Pierroz has worked in this popular winter-sports resort in an equally popular restaurant. The holder of one Michelin star, four red chef's hats and 19 points in Gault-Millau, and three stars in Bottin Gourmand, he was awarded the "Golden Key of Gastronomy" in 1980 and named "Chef of the Year" in 1992. Roland Pierroz trained in Lausanne (Switzerland) and London, and is a member of Relais et Châteaux and Relais Gourmands, as well as vice-chairman of the Grandes Tables Suisses. A native of the Valais, he enjoys hunting and playing golf.

Jacques and Laurent Pourcel

born September 13, 1964

Restaurant: **Le Jardin des Sens**
Address: 11, avenue Saint Lazare
34000 Montpellier, France
Tel. (0)4 67 79 63 38; Fax (0)4 67 72 13 05

Though specializing in different areas, these inseparable twins underwent the same training, serving apprenticeships with Alain Chapel, Marc Meneau, Pierre Gagnaire, Michel Bras, Michel Trama and Marc Veyrat. Together with their business partner, Olivier Château, they opened the *Jardin des Sens* in a house made of glass and stone in 1988, since when they have collected stars in various guides: two from Michelin and three red chef's hats in Gault-Millau (17). Both chefs are Maîtres Cuisiniers de France and members of Relais Gourmands.

Stéphane Raimbault

born May 17, 1956

Restaurant: **L'Oasis**
Address: rue Honoré Carle,
06210 La Napoule, France
Tel. (0)4 93 49 95 52; Fax (0)4 93 49 64 13

After working for several years in Paris under the watchful eye of Émile Tabourdiau at *La Grande Cascade*, followed by a stint with Gérard Pangaud, Stéphane Raimbault spent nine years in Japan, where he ran the *Rendez-vous* restaurant in the *Hotel Plaza d'Osaka* in Osaka. After returning to France in 1991, he took over *L'Oasis* in La Napoule, with his brother as pastry chef. The recipient of two Michelin stars and three red chef's hats in Gault-Millau (18), he was also a finalist for the title of Meuilleur Ouvrier de France. In addition, he is a Maître Cuisinier de France and a member of Traditions et Qualité.

Paul Rankin

born October 1, 1959

Restaurant: **Roscoff**
Address: 7, Lesley House, Shaftesbury Square Belfast BT2 7DB, Northern Ireland
Tel. (0)1232 331 532; Fax (0)1232 312 093

Paul Rankin has had an international career, working first in London with Albert Roux in *Le Gavroche*, then in California and Canada. It was not, however, in Canada, but on a cruise in Greece that he got to know his Canadian wife Jeanne, whose skills as pastry chef have delighted diners at *Roscoff* since 1989. Named "Best Restaurant in the United Kingdom" by the Courvoisier guidebook in 1994–5, it is only a wonder that Roscoff has just one Michelin star. Paul Rankin also presents the BBC television program "Gourmet Ireland". Our chef loves traveling and wine, plays soccer and rugby and practices yoga.

Jean-Claude Rigollet

born September 27, 1946

Restaurant: **Au Plaisir Gourmand**
Address: 2, rue Parmentier
37500 Chinon, France
Tel. (0)2 47 93 20 48; Fax (0)2 47 93 05 66

Jean-Claude Rigollet began his career at *Maxim's* under Alex Humbert, then arrived in the Loire valley, working first at *Domaine de la Tortinière* in Montbazon (1971–7), then at the famous *Auberge des Templiers* of the Bézards (1978–82), not far from Montargis. In 1983 he became chef at *Plaisir Gourmand* in Chinon in the Touraine, the home of Rabelais. He received one Michelin star in 1985. Although he comes from the Sologne, Jean-Claude Rigollet also cooks in the style of the Touraine, and his wine cellar is testament to his extensive knowledge of regional wines.

Michel Rochedy

born July 15, 1936

Restaurant: **Le Chabichou**
Address: Quartier Les Chenus,
73120 Courchevel 1850, France
Tel. (0)2 47 93 20 48; Fax (0)2 47 93 05 66

Michel Rochedy received his earliest professional instruction from André Pic, the celebrated chef from Valence, from 1954–6. Originally from the Ardèche, Rochedy arrived in Savoy in 1963 and succumbed to the charms of that region. His restaurant *Chabichou*, which specializes in Savoy cuisine, has earned him two Michelin stars and three red chef's hats in Gault-Millau (17). A Maître Cuisinier de France and member of Eurotoques, he is also the chairman of the tourist information board of Courchevel. In his spare time, Michel Rochedy enjoys art and literature, fishes, and plays soccer and rugby.

Joël Roy

born November 28, 1951

Restaurant: **Le Prieuré**
Address: 3, rue du Prieuré,
54630 Flavigny-sur-Moselle, France
Tel. (0)3 79 26 70 45; Fax (0)3 86 26 75 51

In 1979, while still in the employ of Jacques Maximin at the Hôtel *Negresco* in Nice, Joël Roy won the Meilleur Ouvrier de France competition. Shortly afterwards, he became head chef at the *Frantel* in Nancy. In 1983 he opened *Le Prieuré*, which looks like a modern cloister with its arcades and garden. His one-Michelin-starred establishment is in the Lorraine, a region he loves for its traditions and natural beauty. An expert on fish, he is especially fond of river angling, and also enjoys cycling in his spare time.

Santi Santamaria

born July 26, 1957

Restaurant: **El Racó de Can Fabes**
Address: Carrer Sant Joan, 6
08470 San Celoni, Spain
Tel. (9)3 867 2851; Fax (9)3 867 3861

Since 1981, Santi Santamaria has taken great pleasure in serving specialties from his native Catalonia to his discerning clientele. His restaurant, which is just a stone's throw away from Barcelona, at the foot of Montseny national park, has been awarded three Michelin stars and 8/10 in Gourmetour. In addition, Santi Santamaria is a member of Relais Gourmands and Traditions et Qualité. Our chef also organizes gastronomic seminars, on herbs in the spring and on mushrooms in the fall. These gourmet workshops are always a great success. In his free time, Santi Santamaria enjoys reading.

Ezio Santin

born May 17, 1937

Restaurant: **Antica Osteria del Ponte**
Address: 9, Piazza G. Negri
20080 Cassinetta di Lugagnano, Italy
Tel. (0)2 942 0034; Fax (0)2 942 0610

Ezio Santin's culinary talents have been common knowledge since 1974, when he became chef at the *Antica Osteria del Ponte*. Three Michelin stars, four red chef's hats in Gault-Millau (19.5), one sun in Veronelli and 92/100 in Gambero Rosso: these honors justify the high regard in which he is held by his fellow Italian chefs, who have elected him chairman of Le Soste, an association of the best restaurants in Italy. Ezio Santin enjoys reading in his spare time. An enthusiastic fan of Inter Milan soccer club, he is also interested in modern dance.

Nadia Santini

born July 19, 1954

Restaurant: **Dal Pescatore**
Address: 46013 Runate Canneto sull'Oglio,
Italy
Tel. (0)376 72 30 01; Fax (0)376 70304

Since 1974 Nadia Santini has presided over the kitchens of *Dal Pescatore*, which was opened in 1920 by her husband's grandfather. The outstanding reputation of this restaurant is impressively documented in both Italian and French restaurant guides: two Michelin stars, four red chef's hats in L'Espresso/Gault-Millau (19), one sun in Veronelli and 94/100 in Gambero Rosso. A member of Le Soste, Relais Gourmands and Traditions et Qualité, she was awarded the prize for the "Best Wine Cellar of the Year" by L'Espresso/Gault-Millau in 1993. Nadia Santini is interested in history, especially the history of the culinary arts, from which she draws inspiration. She also loves hiking in the mountains.

Maria Santos Gomes

born August 10, 1962

Restaurant: **Conventual**
Address: Praça das Flores, 45
1200 Lisbon, Portugal
Tel. (0)1 60 91 96; Fax (0)1 387 5132

The *Conventual* is located in the historic Old Town of Lisbon, right by the Parliament. There, in 1982, Dina Marquez engaged the young chef Maria Santos Gomes – to the great delight of Lisbon politicians, who dine there regularly. Much of the restaurant's decor comes from the former cloister of Igreja (hence the restaurant's name). Maria Santos Gomes' inventive cuisine has already earned her one Michelin star; in 1993, she won first prize in the "Portuguese Gastronomy Competition", which always takes place in Lisbon. In addition to cooking, she loves literature, going on walks and traveling.

Nikolaos Sarantos

born December 5, 1945

Restaurant: **Hôtel Athenaeum Inter-Continental**
Address: 89-93, Syngrou Avenue
117 45 Athens, Greece
Tel. (0)1 902 3666; Fax (0)1 924 3000

From 1971–88, Nikolaos Sarantos traveled around the Mediterranean and the Middle East, honing his culinary skills in the various *Hilton* Hotels in Teheran, Athens, Corfu, Kuwait City and Cairo before finally settling down at the *Athenaeum Inter-Continental* in 1988. Nikolaos Sarantos is a member of the jury at international cooking competitions in San Francisco, Copenhagen and Bordeaux. Chairman of the "Chef's Association of Greece", he is also a great sports fan, and a keen tennis, soccer and basketball player.

Fritz Schilling

born June 8, 1951

Restaurant: **Schweizer Stuben**
Address: Geiselbrunnweg 11,
97877 Wertheim, Germany
Tel. (0)9342 30 70; Fax (0)9342 30 71 55

A chef since 1972, Fritz Schilling opened his restaurant in the Main valley near the romantic little town of Wertheim in 1990. His refined and versatile cuisine, which cultivates the best German gastronomic traditions, has already earned him two Michelin stars and four red chef's hats in Gault-Millau (19.5). A member of Relais et Châteaux and Relais Gourmands, his restaurant is one of the best in Germany. In his spare time, Fritz Schilling loves listening to pop music. A passionate driver, he enjoys playing golf and likes most beach sports.

Jean Schillinger

born January 31, 1934
died December 27, 1995

This former Chairman of the Maîtres Cuisiniers de France was a symbol of Alsatian gastronomy: The well-known restaurant *Schillinger* in Colmar, France (1957–95) boasted two Michelin stars, three red stars in Gault-Millau (17) and three stars in Bottin Gourmand. Jean Schillinger, a Knight of the Mérite Order, was the third generation of a family which had been in the restaurant business since 1893. For over 20 years he worked to heighten the profile of French cuisine throughout the world, from Japan to Brazil and Australia.

Jean-Yves Schillinger

born March 23, 1963

Succession in the Schillinger culinary dynasty is guaranteed thanks to this brilliant young chef, who has shown himself in all respects worthy of his predecessors. From 1988–95 he worked side by side with his father in Colmar. Prior to this he had worked in prestigious restaurants such as *Crillon* in Paris, in *Jamin*, where he was Joël Robuchon's sous chef, and even at *La Côte Basque* in New York. He is also a member of the "Young Restauranteurs of Europe", as well as of the Prosper Montagné and the French Haute Cuisineassociations. Jean-Yves Schillinger is very active and especially enjoys golfing, skiing and motorcycling.

Rudolf Sodamin

born April 6, 1958

Restaurant: **Passenger vessel Queen Elizabeth 2**
Home port: Southampton, England

The Austrian Rudolf Sodamin (pictured standing next to his colleague Jonathan Wicks) currently works for the *Cunard Line* shipping company, which owns several other magnificent liners besides the *QE2*. This chef de cuisine/pastry chef has attracted much favorable attention in numerous restaurants in Austria, France, Switzerland and the US. In New York, he worked in the kitchens of the famous *Waldorf-Astoria*. He is a member of the Prosper Montagné and Chefs des Chefs associations. Although Sodamin enjoys jogging, his favorite sport is still skiing in his home town of Kitzbühel.

Roger Souvereyns

born December 2, 1938

Restaurant: **Scholteshof**
Address: Kermstraat, 130
3512 Stevoort-Hasselt, Belgium
Tel. (0)11 25 02 02; Fax (0)11 25 43 28

Since 1983, Roger Souvereyns has presided over the *Scholteshof*. This 18th-century farmstead has a large vegetable garden which used to be tended by his friend and gardener Clément, and which is the source of the wonderful fresh fruit and vegetables used in his cooking. Roger Souvereyns has two Michelin stars, four red chef's hats in Gault-Millau (19.5), three stars in Bottin Gourmand, and 95/100 in the Belgian restaurant guide Henri Lemaire. A member of Relais et Châteaux, Relais Gourmands and Traditions et Qualité, he is a collector of antiques and old pictures. He also loves opera, and enjoys swimming and cycling.

Pedro Subijana

born November 5, 1948

Restaurant **Akelaré**
Address: 56, Paseo del Padre Orcolaga
20008 San Sebastian, Spain
Tel. (9)43 21 20 52; Fax (9)43 21 92 68

Since 1981, Pedro Subijana has had his own restaurant overlooking the Bay of Biscay. Awarded two stars in Michelin and 9/10 in Gourmetour, he was named "Best Cook in Spain" in 1982. Subijana underwent a traditional training at the college of hotel management in Madrid and at Euromar college in Zarauz, and became a cooking teacher in 1970. In 1986 he became Commissioner General of the European Association of Chefs, whose headquarters is in Brussels. He presents food programs on Basque Television and on Tele-Madrid. Pedro Subijana loves music and the movies.

Émile Tabourdiau

born November 25, 1943

Restaurant **Le Bristol**
Address: 112, rue du Faubourg Saint-Honoré
75008 Paris, France
Tel. (0)1 53 43 43 00; Fax (0)1 53 43 43 01

Since 1964, Émile Tabourdiau has worked only in the most famous of restaurants: First at *Ledoyen*, then at *La Grande Cascade*, and finally, since 1980, at *Le Bristol*, located in the immediate vicinity of the Élysée Palace and boasting magnificent large gardens. A former pupil of Auguste Escoffier, Émile Tabourdiau is a member of the "Culinary Academy of France", and was the winner of the Prosper Montagné prize in 1970 as well as Meilleur Ouvrier de France in 1976. He restaurant has one Michelin star. In his spare time he loves painting, and enjoys playing tennis and spending time in his garden.

Romano Tamani

born April 30, 1943

Restaurant: **Ambasciata**
Address: 33, Via Martiri di Belfiore
46026 Quistello, Italy
Tel. (0)376 61 90 03; Fax (0)376 61 82 55

Romano Tamani is the only one of our top chefs to hold the coveted title of Commendatore della Repubblica Italiana, a distinction conferred on him by his native Italy in 1992. This Lombardian, who learnt his craft in London and Switzerland, is without doubt one of the most skillful representatives of Italian gastronomy to be found. Together, he and his brother Francesco have run the *Ambasciata* since 1978. Accolades received include two Michelin stars, three chef's hats in Espresso/Gault-Millau, one Veronelli sun and 90/100 in Gambero Rosso, as well as membership of the prestigious Italian chain Le Soste. It is hardly surprising, therefore, that cooking is Tamani's consuming passion.

Laurent Tarridec

born May 26, 1956

Restaurant: **Le Restaurant du Bistrot des Lices**
Address: Place des Lices,
83990 Saint-Tropez, France
Tel. (0)4 94 97 29 00; Fax (0)4 94 97 76 39

That this Breton, a pupil of Michel Rochedy, could set himself up on the Côte d'Azur of all places, and after only one year (1995) walk off with one Michelin star and three red chef's hats in Gault-Millau (18), is testimony to his extraordinary adaptability. Before this, he honed his skills in Brittany at the *Lion d'Or*, in Paris, and in the Rhone valley at the *Beau Rivage*. Laurent Tarridec is interested in politics, as well as anything related with the sea. He also skis, rides a motorcycle, and, since living in Saint-Tropez, has discovered the game of boules.

Dominique Toulousy

born August 19, 1952

Restaurant: **Les Jardins de l'Opéra**
Address: 1, place du Capitole
31000 Toulouse, France
Tel. (0)5 61 23 07 76; Fax (0)5 61 23 63 00

Dominique Toulousy has only been resident in Toulouse since 1984. Hanging out his shingle on the Place du Capitole, he reaped accolades by the dozen: "Golden Key of Gastronomy" (1986), three red chef's hats in Gault-Millau (18) and two Michelin stars, as well as the title of Meilleur Ouvrier de France (1993). Before this, he had his first successes in Gers, a region known for its generous cuisine. Dominique Toulousy is a member of the "Young Restaurateurs of Europe", the Prosper Montagné association, Eurotoques, and Traditions et Qualité. He enjoys poring over old cookbooks and loves gardening, tennis and swimming.

Gilles Tournadre

born June 29, 1955

Restaurant **Gill**
Address: 8 & 9, quai de la Bourse
76000 Rouen, France
Tel. (0)2 35 71 16 14; Fax (0)2 35 71 96 91

Even a Norman can occasionally be persuaded to leave his native region in order to learn his craft: Gilles Tournadre started out his career at *Lucas Carton*, followed by the *Auberge des Templiers* of the Bézards and *Taillevent*, before finally winding up – on his own two feet – in Bayeux, and lastly in 1984, back in his home town. His career successes have justified all these changes: the young gastronome can boast two Michelin stars and three red chef's hats (17 points) for his restaurant right near Rouen cathedral. A member of the "Young Restaurateurs of Europe", this enthusiastic sportsman loves judo, golf and motor sports, and is also a passionate conservationist.

José Tourneur

born January 4, 1940

Restaurant: **Des 3 Couleurs**
Address: 453, avenue de Tervuren
1150 Brussels, Belgium
Tel. (0)2 770 3321; Fax (0)2 770 8045

The three colors which José Tourneur chose in 1979 as the logo and name of his restaurant are those of the Belgian national flag. The restaurant, which is wholly dedicated to Belgian cuisine, has one Michelin star and was awarded 88/100 in the Belgian restaurant guide Henri Lemaire. A self-taught cook, Tourneur gained further experience in Brussels and Nice, won the Prosper Montagné prize in 1969, and was chef de cuisine at the Brussels *Carlton* from 1969–79. He is also a member of the "Order of the 33 Masterchefs of Belgium", the "Culinary Academy of France", and the "Vatel Club". His other interests all revolve around the sea: he loves ships, and enjoys fishing and waterskiing.

Luisa Valazza

born December 20, 1950

Restaurant: **Al Sorriso**
Address: Via Roma, 18
28018 Soriso, Italy
Tel. (0)322 98 32 28; Fax (0)322 98 33 28

Taking their cue from the name of the restaurant which she and her husband Angelo have run since 1981 in their home town in the Piedmont region, the food critics have all "smiled" on Luisa Valazza, awarding Al Sorriso two Michelin stars, four chef's hats in Espresso/Gault-Millau (19.2), one sun in Veronelli and 90/100 in Gambero Rosso. Our chef, who is also a member of the Le Soste chain, remains modest in the midst of this avalanche of praise, carefully cooking the recipes she has amassed since 1971 in the *Europa* in Borgomanero. Luisa Valazza is passionately interested in art, especially painting and literature. A keen museum-goer, she is also an enthusiastic practitioner of winter sports.

Guy Van Cauteren

born May 8, 1950

Restaurant: **T'Laurierblad**
Address: Dorp, 4
9290 Berlare, Belgium
Tel. (0)52 42 48 01; Fax (0)52 42 59 97

Before opening his restaurant *T'Laurierblad* ("The Bay leaf") in 1979, Guy Van Cauteren was taught by some of France's most outstanding chefs: Alain Senderens at *Archestrate* in Paris, and the Allégriers at Lucas Carton (1972–4). He then spent several years cooking at the French Embassy in Brussels (1974–9). Since then, he has acquired two Michelin stars, three red chef's hats in Gault-Millau (17) and 89/100 in the Belgian restaurant guide Henri Lemaire. In addition, he was the fortunate recipient of the bronze Bocuse in 1993, and holds the title of Maître Cuisinier de Belgique. Guy Van Cauteren collects old books and enjoys traveling. In his spare time, he relaxes by cycling.

Freddy Van Decasserie

born October 10, 1943

Restaurant: **La Villa Lorraine**
Address: 75, avenue du Vivier d'Oie
1180 Brussels, Belgium
Tel. (0)2 374 3163; Fax (0)2 372 0195

Freddy Van Decasserie started off at *La Villa Lorraine* in 1963 as a kitchen boy and worked his way up the hierarchy until finally becoming head chef and the recipient of numerous awards: two Michelin stars, three red chef's hats in Gault-Millau (18), three stars in Bottin Gourmand and 92/100 in Henri Lemaire. He is a Maître Cuisinier de Belgique and a member of the "Culinary Academy of France" and Traditions et Qualité. In his spare time, he stays fit by being a "training partner" to the racing cyclist Eddy Merckx . He also swims and goes to the occasional soccer match.

Geert Van Hecke

born July 20, 1956

Restaurant: De Karmeliet
Address: Langestraat, 19
8000 Bruges, Belgium
Tel. (0)50 33 82 59; Fax (0)50 33 10 11

Geert Van Hecke was introduced to his craft by Freddy Van Decasserie at the *Villa Lorraine* in 1977, then served a stint with Alain Chapel at the famous *Cravache d'Or* in Brussels, finally opening his own restaurant in a renowned historic house in the heart of Bruges, the "Venice of the North". To date, his cooking has earned him two Michelin stars, three stars in the Bottin Gourmand, three red chef's hats in Gault-Millau (18) and 92/100 in Henri Lemaire. A winner of the "Best Chef in Belgium" award, he is also a member of Traditions et Qualité. It was not sheer coincidence which led him to settle in Bruges, a well preserved medieval town and popular tourist destination, as he is interested in art and enjoys visiting museums.

Gérard Vié

born April 11, 1943

Restaurant: **Les Trois Marches (Trianon Palace)**
Address: 1 boulevard de la Reine
78000 Versailles, France
Tel. (0)1 39 50 13 21; Fax (0)1 30 21 01 25

The incomparable chef of the *Trois Marches* (since 1970) started his career at the tender age of 13 at *Lapérouse*. There followed stints at *Lucas Carton* and the *Plaza-Athénée* in Paris and *Crillon Tower's* in London, as well as three years with the *Compagnie des Wagons-Lits* (1967–70). Today, Gérard Vié can boast two Michelin stars and three red chef's hats (18). Recipient of the "Silver Table" award from Gault-Millau in 1984, he was presented with the "Golden Key of Gastronomy" in 1993. An enthusiastic fan of the theater, opera and movies, he collects paintings and is a Chevalier des Arts et Lettres. He also loves hiking and swimming.

Jean-Pierre Vigato

born March 20, 1952

Restaurant **Apicius**
Address: 122, avenue de Villiers
75017 Paris, France
Tel. (0)1 43 80 19 66; Fax (0)1 44 40 09 57

Jean Pierre Vigato started off as a cellarman and served an apprenticeship in various restaurants before his first major successes at *Grandgousier* in Paris from 1980–3. In 1984 he set up on his own, opening *Apicius* in his native Paris. The restaurant, named after a famous Roman epicure, was awarded its first Michelin star in 1985, and its second two years later. It also boasts three red chef's hats in Gault-Millau (18). A member of Relais Gourmands, Jean-Pierre Vigato was Gault-Millau "Best Chef of the Year" in 1988, and chef at the French Pavillion at the 1992 World's Fair in Seville, Spain.

Gianfranco Vissani

born November 22, 1951

Restaurant **Vissani**
Address: 05020 Civitella del Lago, Italy
Tel. (0)744 95 03 96; Fax (0)744 95 03 96

With a rating of 19.6 and four chef's hats, Gianfranco Vissani got a near-perfect report card from Espresso/Gault-Millau – the best in all of Italy. Two Michelin stars, one Veronelli sun and 87/100 in Gambero Rosso complete the guidebook honors showered on the restaurant run by Vissani since 1980 as a family concern together with his wife, mother and sister. One of the selling points of his establishment is his own-production olive oil, an indispensable seasoning in his Mediterranean cooking. In his spare time, this gourmet collects clocks and relaxes by listening to classical music or reading. In addition, he is an unconditional fan of the AC Milan soccer club.

Jonathan F. Wicks

born June 14, 1962

Restaurant:**Passenger vessel Queen Elizabeth 2**
Home port: Southampton, England

From 1980–7, Jonathan Wicks (pictured seated next to his colleague Rudolf Sodamin on page 328) worked at a number of prestigious London restaurants, including the *Mayfair Intercontinental*, the *Grosvenor House* in Park Lane, and the *Méridien* in Picadilly, where he made his way up the ranks to sous-chef. In 1987 he became chef aboard the luxury ocean liner QE2. The home port of the vessel is Southampton, but the constant change of scenery suits this travel-loving gourmet to a T. Although rugby is the main sport in his home town of Bath in England, Jonathan Wicks plays American football and sails in his spare time. He also collects valuable porcelain plates and loves having breakfast in bed.

Heinz Winkler

born July 17, 1949

Restaurant: **Residenz Heinz Winkler**
Address: Kirchplatz 1,
83229 Aschau im Chiemgau, Germany
Tel. (0)8052 17990; Fax (0)8052 179 966

At only 31 years of age, Heinz Winkler already boasted three Michelin stars: how on earth did he do it? Perhaps by training at the *Victoria* in Interlaken, under Paul Bocuse, and at *Tantris* in Munich, before opening the *Residenz Heinz Winkler* in 1991. To crown it all, this gastronome has three white chef's hats (18) and was "Chef of the Year" in 1994 in Gault-Millau. Heinz Winkler is a member of Relais et Châteaux, Relais Gourmands, Traditions et Qualité, and the Italian chain Le Soste. He enjoys poring over old cookbooks, playing golf and skiing.

Harald Wohlfahrt

born November 7, 1955

Restaurant: **Schwarzwaldstube**
Address: Tonbachstrasse 237,
72270 Baiersbronn, Germany
Tel. (0)7442 49 26 65; Fax (0)7442 49 26 92

Harald Wohlfahrt started work at the *Schwarzwaldstube*, the restaurant of the Hotel *Trauben-Tonbach* in the heart of the Black Forest, in 1976, and has been chef there since 1980. He learned his trade at *Stahlbad* in Baden-Baden and *Tantris* in Munich. Voted "Chef of the Year" in 1991 by Gault-Millau, he currently boasts three Michelin stars and four red chef's hats (19.5). He is also a member of Relais Gourmands and Traditions et Qualité. While his main interests, unsurprisingly, are eating- and cooking traditions, Harald Wohlfahrt is also an outstanding athlete, with swimming, soccer and cycling being his favorite sports.

Armando Zanetti

born December 11, 1926

Restaurant: **Vecchia Lanterna**
Address: Corso Re Umberto, 21
10128 Turin, Italy
Tel. (0)11 53 70 47; Fax (0)11 53 03 91

A native Venetian, Armando Zanetti ran the *Rosa d'Oro* in Turin from 1955–69 before opening the evocatively named Vecchia Lanterna ("Old Lantern") restaurant in the same city in 1970. Today, our chef, who devotes himself chiefly to the traditional cuisine of his native country, now proudly boasts two Michelin stars and four chef's hats in Espresso/Gault-Millau (19.2/20). In his spare time, Armando Zanetti tirelessly researches European cuisine of bygone eras. He derives especial pleasure from trying new dishes, both his own and those of his fellow chefs.

Alberto Zuluaga

born March 31, 1960

Restaurant: **Lopez de Haro y Club Nautico**
Address: Obispo Orueta, 2
48009 Bilbao, Spain
Tel. (9)4 423 5500; Fax (9)4 423 4500

As a Basque from the Spanish province of Vizcaya on the Bay of Biscay, Alberto Zuluaga is especially proud to be able to exercise his profession in the true capital of his native province. He has been chef of the five-star luxury restaurant *Club Nautico* in the banking district of Bilbao since 1991. Before this, from 1987–91, he cultivated his love of Basque cuisine and culinary traditions at the *Bermeo* in the same city, earning the title of "Best Cook in Euzkadi" (the Basque Country) in 1988. It goes without saying that our chef enjoys playing Basque boules in his spare time, but he also likes car racing. He is also an enthusiastic mushroom hunter when time allows.

Glossary

ALMOND AND SUGAR MIXTURE: Mixture of equal parts by weight rather than volume) of ground almonds and refined sugar by weight.

ANGELICA: An herb, which is related to parsley, with a slightly bitter flavor. The stalk of the angelica plant is usually dried and candied and used as a garnish for tortes or other sweet dishes.

APRICOT GLAZE: Hot, strained apricot jam can be spread onto pastries, either as a glaze or as an isolating layer underneath glazes and cream or fruit fillings.

BAIN-MARIE: See double boiler.

TO BAKE: To cook food surrounded by the dry heat of an oven.

TO BAKE WITH OR WITHOUT STEAM: Most professional ovens, but few home ovens, are outfitted with a special vent which traps moisture in the oven when closed, but allows steam to escape when opened, creating a drier heat similar to home ovens. When a recipe specifies to bake with steam, one can create a similar effect at home by placing a shallow pan filled with water in the oven. To achieve better results when baking in a convection (or fan) oven, which creates a very dry heat, always add a source of moisture.

TO BAKE BLIND: To bake a pastry shell without a filling. The bottom should be pricked with a fork to release steam, then covered with waxed or baking paper and filled with dried beans, rice or metal baking beans, which prevent the bottom from buckling and the sides from collapsing.

TO BIND: Adding any of a number of substances, including flour, cornstarch, eggs, egg yolk, gelatin or cream, to a hot liquid in order to make it creamier.

BISCUIT: The French word for sponge cake, in Eurodélices biscuit designates a classic sponge cake consisting of egg whites and egg yolks each beaten separately with sugar until light and foamy, then combined and enriched with a small amount of flour, ground nuts and/or baking powder.

TO BLANCHE: Briefly immersing fruits or vegetables in boiling water, then in cold water so they do not continue cooking. This process makes it easier to remove peels and skins, and also preserves the flavor and color of foods before freezing.

TO BLEND: See to fold.

BRITTLE: A mixture of caramelized sugar and nuts, often ground hazelnuts or almonds; crumbled it is a common topping for cakes and desserts, particularly in Europe where it is called krokant.

TO BROWN: In baking, browning usually refers to placing food in a hot oven directly below a strong source of heat for a short time until they gain color. A salamander can also be used for this purpose.

CAKE GLAZE: Cake glaze, called *Tortenguß* in German, is available in most European countries as a ready mix. The commercial mixture is modified starch, the gelling agent carrageenan, with the addition of calcium tartrate. At home one could use 1 heaped tbsp of a mixture of cornstarch and ground gelatin or carrageenan and 2 level tbsp of sugar, to which 1 cup water (or a little more than 1 cup fruit juice) is gradually added over low heat. Stir continuously until the glaze is smooth, then bring to a boil and thicken. use immediately.

TO CANDY: To immerse, marinate or cook fruits, flowers, peel or seeds (e.g. cherries, ginger, lemon peel, orange peel, violets) in one or more increasingly concentrated sugar syrups and then allow them to air-dry. The sugar crystallizes, forming the typical thick crust.

CARAMEL: Caramel is produced when sugar is melted and heated to 320–350 °F/160–177 °C and becomes light to dark brown. To make caramel candy or sauce, other ingredients like water, cream and butter are added, but one must add liquid carefully and gradually to sugar heated to these temperatures.

TO CARAMELIZE: To melt sugar until it becomes caramel; or to coat with caramelized sugar; or to sprinkle sugar on the surface of a cake or dessert and then apply strong heat briefly until the sugar turns into caramel (for example a crème brûlée).

CHOCOLATE COATING: Also known by its French name, *couverture*, chocolate coating is professional-quality chocolate with a high cocoa butter content (around one-third) that makes it particularly suitable for thin, shiny chocolate glazes. It is available in chocolate shops or gourmet supply stores.

CLARIFIED BUTTER: Butter from which the milk solids and water have been removed, leaving pure butter fat. It has a higher smoking point than whole butter but less butter flavor. To clarify butter, melt it slowly in a double boiler without stirring, then remove and discard the foam on the surface and pour off the clear butter without the solids at the bottom of the pan.

TO COAT: In baking, coating generally refers to covering cakes and pastries with a surface layer of chocolate, marzipan or other substance.

CONFECTIONERS' SUGAR: American term for icing sugar.

COULIS: A thick sauce consisting of pureed fruit, sometimes with the addition of lemon juice and sugar syrup.

TO DEEP-FRY: A means of cooking food by swimming it in enough hot vegetable oil or lard to cover the food.

TO DEGLAZE: To use a liquid such as wine, water, or stock (or in sweet recipes fruit juice) to dissolve food particles and/or caramelized drippings left in a pan after food has been roasted or sautéed in it. The liquid is usually used to make a sauce to serve with the food.

DOUBLE BOILER: Also called a bain-marie, a double boiler is two pans that nestle into each other. The bottom pan is filled with simmering water and the top pan rests over, but not in, the hot water, providing a gently source of heat to cook delicate foods like custards and sauces, to melt chocolate, and to dissolve gelatin. See also water bath.

ESSENCE: See extract.

EXTRACT: Baking extracts are the concentrated flavors and scents of fruits, plants and spices, which are suspended in "carriers" (usually alcohol or oil). Some of the most commonly used in baking include vanilla, lemon, bitter almond, rum and arrack.

TO FLAMBÉ: A dramatic presentation that involves pouring high-volume alcohol over food, most often a dessert (crêpes, crème brûlée) and lighting it. The alcohol burns with a blue flame, producing a characteristic flavor that adds to the taste of the dish.

TO FLAVOR: Adding spices, herbs, extracts or alcohol to foods in order to give them a particular taste.

TO FLOUR: Also called dusting, this means coating a greased baking pan with flour, sugar, breadcrumbs, sesame seeds, finely ground almonds or other nuts, or another fine substance.

TO FOLD: Also called blending. A means of combining a light, airy mixture (often beaten egg whites) with a second, heavier mixture. With the lighter mixture on top of the heavier one, use a spatula to cut through both, scrape along the bottom of the bowl and then up the side. Rotate the bowl slightly and repeat until the mixtures are blended. This should be done carefully and gently so that the lighter mixture does not collapse and its volume is retained.

FONDANT: A mixture of sugar, water and cream of tartar cooked until the syrup is reduced, then kneaded and beaten until the mixture can easily be molded. It is used to form decorations, or warmed and used as icing for cakes.

GELATIN: A clear and flavorless substance used to jell liquid mixtures. Gelatin is available in $1/4$ oz envelopes of granules (more common in the United States), or in paper-thin sheets (standard in

Europe). Sheet gelatin should be soaked in cold water for 5–10 minutes, then thoroughly wrung out before, like ground gelatin, being dissolved in a small amount of hot liquid (preferably in a double boiler) before use. To jell 2 cups of liquid, one needs 1 envelope or 4 sheets of gelatin.

GÈNOISE: A type of sponge cake in which whole eggs are beaten with sugar until light and foamy before flour, finely ground nuts or other ingredients are folded into them.

TO GLAZE: To spread a thin layer of eggs, jelly or jam, gum arabic or any other kind of coating onto foods to give them a shiny finish.

GLUCOSE: A thickening syrup which is often added to sugar when it is cooked to ensure that the sugar recrystallizes.

TO GREASE: Brushing a thin layer of butter or some other fat onto baking pans so that the finished pastry is easier to remove from the pan.

HALF AND HALF: Mixture of equal parts milk and cream, widely available in the United States.

HEAVY CREAM: American term for double cream.

INSTANT COFFEE: Soluble coffee with a very intense flavor which is manufactured according to a particular process.

ITALIAN MERINGUE: A variation of meringue made by beating egg whites until stiff and then pouring hot sugar syrup over them while beating continuously until the meringue has completely cooled.

TO KNEAD: To thoroughly combine and work the components of a dough either manually with both hands or with the dough hook of an electric mixer. Kneading by hand, it can take 15 minutes or longer until a smooth, elastic dough is produced.

LIGHT CREAM: American term for single cream.

MARZIPAN: A paste-like mixture of finely 0ground almonds, sugar or confectioners' sugar, and often egg whites. Raw marzipan is available ready-made.

MACERATE: To marinate fruits (especially dried fruits) in alcohol or liqueur until they take on the flavor of the marinating liquid.

MERINGUE: A light mixture consisting of sugar and stiffly beaten egg whites; it can be used as an icing or topping, an element of a mousse or cream, or baked as cookies or bases for tortes. see also Italian meringue.

NOUGAT: Called *praliné* in French, nougat is a paste or cream consisting of finely ground roasted nuts (most often hazelnuts or almonds), sugar and

sometimes honey or cocoa. Light nougats, such as Nougat del Montélimar, contain no cocoa solids.

TO POACH: A means of cooking food by immersing it in liquid just below the boiling point.

PRALINÉ: See nougat.

TO PRICK: Making holes in an uncooked dough (such as short pastry) at regular intervals with a fork before baking, so that it does not form blisters while baking.

TO PROVE: See to rise.

QUARK: A soft, spreadable, unripened cheese extremely popular in German-speaking countries, quark has a flavor similar to cottage cheese, but with the texture of sour cream. Unlike ricotta, it is unsalted, and is milder and less rich than mascarpone. It is used to make cheesecakes, as a substitute for sour cream, in a number of desserts, or simply spread on bread or eaten with fruit. As a fresh cheese, it is best consumed within a short time of manufacture. It is increasingly available in specialist outlets in the US.

TO REDUCE: To thicken mixtures by allowing them to boil until some of the liquid has evaporated, resulting in a thicker consistency.

TO REFRESH: A means of preventing sensitive foods like custards from continuing to cook while cooling slowly by rinsing or submerging the cooking pot or bowl in cold water in order to lower the temperature rapidly.

RENNET: A small, speckled apple well-suited to cooking and baking, it is beloved by chefs and cooks in Europe but not available in the United States. Pippin or Granny Smith are the closest substitutes.

TO RISE: Allowing a yeast dough or yeast mixture to rest covered in a warm place so that it can increase in size.

ROYAL ICING: A decorative icing that consists of beaten egg white, sifted confectioners' sugar and lemon juice.

SABAYON: See zabaglione.

SALAMANDER: A hand-held kitchen tool used to grill or brown food.

TO SOAK: To drizzle a mixture of sugar syrup, spirits, fruit juice or other ingredients onto sponge cake bases, pastries etc. Until they are completely drenched. Smaller pastries can also be briefly dipped into the soaking liquid.

SUGAR SYRUP: A solution of sugar and water that has briefly been boiled, sugar syrup can be made in various concentrations and is used for countless purposes in baking and confection-

making. In Eurodèlices, the sugar syrup called for is a heavy syrup of equal parts sugar and water, unless otherwise specified. The sugar is heated to a temperature of 212 °F/100 °C, or to 28 °Beaumé (the equivalent of 30 °Beaumé once cooled). The concentration, or density, of the syrup is measured in degrees Beaumé using a sugar scale, which was invented by the French chemist and engineer, Antoine Beaumé (1728–1804).

TO TEMPER: A method of preparing chocolate to be used for decorative work or coating by slowly melting chocolate, then allowing it to partially cool, then reheating it very briefly. This complicated process serves the purpose of preventing the cocoa butter contained in the chocolate from crystallizing, which would severely detract from the appearance of the finished product.

TO THICKEN: To slightly thicken liquid mixtures either by stirring in egg yolk and cream, milk or butter; or by cooking a cream or sauce without allowing it to boil, stirring constantly, until it coats a wooden spoon, i.e. reaches a thick but still liquid consistency. Also see reduce.

TURNING: *Tourage* in French, a particular sequence of folding dough into thirds, rolling it out, and folding it into thirds again when making puff pastry. The more frequently this process is repeated, the more puffy layers the dough has. Flaky puff pastry is folded and turned four to six times, and must be refrigerated between each turn.

VANILLA SUGAR: Sugar infused with the flavor of vanilla bean, or containing some ground vanilla bean. It is easy to produce sugar with the distinctive vanilla fragrance at home by placing one or more vanilla beans in a jar filled with superfine sugar. After a week or two the sugar is permeated with the aroma of vanilla.

VANILLIN SUGAR: Sugar containing vanillin, an artificial vanilla substitute.

WATER BATH: Similar to a double boiler, foods cooked in a water bath are placed in a larger pan partially filled with water while baked in an oven.

YEAST MIXTURE: Also called yeast starter, a yeast mixture is the first stage in preparing many yeast dough recipes. Generally, it consists of the yeast, a portion of the flour and liquid, and a little sugar. This is worked into a soft dough and allowed to rise in a warm place, covered, until its volume has doubled. It is then kneaded with the other ingredients to form the yeast dough.

ZABAGLIONE: Also known by its French name, *sabayon*, this extremely light, frothy custard consists of egg yolks, sugar and wine that are whisked together in the top half of a double boiler.

Index